Router Jigs & Techniques

Router Jigs & Techniques

PATRICK SPIELMAN

■■■■■

Jig & Fixture Drawings by
Mark Obernberger

 Sterling Publishing Co., Inc.   New York

DEDICATION

To my Patricia—the best

Edited by Michael Cea

Library of Congress Cataloging-in-Publication Data

Spielman, Patrick E.
　　Router jigs and techniques / Patrick Spielman.
　　　　p.　　cm.
　　Includes index.
　　ISBN 0-8069-6694-7 (pbk.)
　　1. Routers (Tools) 2. Jigs and fixtures.　　I. Title
TT203.5.S635 1988
684'.083—dc 19　　　　　　　　　　　87-33674
　　　　　　　　　　　　　　　　　　　　　　CIP

　　　　　　5　7　9　10　8　6

Copyright © 1988 by Patrick Spielman
Published by Sterling Publishing Co., Inc.
387 Park Avenue South, New York, N.Y. 10016
Distributed in Canada by Sterling Publishing
% Canadian Manda Group, P.O. Box 920, Station U
Toronto, Ontario, Canada M8Z 5P9
Distributed in Great Britain and Europe by Cassell PLC
Artillery House, Artillery Row, London SW1P 1RT, England
Distributed in Australia by Capricorn Ltd.
P.O. Box 665, Lane Cove, NSW 2066
Manufactured in the United States of America

CONTENTS

Acknowledgments

This book exists because of the support and assistance given to me by a select core of multi-talented individuals and some very helpful companies.

First, much love and gratitude go to my lovely wife, Patricia (Mrs. Pat), and to our son Bob. Both handled the hectic details of our growing businesses, leaving me free to give this work my best effort. Bob's personal interest in this book, his contribution of jigs and fixturing ideas, and his creative suggestions, are all valued and appreciated.

A hearty thank-you goes to our Key Man, Mark Obernberger, an expert craftsman and a very talented technical artist. Every reader is sure to appreciate his clear and easy-to-read jig and fixture drawings that are a distinctive feature of this book. Again, a special note of thanks is extended to Julie Kiehnau, an exceptionally talented typist who miraculously transforms my crude scribbles into clear, crisp copy.

Sincere gratitude is expressed to Steve and Mark O'Brien of Onsrud Cutter, Inc., for sharing their router-bit expertise and printed materials. They also reviewed those related chapters in this book.

A big thank you goes to Allen Nielsen and Steven Holley of Ryobi America Corp., and to Richard Schmidt of Porter-Cable Corp., for their generous assistance and prompt response to every query and request. Rob Van Nieuwenhuizen of Furnima Industrial Carbide provided some beautiful line-art illustrations of router bits. Thank you, Art Betterley, for cluing me in about your router jigs for laminate work. Thanks, Dave Freeman, of Amana Tool Co., and Richard Byrom, of Byrom International Corp., for the help and special insight about router bits. Thank you, Gary Compton, Don Duffey, and Greg Guess, of the Robert Bosch Tool Corp., for your important contributions.

Other individuals and companies that responded beyond my expectations with assistance in one form or another include the following:

Mike Barrett, True-Cut Saw and Tool Co.
Jerry Coleman, Porta-Nails, Inc.
Glen Davidson, Welliver & Sons Inc.
Delta International Machinery Corp.
Mark Duginske, Cabinetmaker
Barry J. Dunsmore, Freud U.S.A., Inc.
Zach Etheridge, Highland Hardware
Jim Fink, Shopsmith, Inc.
Guenter Fisher, G. & F. Precision, Inc.
Clay Furtaw, Black & Decker (U.S.), Inc.
Norman Griset, Griset Industries, Inc.
Ken Grisley, Leigh Industries, Inc.
Mark Hurwitz, Milton W. Bosley & Co., Inc.
David Keller, Keller & Co.
Michael Lovett, Omark Industries
John McConegly, J.D.S. Company
Julia Moore, Nevamar Corp.
Terry Mote, Allen Company

Mitch Olson
Charles Onsrud, C.R. Onsrud, Inc.
Pasco Robles Carbide, Inc.
Poitras Machinery Co.
Jim Roberts, Black & Decker (U.S.), Inc.
Ellen Safranek, Safranek Enterprises, Inc.
Ken Spitulski, Kencraft Co.
Robert Steck, Sears

Steve and Julie Sussek, S/J Fine Wood-
works Co.
Don Thomas, Woodmachine Co.
Roy Thompson, Makita U.S.A., Inc.
John Totten, Ring Master, Inc.
Brad Witt, Woodhaven Co.
Steve Witt, Progressive Technology, Inc.

Introduction

Since the 1983 publication of my popular book, *Router Handbook*, there has been a flood of new technical advances and convenience devices related to router tooling and techniques. One supplier of routers and bits calls this the "router revolution." One result of this revolution is that the plunge-type routers, which were essentially unknown and untried in the United States less than a decade ago, are now widely used. They are predicted to beome the most popular of all woodworking tools (Illus. 1 and 5), though there is no doubt that hand-held standard routers will still be around for some time because of their adaptability to secondary uses such as power units for router tables, pin routers, etc. This book deals with both types of routers.

During the past couple of years, some very promising improvements have been made to routers in general. These very versatile, safe, and easy-to-handle woodworking tools can to-day be used to handle many new materials and new jobs. This has caused manufacturers to introduce special new bits and particular router features to fully utilize this tool's potential. For example, note how much bigger and more powerful hand-held routers are becoming. (See Illus. 3–5.) This added power, coupled with speed-changing features, has stimulated some manufacturers to produce and market bigger, shaper-like bits (Illus. 6). As a result, there are now extremely large bits and extremely large

Illus. 1. *The plunging feature of this router permits very accurate, small circular cuts to be made easily with the help of this shop-made, special base discussed in Chapter 19.*

Illus. 2.   *The plunging router is ideal for all hand-held template routing jobs, such as when using these "foolproof" lettering templates shop-made from the full-size patterns given in Chapter 25.*

Illus. 3   *Porter-Cable's new 5-speed Model 518 Speedtronic 3 horsepower router offers a choice of 10, 13, 16, 19, and 22,000 RPM with a touch of the control. This new router also operates much quieter than standard routers, and handles large bits at lower speeds. It weighs almost 19 pounds.*

Illus. 4.   *A closeup look at the digital readout on Porter-Cable's new microprocessor-controlled router confirms the speed selected.*

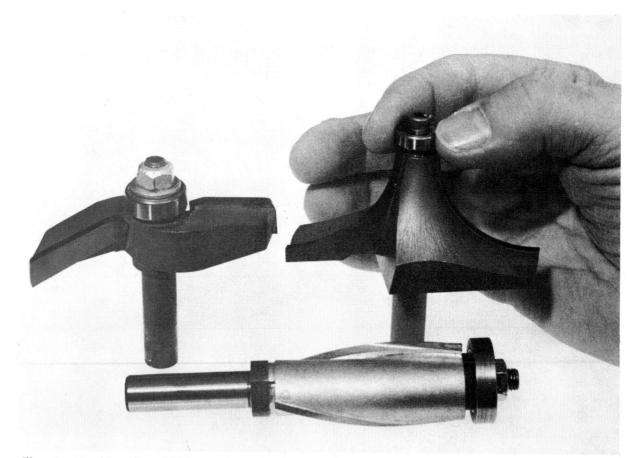

Illus. 6.   New big and special bits permit us to make unusual cuts with the hand-held router but, at the same time, dictate an even greater concern for operator safety and awareness.

routers that supposedly allow us to do more. This is both good and bad, the disadvantage being that the big bits can easily be misused. An unknowing novice might install one in a smaller, lightweight, high-speed router not designed for such extreme tooling, a potentially very hazardous situation. User Beware warnings should be engraved on some bits and on certain routers.

Chapter 4 illustrates many new special bits, and some are large. However, when they are properly used in the bigger, more powerful, routers with optional slower RPM adjustments, a wide variety of new routing options are available.

You'll also find in this book some new ideas and uses for those smaller trimming routers primarily designed for decorative laminate work. (See Illus. 7–9.)

In Chapters 1–3 I discuss recent technical advances in router bits (Illus. 10 and 11) and give advice on how to determine bit quality. Since it is essential that new safety concerns are addressed, one chapter is devoted to safety-related devices. Of particular interest are a device for slowing down router spindle speeds and foot switches, two accessories that improve safety conditions and give you better overall control of the routing process.

Illus. 7.   This Bosch tilting-base laminate trimmer weighs just over 3 pounds.

Illus. 8.   Makita's new Model 3700D cordless trimmer has a spindle speed of 8,000 RPM and weighs about 2½ pounds.

Illus. 9. *A small trim router used with this easy-to-make base produces toy wheels of various designs and sizes. See Chapter 22.*

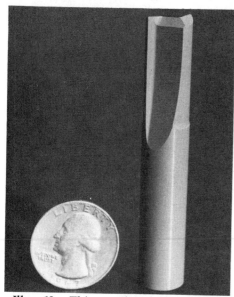

Illus. 10. *This new ½-inch bit, made from a ceramic composite material by Onsrud Cutter, measures 2¾ inches in overall length.*

Illus. 11. *The first adjustable router bit. It will cut various-size dadoes, grooves, mortises, etc.*

Part III is devoted to commercially made devices, and in Chapter 9 I introduce a device that, used with the router, produces dowels in various sizes from wood scraps.

Cabinetmakers will want to read about the "mitre-fold" device discussed in Chapter 7. This remarkable routing tool easily mitre-cuts the thin edges of decorative laminates to eliminate the traditional, unsightly dark line, a job that has previously been considered impossible.

Other chapters describe the latest in pin routers and router tables, as well as several new router machines that are used for joint-making techniques. You will also learn how to convert the new Ryobi radial arm saw into a potent pin router and joint-making machine.

A major part of this book is devoted to shop-made jigs and fixtures. Many different kinds of router bases that can be made for special uses are illustrated and described. Also included are some adjustable jigs and guides for making any number and size of geometrical-routed patterns, including squares, rectangles, circular (Illus. 9) and elliptical configurations. Note the jig for cutting ovals shown in Illus. 12.

The entry motion of the plunge router makes it ideal to use on some boring applications. When you use any of several shop-made jigs, you will be surprised by the preciseness of the results and the practical boring techniques you can incorporate. Plunge-router boring gives new life to the traditional dowel joint (Illus. 13), and this application is discussed in Chapter 24.

In Chapter 25, you will learn how to make some foolproof lettering templates for wooden-sign work. In Chapter 23, shop-made jigs and fixtures used for making many different kinds

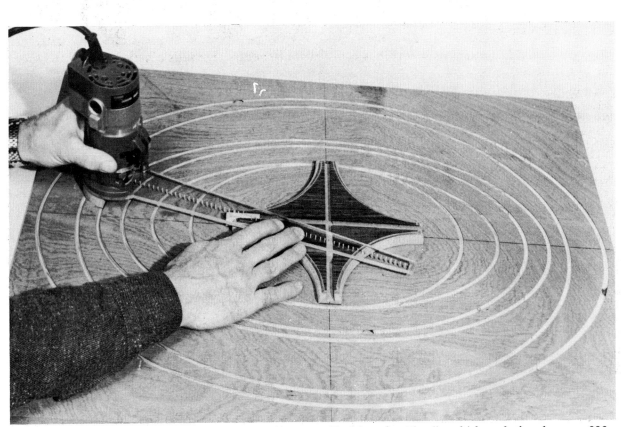

Illus. 12.   Making perfect oval cuts in various sizes is a snap with this oval-cutting jig, which can be found on page 229.

Illus. 13.   This corner joint was made with a homemade jig; a plunge-router boring technique was used to make the perfectly aligned dowel holes. Refer to pages 260–263.

of joints and joinery cuts are discussed. In Chapter 27, I describe inexpensive approaches, and provide a number of original ideas, for making your own vacuum clamps and templates just like those used in industrial settings.

In the final part of the book detailed plans are presented for the "ultimate" router table—one that is designed for contemporary use, and which is far more functional than any router-table design previously published. This router table is designed to handle, if you wish, the heaviest and largest hand-held routers available. Even if you don't have one of the big routers, it still might be a good idea to build a table to handle one because sometime in the future you might want to switch to a larger router.

In the last section, I show how to make the router table in step-by-step stages, starting with a basic floor-standing unit that provides shaper-like routing features. (See Illus. 14.) Also included are plans and instructions for making a number of optional attachments and accessory items (jigs and fixtures) to be used with this unit. These include a simple, but unique, mitre gauge, an adjustable split fence, a vacuum work-clamping plate, a swivel vacuum work-holding chuck, a horizontal

Illus. 14.   Chapter 31 shows how to make and use this horizontal joint-making device, just one of several unique attachments for the Ultimate Router Table shown here.

router joint-maker, and a combination unit that functions as both a swinging router (Illus. 15) and a tiltable spindle pin router. Chapter 33 includes plans and instructions for making the pin router (Illus. 16) for use on the Ultimate Router Table. The pin router is one of my favorite attachments because of its unique safety features.

All plans and specifications for the jigs and fixtures in this book are sized and designed to fill a particular need or liking of mine. Changes and individual modifications are obviously encouraged to make the jigs or fixtures more functional, as dictated by individual requirements.

Patrick Spielman
Spielmans Wood Works

Illus. 15. This accessory to the Ultimate Table doubles as a swinging router and tilting pin router.

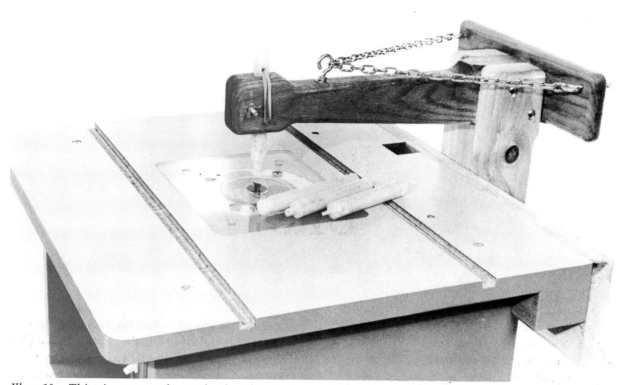

Illus. 16.   This pin-arm attachment for the Ultimate Router Table makes template-routing safe and easy. Plans and instructions for making both are given in Chapters 28 and 33.

Part I
Bits

An onslaught of new ideas in router-bit design and manufacture has hit the market in recent years. Some of these developments are sound, and allow the woodworker to choose bits of value that will prove helpful and practical; others do not.

Overall bit performance, in particular edge durability, has been improved by reputable manufacturers. Major developments include new materials, coatings, and edge tippings, along with refined geometric cutting designs.

These developments, plus the vast selection of new cutting profiles available today, make the router more productive and versatile than ever.

Research in material microstructures and cutting feeds and speeds has uncovered some unusual reasons why bits dull. This information provides a block of knowledge important to selecting and buying router bits, and is discussed in chapters 1–3, which also outline the new options and advances in router-bit technology.

1

Bit Developments and Innovations

Besides the vast array of new shapes that can now be cut because of the many different bit profiles available, manufacturers are coming up with other ideas that are noteworthy.

Today, special bits are designed to cut certain materials. For example, a stellite steel-alloy material that's high in chrome and nickel, called Tantung®, has been found to outlast carbide for machining oak and similar dense hard woods at much less than the cost of industrial tooling like polycrystalline diamond (a diamond bit costs about 15 times more than a carbide counterpart; Tantung® is only slightly more expensive than carbide). It will do certain jobs better than the steadfast carbide.

Onsrud Cutter, of Libertyville, Illinois, has been one of the leaders in developing special tooling to match specific-material cutting jobs. This approach to router use makes good sense, because in the routing process the bit should match the type of router being used and the material that has to be cut.

Ceramic Bit One of the more interesting developments coming from Onsrud Cutter's R & D (research and development) laboratories is a new "ceramic" bit, which is made of a super-tough ceramic composite material that is far different than the kind of ceramic used to make pots and vases. (See Illus. 17.) This bit

Illus. 17. This new bit, developed by Onsrud Cutter, is made from solid rounds of a ceramic composite material. It's now made in the straight-flute style, as shown, and spirals as well.

was primarily developed for cutting the toughest kinds of abrasive woodworking materials, such as particle board and MDF (medium-density fibreboard). Research has shown that it has a normal life span up to six times as great as typical carbide bits, and may only cost 50% more. The hulls from rice actually produce the silicon carbide fibres ("whiskers") that reinforce the ceramic compound, much like metal rods reinforce concrete.

Stamped Sheet-Steel Bits Another unusual innovation is a new method of manufacturing "lower-end bits" from stamped sheet steel. (See Illus. 18 and 19.) Manufactured by Omark Industries, of Woodburn, Oregon, these ¼-inch-shank bits are claimed to be of a heat-

20

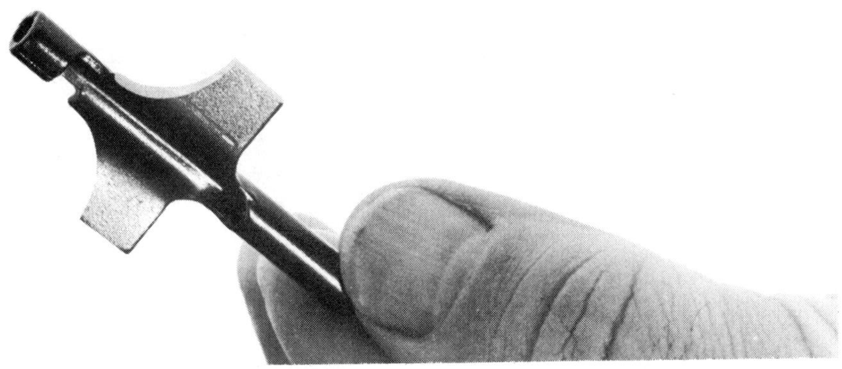

Illus. 18. This low-priced router bit, made of stamped sheet-steel, is available in many configurations. Note its hollow tubular pilot and hollow shank.

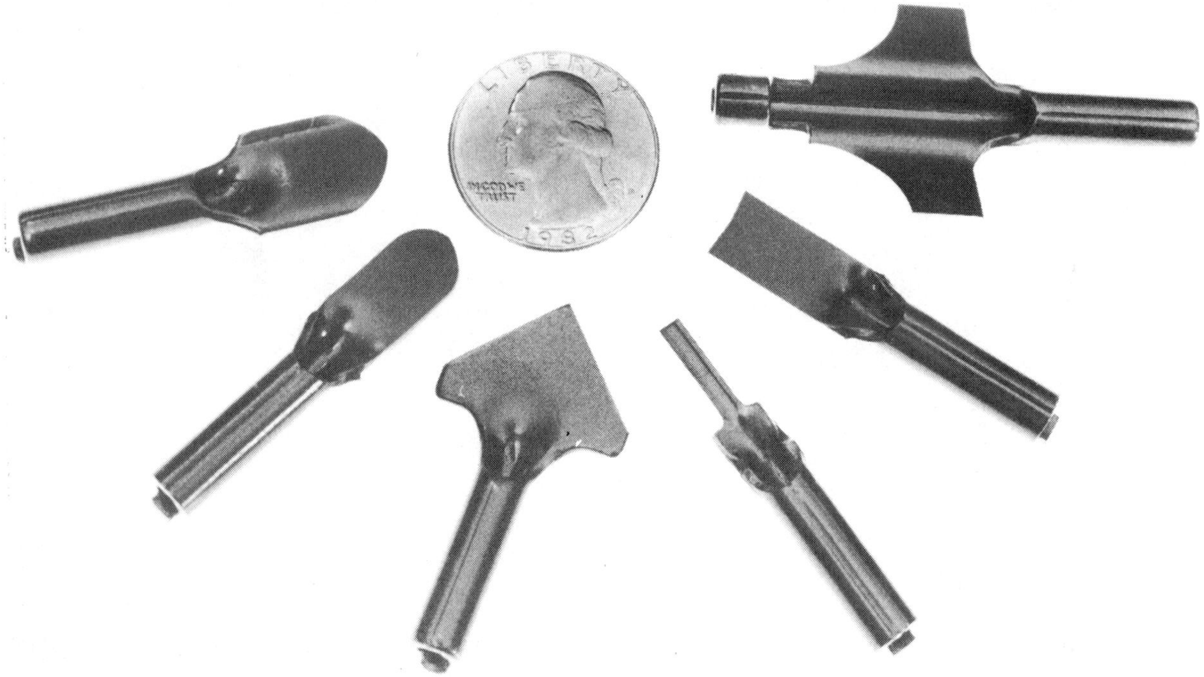

Illus. 19. Stamped-sheet metal bits are available in most standard cutting profiles, including those shown here.

treated alloy steel that keeps its sharpness "as long as any comparable high-speed steel router bit." All of the shanks and those bits having integral pilots are hollow-formed sheet steel. The hollow pilot runs cooler and does not have the same tendency to burn the wood as do typical high-speed bits with solid pilots.

The sheet-metal bits cut surprisingly well, to a maximum depth of cut of 1/8 inch. Typical prices range from $1.50 to $5.50 per bit, depending upon style and local pricing. These bits are sold under the Dura-Sharp trade name.

European-Style Safety Bits The safety-design commission in West Germany (known as Holtzberufsgenossenschaft), which tests and recommends safety measures for the protection of operators using hand-held routers, has developed a new safety-bit design that limits the amount of feed into the wood per revolution to 1/32-inch (1.5-mm) per cutting edge and makes it impossible for the bit to dangerously pull the router into the work. (See Illus. 20.) This concept should find good markets, and should be especially popular with woodwork-

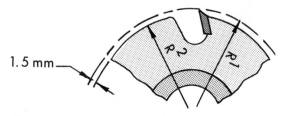

Illus. 20. *The safety bit. This illustration shows how the depth of cut per edge is limited to ½₃₂ inch (1.5 mm) per revolution.*

ing beginners and in educational institutions where maximum safety procedures are desirable.

A new "Truk" shank bit furnished by Byrom International should not be taken lightly. A side-by-side comparison of the heavy-duty 5/16-inch diameter "Truk" shank and the standard ¼-inch shank diameter reveals great differences in design. (See Illus. 21.) The "Truk" shank bit design has merit, especially when the bit is used with the larger-diameter and heavier edge-forming bits. The larger 5/16-inch shank obviously carries a heavier feeding load while reducing vibration and chatter. Bits with 5/16-inch shanks have become widely used in Europe (as 8-mm shanks), where they are, according to Byrom, the standard for portable hand-held routers.

Illus. 21. *The new safety bit on the right, by Byrom International, has several unique features. It has a Teflon™ coating and a 5/16-inch (8-mm)-diameter "truk" shank. Compare it to the conventional ¼-inch shanked bit on the left.*

Teflon®-Coated router bits These bits are another promising concept. (See Illus. 21 and 22.) We know that the Teflon used on frying pans prevents anything from sticking to their surfaces. This coating also keeps wood pitch and glues from adhering and building up on the bit, and allows the chips to flow freely from the bit as it cuts, which eliminates the need to clean bits often. It's reported that skilled router operators feel an easier cutting action.

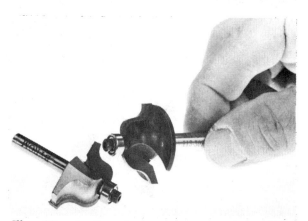

Illus. 22. *Another view comparing a typical carbide-tipped Roman Ogee, at left, to Byrom International's new carbide-tipped safety bit with truk shank (5/16 inch) and Teflon coating.*

Adjustable Router Bits These types of bits have just been developed. The bit shown in Illus. 23 is one of three that come in different adjustment ranges. One bit adjusts from ½ to ¾ inch, another from 5/8 to 7/8 inch, and the largest bit adjusts from ¾ to 1 inch.

With just a turn of the adjustment gear, you can increase or decrease the cutting diameter of your bit. It's easy to make a routed dado, groove, or mortise accommodate the exact size of the lumber thickness, which makes it easy to make perfect fits when you work various materials like vinyl and laminate overlay materials.

This tool consists of a single-edge carbide-tipped bit unit complete on an arbor with a worm-gear drive adjustment, counterbalance,

Illus. 23.   This adjustable router bit comes as a complete unit, as shown. It has a single carbide-tipped cutting edge on an arbor with counterbalance and a modified collet that fits some Porter Cable routers and some older and equivalent Rockwell models.

wrenches, and modified collet, that fits most heavy-duty Rockwell and Porter-Cable routers. It is available from Safranek Enterprises Inc., of Atascadero, California.

Large Bits   Large bits of various cutting configurations, as shown in Illus. 24–26, are available in many profiles, and are apparently selling well. However, I regard them as extremely dangerous. It is quite possible to misuse them. Many of these huge bits have cutting diameters of well over 3 inches with some cutting to almost 4 inches, and they certainly cannot be used on conventional hand-held routers!

The first really large bits were the panel raisers. The larger the bit, the more that is revealed on the raised panel and the more professional the finished project looks, two reasons why these large bits are becoming so popular. They are used to make the router do the work of a shaper, an idea many experts openly question. If you decide to use them, be extremely careful; use the appropriate fix-

turing in a router table, take shallow cuts at a slower RPM, and pay attention throughout the job. Refer to Chapter 4 for a discussion of more panel-raising bits, and review pages 68–70 before purchasing or using large panel-raising bits.

Some domestic manufacturers I've spoken to concerning the possible hazards associated with the large bits refuse to manufacture them. They limit the maximum cutting-edge diameters on their bits to five times the shank diameter. In other words, a $1/2$-inch shank on a bit used by the general woodworking public (which includes both "weekenders" and professionals) would only carry a $2\frac{1}{2}$-inch-diameter bit.

Just to give you an idea of how potentially dangerous these large bits are, let's look at the following examples: The cutting edge of a $3\frac{3}{4}$-inch-diameter bit rotating at 22,000 RPM travels at 245.5 miles per hour. The speed of the cutting edge of the same bit traveling at 24,000 RPM increases to 268 miles per hour. As a comparison, a tooth on a 10-inch-diameter saw

Illus. 24. This 3-wing panel-raising bit, available from Xylophiles Company of Lexington, Kentucky, has a 3½-inch-diameter cutting circle and a ½-inch shank. Note how large it is compared to the quarter.

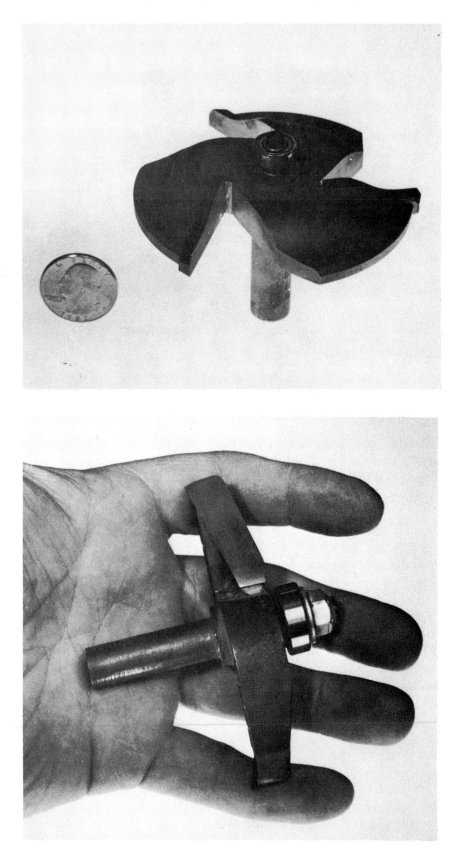

Illus. 25. Here's an even larger panel-raising bit that has a 3¾-inch cutting circle. (See Illus. 105, page 69). Just looking at this bit should suggest extreme caution when using it.

Illus. 26. Here a big round-over bit from True-Cut Saw and Tool Company of Hamilton, Montana, that cuts a whopping 1½-inch radius on a ½-inch shank.

blade typically moves at a speed of around 113 miles per hour. Imagine holding onto a tool that has a cutting force of more than twice that of a rotating 10-inch saw blade.

Large diameter bits require larger shanks, heavier machines (heavy-duty routers), and much slower RPM's (routing speeds) than most hand-held routers normally provide. If using these big bits, I strongly recommend a router such as the Porter-Cable model 518, which is a 5-speed, 3-horsepower heavy-duty router. This router has speed options ranging from 10,000 to 22,000 RPM, with settings of 13, 16, and 19,000 RPM in between. Refer to page 11 for more information on this router. Also, see Chapter 28, which describes a router table designed to hold a router unit of this size and capabilities.

2

Bit Quality

With the number of domestic and worldwide router-bit manufacturers and importers growing at such a rapid pace, one might think all of this competition would be good for the woodworking consumer. What is happening is that reputable, brand-name manufacturers, who are trying to improve the performance and durability of their bits through continuous research and testing while simultaneously fighting off the competition of lower-priced, low-quality imitations, are now finding themselves in tenuous situations. Frankly, I think these manufacturers deserve our support and business.

I've always felt that a tool is a good value if it is well made—quality is more important than cost. Another important consideration is my personal safety. How do I know that the less expensive bit is not made from low-grade steel or carbide with an internal flaw that might cause the bit to snap during normal use? Poor-metal quality and inferior workmanship can make a bit dangerous. Reputable manufacturers use certified metals, have stringent inspection and testing standards for the raw materials, and test the end product.

Some very inferior-quality bits are being made and sold today. Most woodworkers buying these bit are being victimized because they are only considering expense instead of quality

and safety. In fact, most woodworkers do not know what we are buying in terms of bit quality. It's difficult to tell the quality of a bit simply with a casual look at the tool. For example, how do you really know you are getting good-quality steel when you buy a new router bit, or a new saw or chisel for that matter? Unless you actually use the tool for a fair amount of time, grind it, or subject it to microanalysis, you really don't know how good the raw material actually is.

Sales representatives usually are not trained woodworkers, and they certainly are not the tool manufacturer. In fact, they often do not know the best cutting tool for specific applications. Their recommendations to the retailer, your local supplier, and eventually to the woodworking consumer are based only on the names, numbers, and prices in a catalogue. Sadly, all too often price is the only factor determining whether or not a supplier will carry a line of bits. If the retailer can sell a tool for less than his competition, and make a higher profit regardless of its quality or whether it is the best tool for that particular job, he will.

In this chapter I will point out and discuss the features in a bit you should understand when determining bit "quality."

Comparing Bits If you were to place two bits of the same general size and type side by side, you would not notice very obvious differences between them. In Illus. 27, two brand-new bits are compared. They look very much alike, and have the following identical specifications: they are $\frac{1}{4}$-inch carbide-tipped, and have a 2-inch flute, 1-inch cutting length, and $2\frac{3}{8}$-inch overall length. One bit is of American manufacture and the other is an Asian import.

However, a closer look at the import reveals the following deficiencies: (1), the cutting-edge length is actually $\frac{1}{8}$ inch short, as is the overall length; (2), the braze is insufficient to the point where it is dangerous (Illus. 28); (3), the shank is .00075 out of round and undersized; (4), the carbide is unsupported at the cutting tips, and thus very fragile; (5) the carbide is much thinner, reducing the number of times it can be sharpened; (6), there is pitted steel in the flute of the import; and (7), the ends of the carbide tipping are not ground for vertical plunge-entry cutting, which is certain to cause strain, overheating, and premature dulling. Illus. 29 reveals some of these deficiencies.

The American-made bit shown in Illus. 27 has been hardened, vapor-blasted, and then ground at the face and relief side. Vapor-blasting of the shank actually roughens it so that it grabs (holds) better in the collet than a smoothly ground shank. The import (assuming it has been properly tempered) has been ground to cutting-edge sharpness and to bring the shank to within its size tolerance.

Although the illustrations do not show it, one can visually observe that coarser-grit abrasive was used to grind the back of the carbide edge on the import bit. This leaves a microscopic, ragged cutting edge, even if the faces of the carbide on both bits appear to be equally honed with fine-grit abrasive.

It's difficult to detect with the naked eye if 180-, 220-, grit, or finer abrasives have been used in sharpening a bit. Coarse-abrasive dia-

Illus. 27. Two $\frac{1}{4}$-inch carbide-tipped bits that at first glance appear to be similar in quality. The upper one is an American-made bit, and the lower one is an Asian import.

Illus. 29. Still another look at the tips and flutes. Note that the carbide is not supported at the tips, leaving it fragile and dangerous at these points.

Illus. 28 (left). Another look at these same bits. Note the braze of the import carbide bit on the left. It has voids, is rough, and is irregular.

mond wheels will cut faster. Was the bit ground with the recommended 500-to-600-grit abrasive? Illus. 30 compares two edge grindings at 60 times magnification. One bit is a low-quality Asian import, and the other a high-quality United-States-made bit. Illus. 31 compares two other carbide grindings at 100 times magnification, and shows that differences in edge finishes of new bits do exist.

Incidentally, when you send out bits for sharpening, insist that they be finished with 400–600-grit abrasive, and that the grinding be done with coolant or on a "flood"-type grinder. Wet-grinding eliminates any chance of heat buildup and thermal expansion that might cause minute cracking.

Unless a bit is chipped or nicked, it is not necessary to remove a lot of carbide thickness.

A dull cutter, if properly indexed in the grinder, can be resharpened without removing more than .008 inch (20 mm).

In addition to the qualities that we can see with the naked eye, there are many other unobservable qualities that are of primary importance. First of all, a good bit needs high-quality, inspected steel. Proper steel heat-treating is a special skill and, actually, a precise operation that achieves maximum hardness and toughness. Unfortunately, you cannot determine steel quality just by looking at a bit.

Subtle changes in grinding angles (tool geometry) can have a dramatic effect on tool performance. (Illus. 32 gives basic bit geometries.) Lower geometry on the rake angle can make a bit difficult to feed. In such cases, weaker tools are likely to bend or break when used.

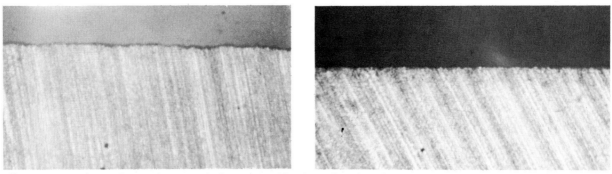

Illus. 30 A and B. Comparing, at 60 times magnification, the edge-sharpness grinding of an imported bit, left, to a creep-grinding technique, right, by Onsrud Cutter.

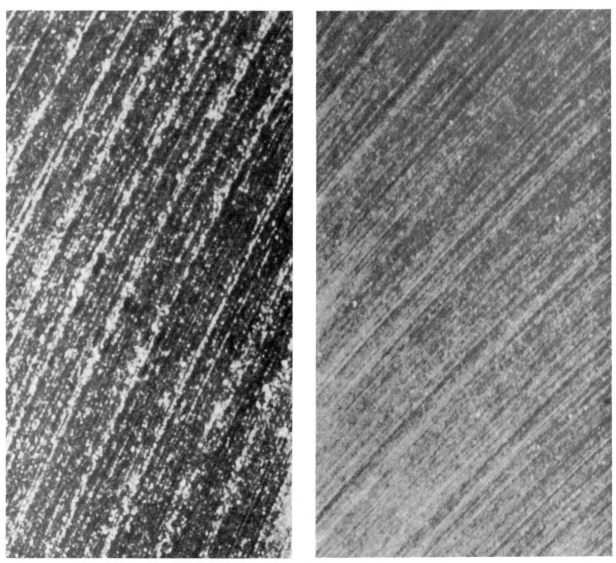

Illus. 31. This 100 times magnification compares 600-grit diamond-edge honing, at right, to conventional grinding with coarser abrasives. (Courtesy of Bosch Power Tools.)

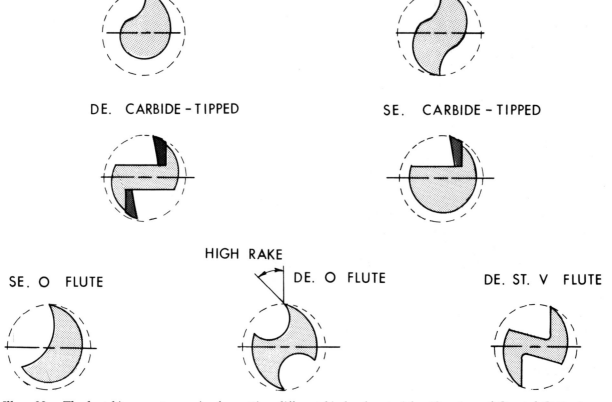

Illus. 32. The best bit geometry varies for cutting different kinds of materials. (Courtesy of Onsrud Cutter.)

Some other factors that comprise good bit design include the following:

1. Good clearance and relief grinding without weakening the tool. This prevents the bit from riding or rubbing in the cut, and eliminates the heat from friction that shortens bit life.
2. Smooth, polished flute finish to provide for maximum chip discharge.
3. Cutting edges concentric with shank and body of the bit to eliminate "whipping action."
4. Optimum hook (rake) angle to permit aggressive feeding where necessary.
5. Optimum flute-area design for maximum chip flow.
6. Optimum relationship between cutting-edge length and cutting-edge diameter. (A 3- or 4:to:1 ratio of cutting-edge length to shank diameter is the *maximum* (a ratio of 2:1 is recommended).
7. Optimum ratio between shank diameter and cutting-edge diameter (The cutting-edge diameter normally should not exceed more than five times the shank diameter.)
8. Perfect shank roundness. Out-of-round shanks inhibit good chucking and can cause "bit whip"—a vibrating action that is extremely dangerous, especially when considering normal speeds of 20,000 RPM and more.
9. Attention to end sharpness and end-cutting geometry to permit free vertical-plunge entry into the workpiece.

Proper grinding must also be skillfully employed to ensure that the material is not burned; burning actually restructures the steel during manufacturing.

Carbide Grades and Quality of Material The grade of the carbide or quality of the material used vary substantially from manufacturer to manufacturer. Router bits may be made from solid carbide, or from tool steel tipped with carbides; classified as C-2, C-3, C-4, C-5, etc. The problem is that within each grade or classification there can be a vast difference in quality. In other words, there is standard and substandard C-2 carbide, standard and substandard C-3 carbide, etc.

There are some things you should know about carbide grades. First, as the number of the carbide increases from C-2 to C-3 and up, the material becomes harder; however, it also becomes increasingly brittle. C-2 is a good general-purpose grade that can be brazed easily. C-4 is much more difficult to braze, so C-4 tooling for high-speed routing could be extremely dangerous if the brazing fails. The essential differences between C-2, C-3, and C-4 have to do more with the mixtures of materials than the grain sizes of carbide powders.

Considerable differences in carbide-material qualities can be observed when studying carbide microstructure. The specific quality of carbide is best determined by examining its microstructure, which can be correlated to the eventual performance quality of the tool. The examination is best done at a magnification of 1,500. Illus. 33 shows some very high-quality micrograin carbide inspected at a magnification of 1,500. Compare this structure to the magnification of cheaper, lower quality carbides shown in Illus. 34 and 35. Coarse-carbide structure and free carbon in the carbide make it difficult to achieve a keenly sharp edge, regardless of how fine or precise the sharpening equipment might be, plus, edge life will be substandard due to these conditions.

High-speed steel and carbide-bit performance can be further improved for certain cutting jobs with the addition of some special coatings. For example, Diamond Black™ improves bit performance when some aluminum materials are being cut. Titanium Nitrate (TiN), which gives high-speed steel bits

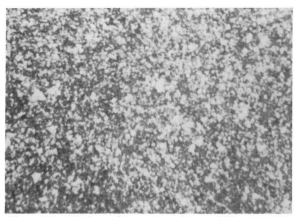

Illus. 33. High-quality micrograin carbide at 1,500 times magnification. (Photo courtesy of Onsrud Cutter.)

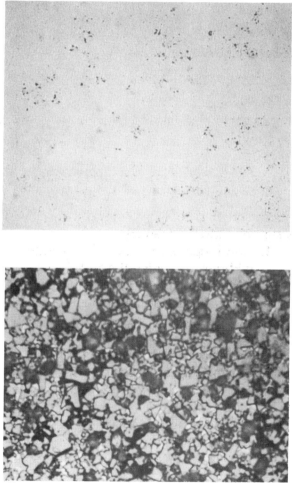

Illus. 34 A and B. Cheap carbide with excessive porosity due to carbon deficiency is shown at 100 times enlargement, above, and at 1,500 times enlargement, below. (Photos courtesy of Onsrud Cutter.)

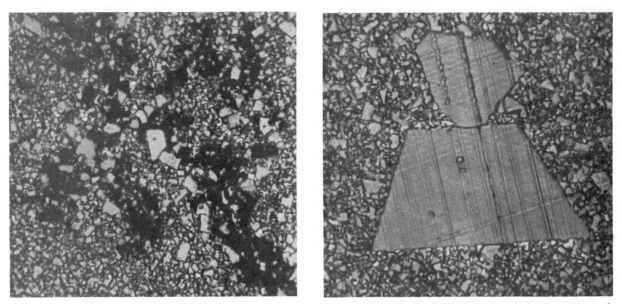

Illus. 35. Examples of substandard carbide composition enlarged 1,500 times shows coarse carbide structure and free carbon crystals. (Photo courtesy of Onsrud Cutter.)

a gold-colored appearance, improves the edge durability of tooling used for routing ferrous metals. One common application is in routing openings in metal-covered doors. A boride coating is a carbide-tool treatment used to improve the cutting quality of tools in very hard and fibrous materials.

As you can tell from what you have just read, we are now in the era of high-tech tooling. The reasons for the preceding discussion are not to confuse or frighten you, the would-be purchaser of router bits, but rather to make you aware of all that is happening in the field that plays a part in the production of quality bits. Use this information as a guideline when determining what bits to buy.

3
Selecting Bits

Now that you know what goes into making a quality bit, the next step is selecting the right type to use. One recent survey revealed that approximately 40 percent of those using router bits did not select the right type of router bit for the kind of work material being cut. If true, these are astonishing figures, because almost four out of every 10 woodworkers is not getting the optimum performance from his router or experiencing full satisfaction from woodworking.

I do know from personal experience that changing to a different kind of bit can make a dramatic difference. For example, I quickly found that the upcutting spirals of high-speed steel bits cut grooves in hard wood cleaner and easier than standard two-flute carbide-tipped bits. And high-speed steel is much less expensive. In fact, the cutting performance of good, high-speed steel bits has been grossly overlooked since the introduction of carbide-tipped tooling. They can be sharpened to a keener edge than carbide, and HSS bits will hold their keen edge longer when you machine most hard woods and aluminums, and many plastics.

The bit-selecting process can be very confusing because there are so many styles and kinds of bits to choose from. To further complicate things, there are even more new materials available today that can be routed if you have the right tooling.

Selecting or using the wrong bit type usually results in a "short life" for the bit; it may be dulled or it may be inadvertently destroyed. There is a lot of difference between dulling a bit and destroying it. Dulling means it can be resharpened, but a destroyed bit is economically beyond repair. A cheap bit is more easily destroyed if it is used in the wrong application. It may deflect (bend), break, chip, or quickly over-heat, changing it's metallurgical composition so that it will never hold a new edge.

To select the right type of bit to use, you have to understand some of the essentials of the bit geometry options you will choose from. The number and type of flute, the material composition, and the kind of edge (straight, shear, or spiral) are the primary considerations. Some of the common abbreviations for describing router bits are given in Table 1. Illus. 36 graphically compares some of the flute-design options in both high-speed steel and carbide tooling.

Onsrud Cutter, of Libertyville, Illinois, publishes an informative pamphlet that includes excellent advice on tool selection and

Router Bit Abbreviations

HSS	High-Speed Steel	DE	Double Edge
CT	Carbide-Tipped	ST	Straight Flute
SC	Solid Carbide	SP	Spiral Flute
CED	Cutting Edge Diameter	V	Flute
CEL	Cutting Edge Length	O	Flute
SE	Single Edge		

Table 1. Abbreviations frequently used by manufacturers to describe bit structure and geometric function.

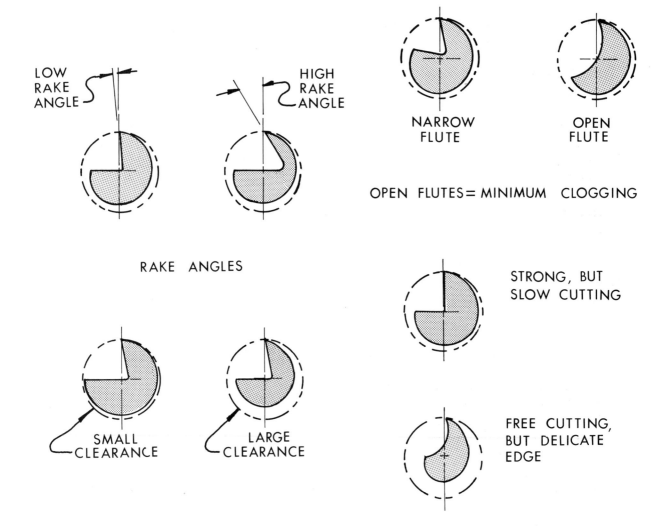

Illus. 36. Design functions of rake angles, clearances, and flutes. (Adapted from drawings by H.M. Staats, Onsrud Cutter Company.)

use. The following are some of the essential points presented in that publication:

1. Use HSS bits for aluminum, natural woods, and most acrylic plastics.
2. Use CT (carbide-tipped) bits for laminated and composition-wood materials, and for machining other abrasive- or resin-based products.
3. Use solid carbide bits for cutting small diameters and where the bit is exposed to hotter cutting conditions.

   Special coatings such as diamond, boride, etc., should only be considered when economics warrants it.
4. Use single-edge tooling when feeding speeds are more important than the finished-cut quality.
5. Use double-edge bits when the finished-cut quality is the important consideration.
6. Use upcut spirals for grooving and slotting or where fast chip removal is required.
7. Use downcut spirals when cutting completely through the thickness of the material and when you want the chip-flow direction to be away from the operator.
8. For natural woods, use HSS spiral-, straight-, or sheer-edge bits.
9. Use spiral, straight, or shear carbide bits for composites, particle board, plywood, and MDF (medium-density fibreboard).
10. Use shear-cutting edge-tooling when problems with the quality of the finished cut arise or when your router is undersized in horsepower.
11. Always use bits with the shortest possible cutting-edge length.
12. Always use bits with the largest shank diameter possible.
13. Only use adapter bushings to reduce collet size for short-run jobs, not for production-routing.
14. When possible, use a coolant when routing. Heat caused by the friction between the tool edge and workpiece plays the greatest part in curtailing tool life.
15. The denser the material, the faster the feed rate should be to minimize heat. Use the fastest possible feed in particle board, fibreboard, and plywood.
16. Proper rake and clearance angles are as important to good cutting as cutting-edge sharpness.
17. Larger cutting-edge diameters require larger shank diameters.
18. Small-diameter router bits have limited clearance and chip-removal capacities (because of the size of the tool). Avoid overfeeding of all bits, which can result in overloading the bits, which, in turn, can cause the bits to bend or break.

Remember that all materials are not equal. Some brands of particle boards, for example, may have higher levels of abrasive impurities imbedded in the composite than other brands. This can affect tool-edge durability. Remember, the quality of the cut surface is always important. Also, practical feeds and speeds must always be a consideration in tool use. However, when cutting tough materials, remember that the faster the feed, the longer the edge stays sharp. The cutting edges should contact the workpiece as seldom as possible.

In the selection process you should take into consideration all of the factors involved in the total routing process, and make compromises. The type and kind of bit-driving force—namely, the router itself—is a fixed, but critical, element. The RPM, horsepower, collet size, and integrity (accuracy, holding ability, etc., of the router) must all be considered, along with the kind of material to be cut, the width, length, and depth of cut, the feed method or feed rate, vertical-plunging entry requirements, the type of fixturing involved and other nonstandard conditions unique to the job at hand.

Table 2 is a router-bit selection chart that provides a list of routable materials and various

Table 2. Router bit selection chart.

Solid Woods		Plywoods & Composites	Plastics			Aluminum		Brass, Copper & Bronze
Softer, Lower Densities	Heavier, Denser Hard woods		Softer	Medium Hard, Rigid	Tough, Fibrous	Soft	Medium to Hard	
Pine Butternut Redwood Willow & Similar Species	Birch Cherry Maple Oak Walnut Teak & Similar Woods	Hardboards Plywoods *Particle Boards MDF (Medium-Density Fibre-boards) & Similar Materials	ABS Polycarbonate (Lexan) Polystyrenes PVC	Acrylics (Plexiglas®, etc.) Nylon Melamine (Decor. Laminates) PVC	Aramid Carbon Epoxy Fibreglass & Similar Materials			
HSS, SE O Flute HSS, DE V Flute *HSS, SE Spiral HSS, DE Spiral	HSS, DE V Flute ST or Shear Edge CT, DE V Flute SC, DE, ST or Spiral HSS, DE, or SE Spirals	CT, DE, ST Flute & Spirals or Shear Edge SC, DE, ST Flute SC, SE, ST Flute SC, SE, DE or Multiple Flute	HSS, SE O Flute HSS, DE, O Flute SC, SE, O Flute	HSS, DE V Flute CT, SE, V Flute CT, DE, V Flute SC, DE, V Flute	CT, SE, V Flute CT, DE, V Flute SC, 3-Edge ST Flute SC Burrs	HSS, SE O Flute HSS, DE Spiral	HSS, SE Spiral HSS, DE Spiral	HSS, SE V Flute SC, DE Spiral
The cedars dull steel bits quickly. *Preferred by experienced woodworkers.	Good horsepower required. Continuous feed. HSS bits can be ground to a keener edge than carbide.	Use fastest feeds possible to minimize heat. Use shortest CEL. Largest shank diameter possible. *Bit design should provide for quick chip removal (O Flute preferred).	SE for faster feed. DE for smoother cut. Slower feed may improve finish.	Make deep cuts in multiple passes. Generally should cut at 150 inches per min. Use SE for slower feeds.	Some materials may require special tooling.	Soft alloys do not cut easily. Use coolant mist, slower rpm. Spirals get chips out quickly to disperse heat.	Harder aluminum cuts easier than soft. Use faster feed & short CEL.	Cut thin mtls. sandwiched between wood. Deep cuts in thick mtls. require air & mist coolant.

recommended bit styles. First, select the type of material or materials you intend to be routing. Check the suggested bit-type alternatives listed under each material. (See Illus. 37 and 38.) Decide whether you want to use single- or double-edge bits. This is a personal

Illus. 38. Some bit configurations for cutting plastics. (Photo courtesy of Onsrud Cutter.)

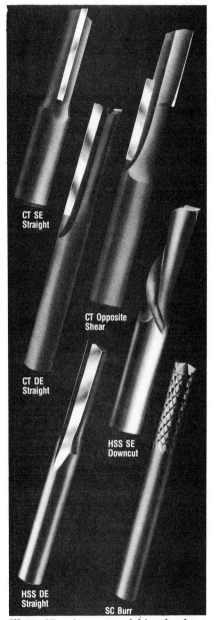

Illus. 37. A group of bits for boat-building materials includes those for cutting aluminum, plywoods, hardwoods, and fibreglass. (Photo courtesy of Onsrud Cutter.)

preference based on your individual requirements; for example, you would use a single-edge bit for faster feeding, and to reduce heat at slower feed rates, and use a double-edge bit to cut surfaces smoother.

Next, decide whether you want to use a HS steel or carbide bit. You would use HS steel for a higher quality of cut surface, and carbide for longer tool life. Finally, determine if the bit can be used for secondary jobs. What other materials are routable with it? For example, you may want to exchange the quality of cut surface on some hard woods that is normally provided by HSS bits for an overall longer bit life provided by a carbide bit.

If the job is a production-type where routing of many identical cuts in identical materials is the objective, it may be necessary to test more than one of the bits given in the group under the material heading in Table 2.

Research on Bit-Dulling Unfortunately, there is no one "super bit" that cuts all materials, stays incredibly sharp forever without servicing, and fits all types and kinds of routers. The prudent woodworking consumer will buy the best bit currently available that, in his judgement, gives him the best-quality job for the price.

New research is challenging some of the established reasons offered for why the best bits dull. An understanding of this information may be of interest and value to you. If you're in a production situation, you may even find it worthwhile and profitable to change your choice of wood material; or, new findings may stimulate you to purchase materials to certain specifications.

As the tool dulls, there is, obviously, a breakdown of the tool material. (See Illus. 39.) It's also apparent that this happens more quickly when routing some types of materials more so than when routing others.

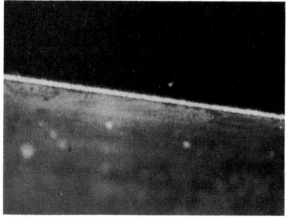

Illus. 39. A worn edge, at 50 times magnification, that resulted from cutting only 2,000 linear inches of MDF (medium-density fibreboard). (Photo courtesy of Onsrud Cutter.)

We have generally assumed that dulling is caused by the abrasive nature of the material. For example, the resins and other components in particle board, fibreboard, and plywood are typically regarded as high-abrasion material. But research by technologist Harold Stewart of the U.S.D.A. Forest Service Laboratory, and tool manufacturers, indicates that tool-edge breakdown is a combination of mechanical abrasion, adhesion, diffusion, fatigue, and corrosion. Even certain chemicals that are found in the water used in adhesive manufacture and used in the production of composite boards can affect the rate of tool-edge wear.

Heat is a major factor. Machining wood is more difficult that machining other materials because wood is such a good insulator. Wood traps and holds the heat at the cutting edge, whereas, when machining metal, for example, the heat is conducted away from cutting action by the metal material itself.

Stewart learned that temperatures in the cutting area can reach 1,000 degrees Celsius! Material heated to these high temperatures undergoes chemical reactions, specifically what is known as "hot corrosion." With carbide tools, a chemical reaction takes place that changes the chemical makeup of the tool-edge material itself. In some test results, the material on the cutting edge was even transformed into a molten state.

Continuing research is needed to determine which species of woods and what additives in adhesives used for the manufacture of wood-composite boards contain chemicals that react with tool materials and cause this chemical breakdown of the cutting edge.

What can the average woodworker do about all this? Not a whole lot, but he can select tools that get the chips out quickly and, consequently, disperse the heat away from the cutting zone, instead of having to recut the chips over and over while they remain in the cutting area. He can also reduce cutting speeds and increase feeds where appropriate to reduce heat. Maybe bits like the ceramic ones discussed on page 20 can one day be used to serve the needs of average woodworkers. These ceramic bits were used for research and development because they have good resistance to high temperature and chemical breakdown. What the future holds is always uncertain, but it is never uninteresting.

4

Special Router Bits

Today there are many more router-bit designs than there were just a few years ago. And new cutting designs and shapes are being developed at a brisk pace. Many of these new bits are "specials" designed to make cuts that in the past were normally done on the spindle shaper. The most popular new bits are the raised panel sets; they include the self-matching stile-and-rail cope cutters and panel raiser, and are offered in number of profile options and combinations. I will explore some of the basic raised-panel systems available, and illustrate different setups involved for their use.

In addition to raised-panel and moulding-edged door-frames systems, there are bits available that will cut all sorts of special joints. These include tooling for making professional drawer joints and finger-joint bits with which you can join wood end to end. There are special glue-joint bits, lock-mitre-joint bits, and bits for making staves for hot tubs and canoe hull strips. There are even bits to "dish"-out trays or plates, and special bits to "stand-up" sign letters in relief or carve them into the background. You will even find some improvements among the familiar standard cutting tools such as trimmers, rabbeting bits, etc.

Just a few words of warning before you purchase some of the expensive, special self-matching bits, such as the "lock-mitre" bits: Some bits of this type can only be sharpened one to three times before they are no longer useful. Every time the bit is sharpened, the "male" cut of the bit grows and the "female" cut shrinks, because of the relief required. Normally, bits with 2 mm of carbide can be sharpened five to eight times, which equates to hundreds of hours in total tool life. (A careless grinding, however, can possibly reduce the overall life of a typical bit by as much as 50 percent, or more.) Consequently, those very expensive bits that demand very critical sharpenings should be given extra-special care and sent only to the best sharpening service available.

The majority of the bits shown in this chapter have been photographed with a 25-cent United States coin that serves as a size reference. Other drawings of bits were provided by Rob Van Nieuwenhuizen, of Furnima Industrial Carbide, Barry's Bay, Ontario, Canada. These drawings are reproduced in full size.

You will note that using large bits requires special precautions, and many of those illustrated should not be used in the typical light-weight, low-horsepower, high-speed router that's designed only to carry bits of smaller sizes.

Illus. 40–104 are included as an overview of the newest "special" bits available today; many of them should whet the interest of all woodworkers. And, if by chance you don't see that certain bit you need, there are companies that specialize in making one-of-a kind bits for a particular job or cutting profile.

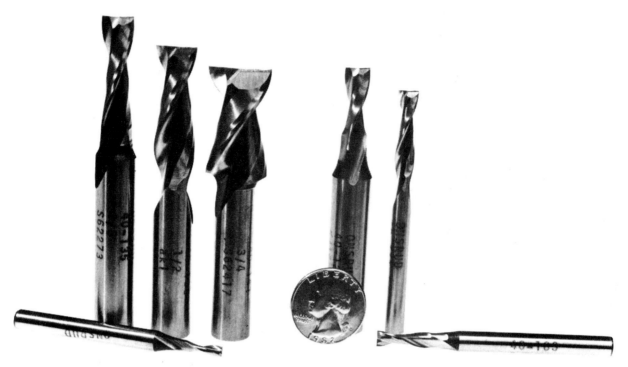

Illus. 40.   Though not all new, this set of HSS double-edge spirals, by Onsrud Cutter, is highly recommended for a variety of grooving, slotting, and mortising jobs.

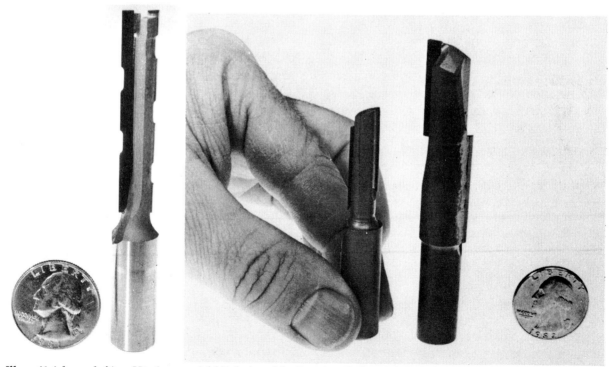

Illus. 41 (above left).   Here's a special bit designed by Furnima Industrial Carbide for cutting deep slot mortises.
Illus. 42 (above right). A couple of stagger-tooth bits, ⅜ and ½-inch, by True-Cut Saw and Tool Company.

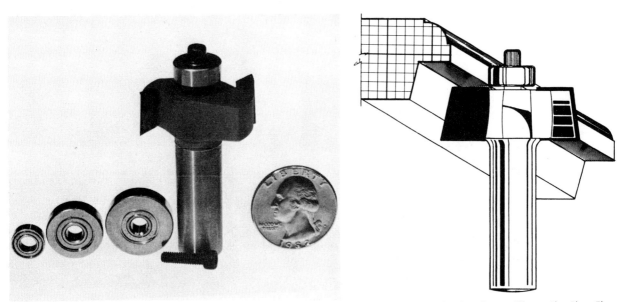

Illus. 43 (above left). Amana Tool Company's rabbet bit with interchangeable pilot bearings will cut ¼-, ⁵⁄₁₆-, ⅞-, and ⁷⁄₁₆-inch rabbet widths. Illus. 44 (above right). A door-lip edge-forming bit by Furnima.

Illus. 45. Rabbeting bit from Paso Robles Carbide, Inc., has interchangeable cutters which cut ⅛-, ¼-, ⅜-, and ½-inch rabbets using the same arbor and ball-bearing pilot. Note the hex-shaped drive that eliminates slippage.

Illus. 46. Assembly detail of Paso Robles Carbide's interchangeable pattern bits on its universal arbor.

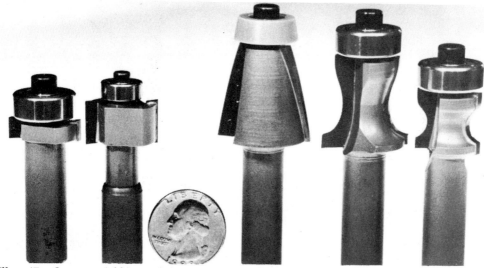

Illus. 47.   Some special bits made by True-Cut Saw and Tool Company for routing Corian® counter-topping material. The two bits on left are for making face inlays. (Various widths and depths are available.)The 10- degree bevel bit with taper bearing for Corian® sink-top application and the two bits at right are for "non-drip" edges on Corian® counter tops.

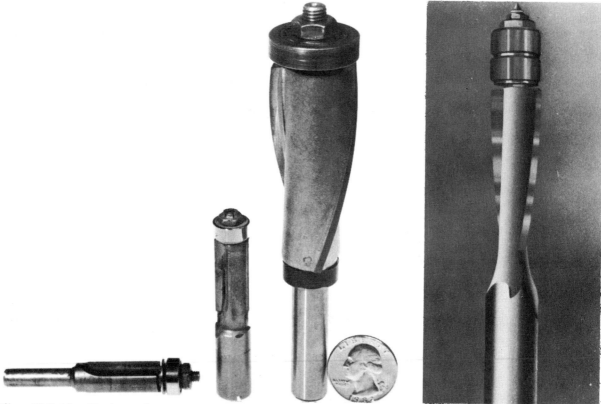

Illus. 48 (left).   Design and growth changes in the ballbearing flush-trim bit. At left: Typical ¼- and ½-inch shank sizes. At right: a heavy-duty face-frame bit manufactured by Paso Robles Carbide in Paso Robles, California, that has a 1⅛-inch cutting diameter, with a cutting-edge length of 2½ inches, and a ½-inch-diameter shank. Illus. 49 (right). A solid-shank carbide spiral trimmer bit by Paso Robles Carbide has a ½-inch-diameter shank and 1½-inch cutting-edge length.

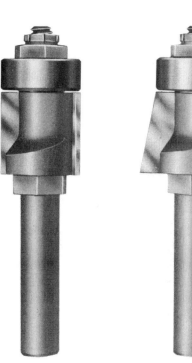

Illus. 50 (left).   Throw-away trimmer bits by Paso Robles Carbide, Inc. These inexpensive, replaceable carbide 2-wing cutters are mounted on hex-drive arbors. When the cutter is dull, throw it away. Illus. 51 (above). A special collar from Byrom International secures shank-mounted bearings.

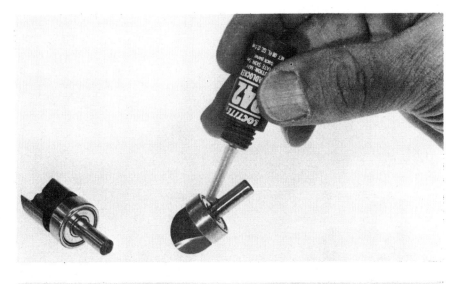

Illus. 52.   A drop of Locktite® (available from most hardware dealers) will hold bearings in place on the shank above the cutter.

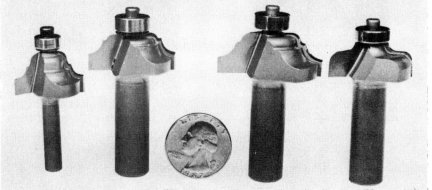

Illus. 53.   Some basic edge-forming bits from True-Cut Saw and Tool Company.

43

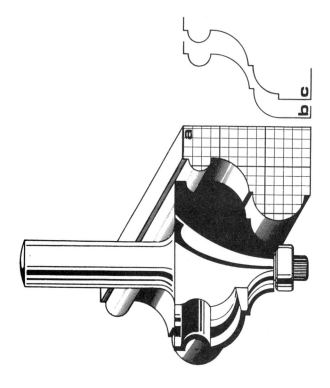

Illus. 54 (left). A basic ogee bit changes the profile cut when you are substituting a smaller diameter bearing. (Drawing courtesy of Furnima Industrial Carbide.)

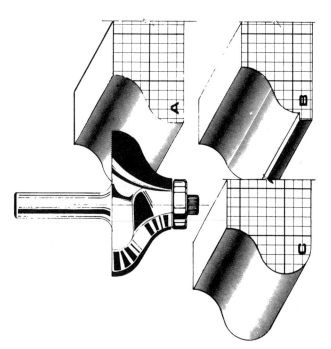

Illus. 55 (right). Furnima Industrial Carbide's French provincial classic bit cuts three bold profiles, as shown. Profile C requires a different, smaller bearing.

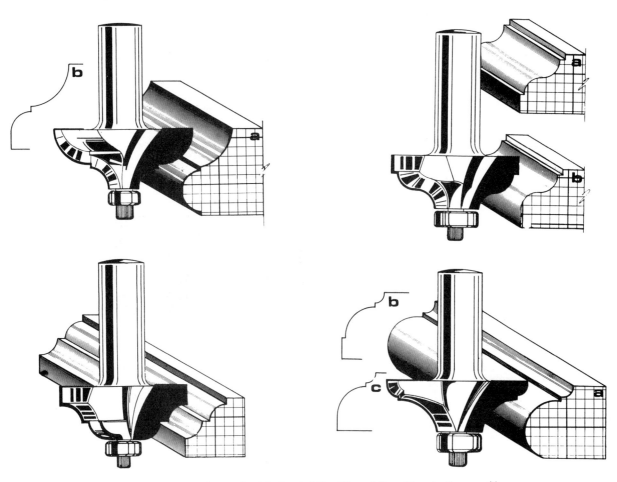

Illus. 56.   More of Furnima's French provincial classic bits. These bits will cut other profiles when used with interchangeable bearings.

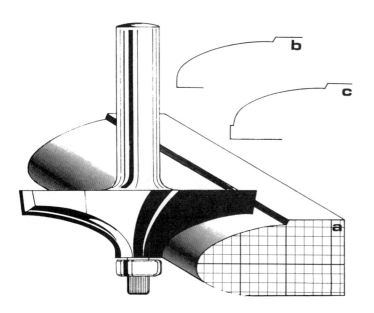

Illus. 57.   Furnima's "thumbnail" bit cuts traditional tabletop edges from either the top only, from the top and bottom, or with an interchangeable bearing, as shown at profile-C, to vary the design.

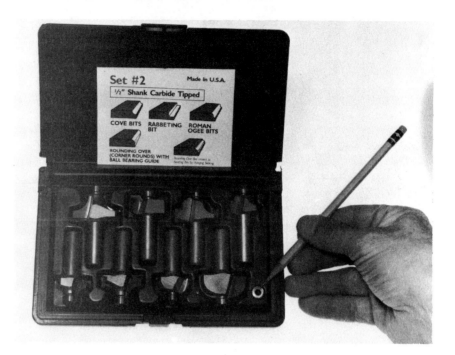

Illus. 58. A set of edge-forming bits from Byrom International comes with interchangeable ballbearings of different sizes to create different profiles.

Illus. 59. Two roundover bits from True-Cut Saw and Tool Company. The bit on the left has a 3½-inch-cutting edge diameter.

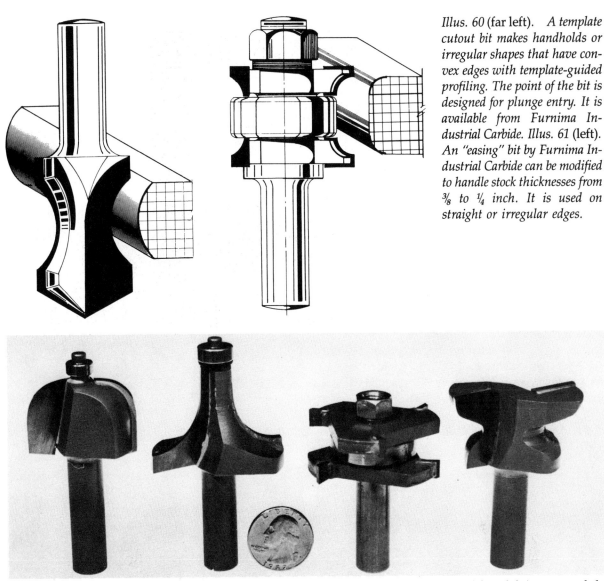

Illus. 60 (far left). A template cutout bit makes handholds or irregular shapes that have convex edges with template-guided profiling. The point of the bit is designed for plunge entry. It is available from Furnima Industrial Carbide. Illus. 61 (left). An "easing" bit by Furnima Industrial Carbide can be modified to handle stock thicknesses from ⅜ to ¼ inch. It is used on straight or irregular edges.

Illus. 62. Some custom standard bits from True-Cut Saw and Tool Company. The second from left is an extended-radius roundover bit. At right are a tongue cutter bit and door-edge bit.

Illus. 63. Half-round bull-nose bits that make external radius cuts.

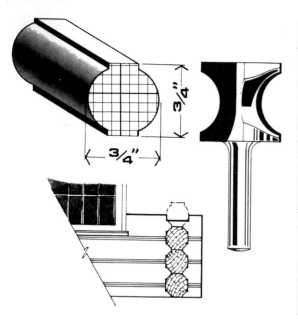

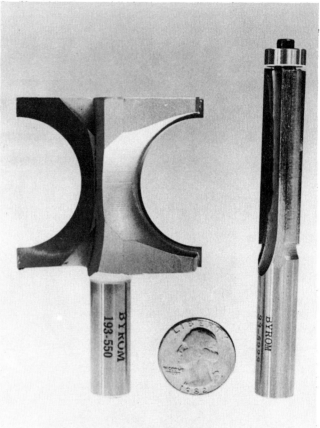

Illus. 64 (above). The Furnima Industrial Carbide toy-log building cutter turns ¾ × ¾-inch scrap stock into mini-building logs. Illus. 65 (right). Two big bits from Byrom International Corporation. At left: bull-nose bit, with a 2¼-inch cutting diameter, that cuts a half round with a ¾-inch radius. At right: A ½-inch-diameter trimming bit, 4 inches overall, with a 2-inch cutting-edge length.

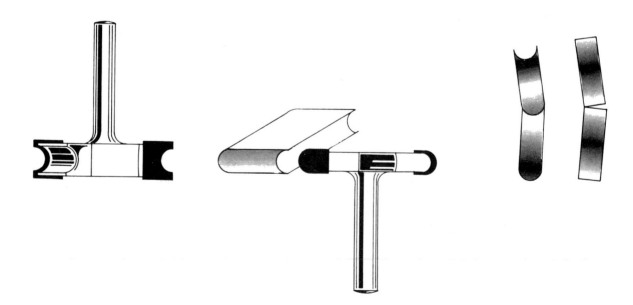

Illus. 66. This canoe strip flute-and-bead-cutter set by Furnima Industrial Carbide prepares ¼-inch-thick strip planking with tight edge joints. Note that the circular edge cuts aid in alignment, and that the flute holds the glue, making it faster and easier to build the strip canoe.

Illus. 67. Another look at Furnima's canoe strip flute-and-bead cutters.

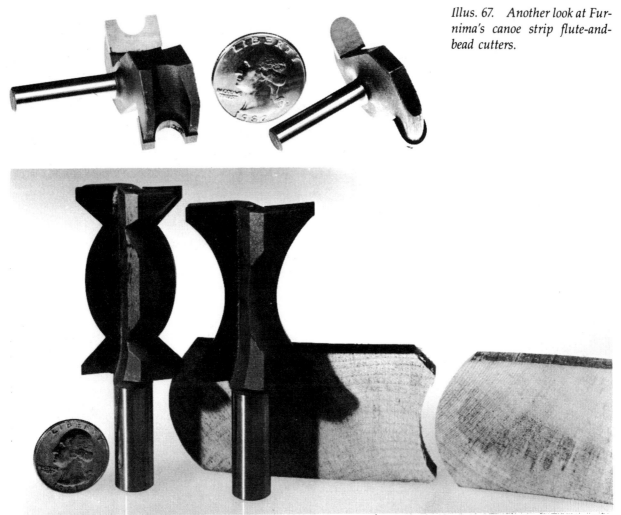

Illus. 68. Two bits that make the matching circular edge joint in the fabrication of staved, circular hot tubs. The stock samples shown are 1¾ inch thick. These bits are available from Furnima Industrial Carbide, Inc.

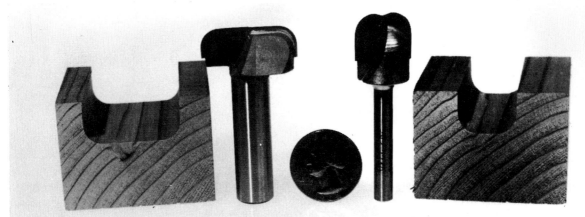

Illus. 69. These dishing bits from Furnima, left, and Byrom International, at right, cut a straight vertical and a flat bottom with a rounded corner, respectively, in one pass. They are useful for trays, boxes, sign-carving, and decorative grooving. Cutting diameters range from ⁷⁄₁₆ and ¾ inch for the Byrom bits to 1 and 1¼ inch for the Furnima bits.

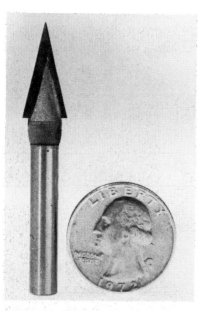

Illus. 70 (left). Sharply pointed carbide bits are available from Furnima Industrial Carbide for incised sign carving. Illus. 71 (above). Structured carbide burrs of the type used for power-carving also work well in routers, but do not produce as smooth a cut surface. These burrs are available in many cutting shapes; most have ¼ inch or smaller shanks.

Illus. 72 (above left). Radius bits from Byrom International have cutting diameters that range from ⅜ inch to the 1¼-inch size shown here. These bits make full inside radius cuts for doors and drawer pulls, etc. Illus. 73 (above right). Freud's Multiform Bit for router-table use cuts 36 standard mouldings. Changing the height of the cut can produce many custom profiles with one or more passes. See Illus. 75 and 76.

Illus. 74 (opposite page). The Furnima 2-bit moulding cutter system comes with instructions for making 52 different profiles, including those shown here. Bits are shown full size, profiles shown at 5% reduction.

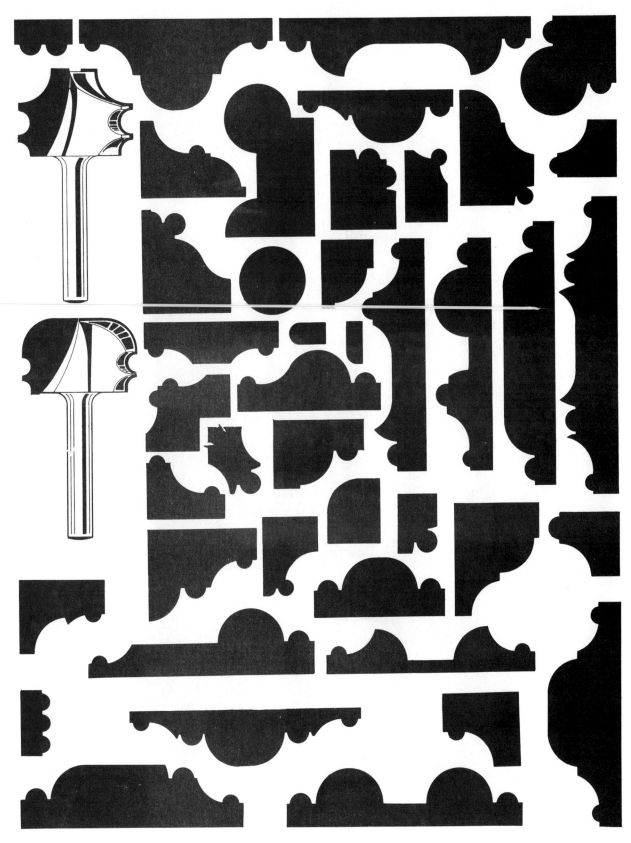

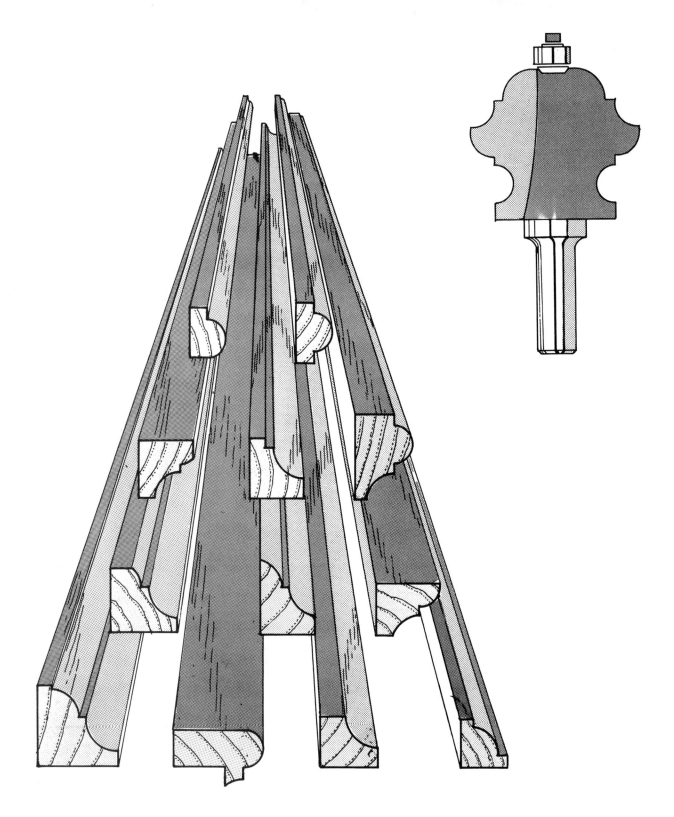

Illus. 75 A and B. (above and following page). *Standard moulding profiles made in one pass using Freud's Multiform Bit.*

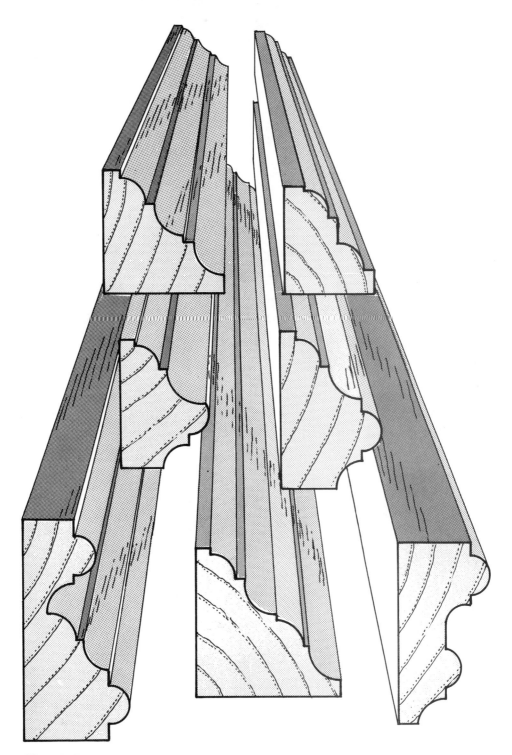

Illus. 75 B.

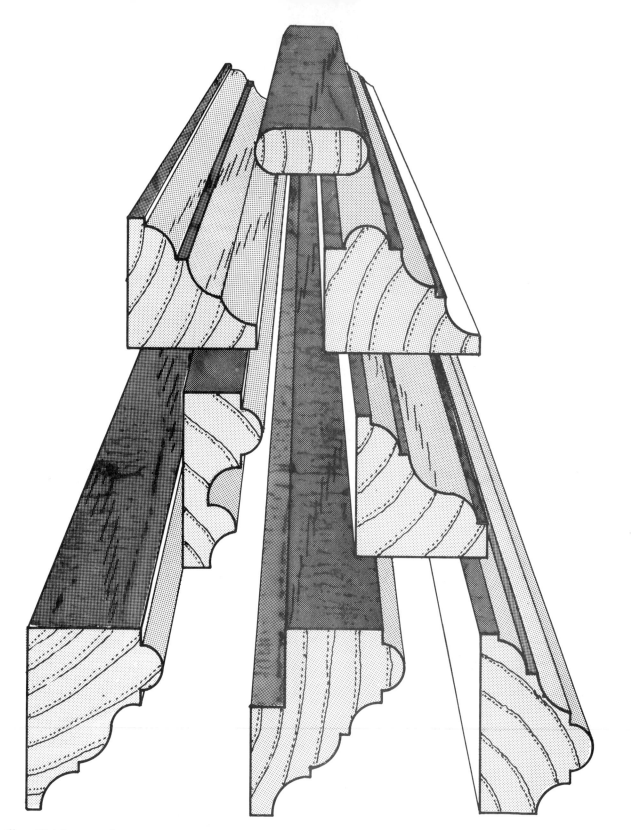

Illus. 76 (above and next page).   *Moulding profiles made with two passes using Freud's Multiform Router Bit.*

Illus. 76 B.

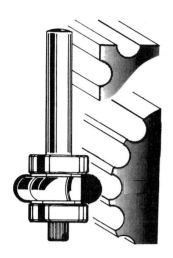

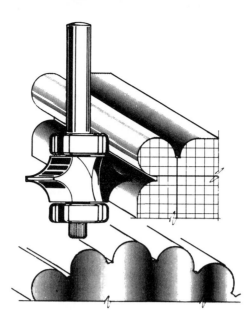

Illus. 77 (far left). A flute cutter is ideal for making flute and cove moulding profiles. You can also use it to make plate rails. It is available from Furnima Industrial Carbide in ¼- and ⅜-inch diameters. Illus. 78 (left). This full bead cutter by Furnima Industrial Carbide is available with 3/16-, ¼-, or ⅜-inch radius to cut ½ or ¾ inch of full beads on round or square table legs, as shown, and similar jobs.

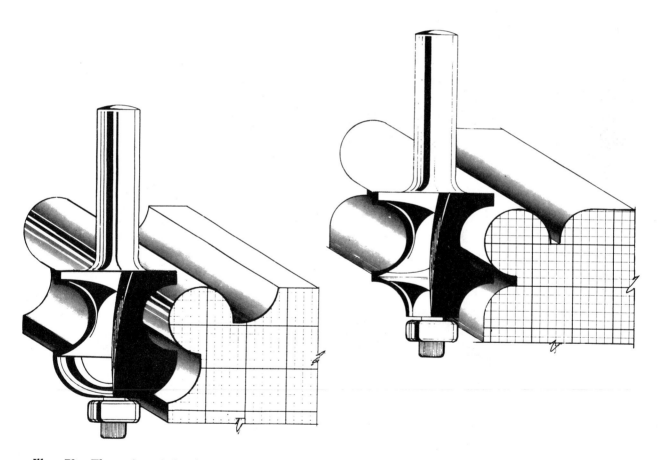

Illus. 79. These giant timber-frame bead bits by Furnima Industrial Carbide were developed for decorating beams and posts in timber-framed and log buildings. They are also called Quirk Cutters, which means a profile with a sudden turn or curved groove that separates a bead or other moulding from the adjoining member.

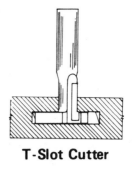

Illus. 80. This T-slot cutter, used for making slotwall and on some pegboard hangers, is available in two sizes from Safranek Enterprises, Inc.

T-Slot Cutter

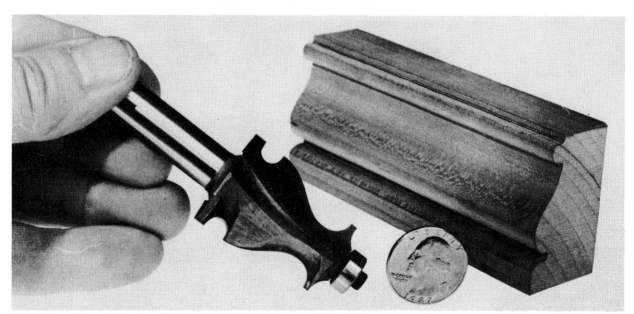

Illus. 81.   One of Furnima Industrial Carbide's face-moulding bits.

Illus. 82.   A 7-piece moulding set from Sears makes the profiles shown in Illus. 84, and many others, in a router table with successive passes when you use the various bits.

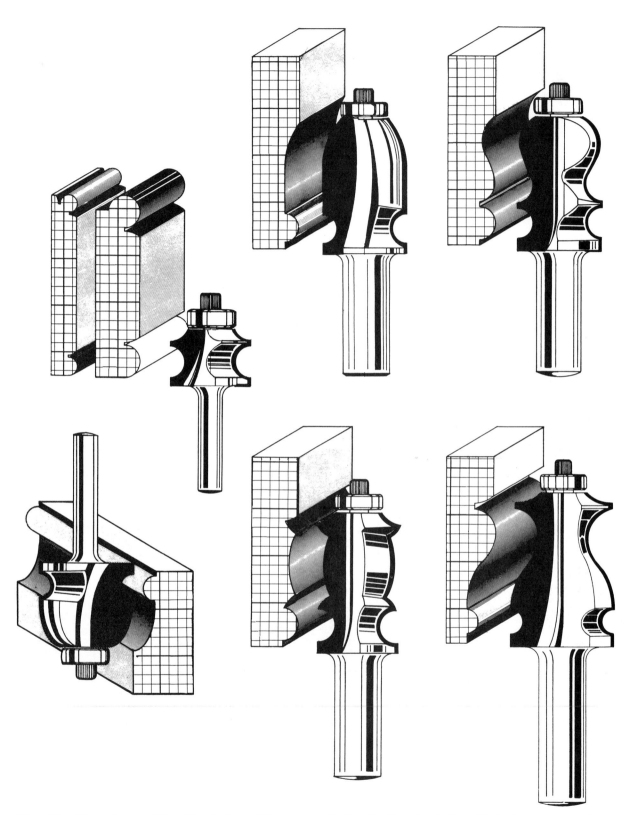

Illus. 83.   These face-moulding bits, in ¼- and ½-inch shank sizes, by Furnima Industrial Carbide, are ideal for architectural base boards, casings, chair rails, etc.

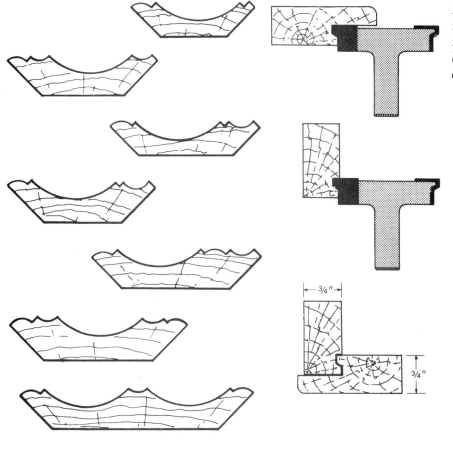

Illus. 84 (far left). Some of the moulding designs that can be made with the Sears moulding-bit set. Illus. 85 (left). Freud's drawer lock bit.

Illus. 86. Some special heavy-duty bits by Freud. Left to right: wedge-grooving bit, drawer-joint cutter, and door-lip bit. See Illus. 84.

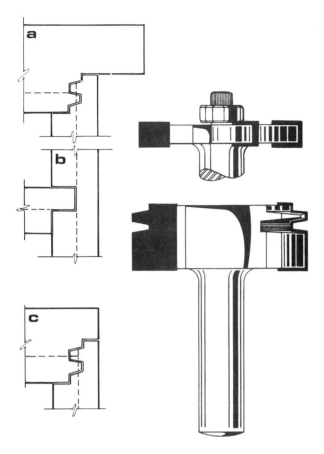

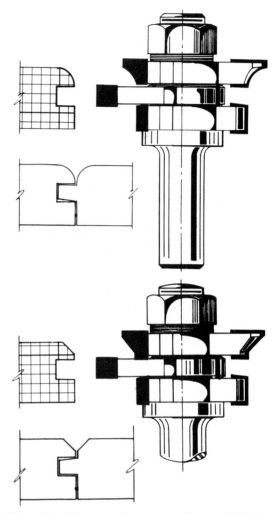

Illus. 87. The Furnima drawer-making system consists of two bits. The lower bit makes self-matching front-to-side joints with either a lipped front, as at detail A, or the flush type, as at detail C. The slot-type cutter above is used to make sides-to-back dado-rabbet cuts and grooves for the drawer bottom.

Illus. 88. Tongue-and-groove radius and V-joint panelling cutters from Furnima Industrial Carbide.

Illus. 89. Furnima's mini-shaper finger-joint bit. This assembly has three 3-wing cutters on a ½-inch threaded router arbor.

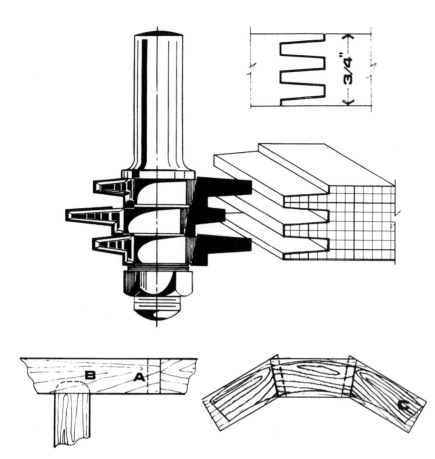

Illus. 90. This finger-joint bit has a 2-inch cutting diameter. It has many uses, as shown: A, Making strong end-to-end joints to replace scarf and spline joints; B, some mortise-and-tenon applications; and C, making strong mitre joints. (Drawing courtesy of Furnima Industrial Carbide.)

Illus. 91. The Sears stile-and-rail cutter bit set includes grooving and moulding cutters, which are used individually one at a time on a ¼-inch arbor with a ball bearing.

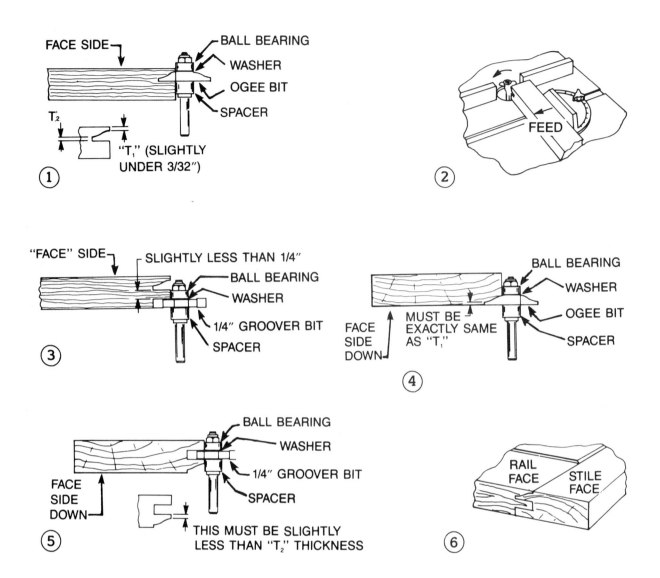

Illus. 92. *The essential steps involved in using the Sears rail-and-stile cutter set are shown as follows:
1, shows setup for first cuts on rail ends (see 2); 3, grooving cutter setup and cut for tongue-on-rail ends; 4, ogee
cutter setup makes moulding cuts on all stiles and rail pieces; 5, grooving setup for all stile and rail pieces; and 6,
assembled joint.*

Illus. 93. Some special bits from Cascade Precision Tool Company include rail-and-stile bits, a lock-mitre bit (above center), door-lip bit (top right), and a large panel-raising bit with a 3½-inch cutting diameter.

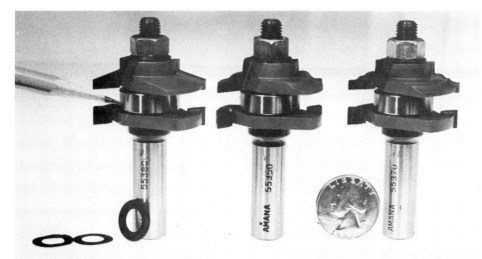

Illus. 94. Amana Tool Company offers several different cutting designs in their reversible stile-and-rail bits. All include ball bearing, grooving, profile cutters, and spacing-adjustment shims on an arbor.

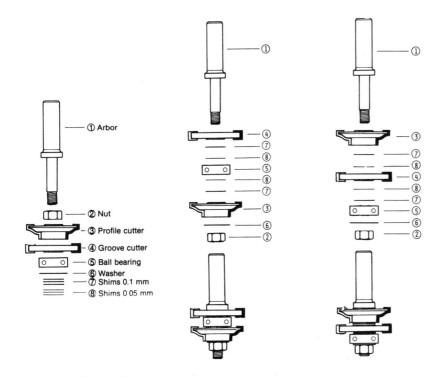

- ① Arbor
- ② Nut
- ③ Profile cutter
- ④ Groove cutter
- ⑤ Ball bearing
- ⑥ Washer
- ⑦ Shims 0.1 mm
- ⑧ Shims 0 05 mm

Illus. 95. Amana's reversible rail-and-stile arbor-mounted cutters. With Amana's raised-panel system, only one bit is required for making the door frame and one bit for raising the panels, i.e., a 2-bit system. The assembly details for the rail-and-stile cutter as shown are as follows: left, basic components provided; center, assembly for cutting the tongue rail end-cope profile; and right, cutter assembly reversed for cutting grooves and moulded edges on all frame pieces.

Illus. 96. Amana's panel-raising bits.

Illus. 97. Amana's panel-raising bits. At left: Cove design. At right: provincial profile.

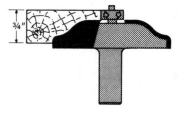

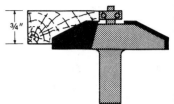

Illus. 98 (above).   Amana's raised-panel bits. At left: Ogee fillet design. At right: their classical design.

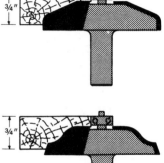

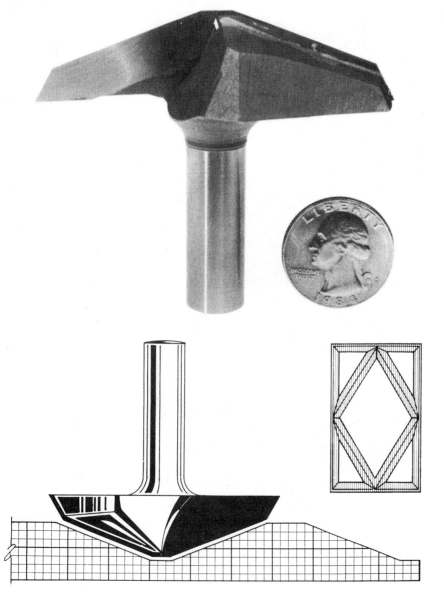

Illus. 99 (above).   The Freud raised-panel bits. Illus. 100 (left). A close look at Furnima's diamond-point panel-raising bit, which has a 2¾-inch cutting diameter.

Illus. 101 (left).   A diamond-point panel-raising bit by Furnima makes the special French provincial diamond-shape panel doors, as shown.

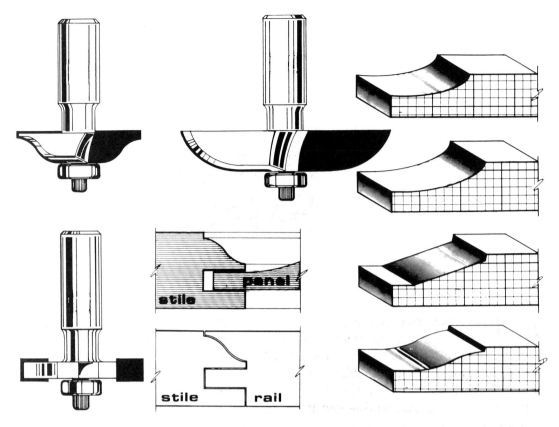

Illus. 102.   The Furnima raised-panel door system is a set of 3 bits. The two bits at the left form the stiles and rails. The large panel-raiser bit is available in the optional shapes shown by the profiles at the right.

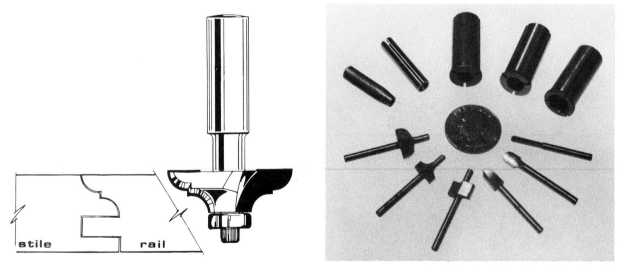

Illus. 103 (above left).   A typical self-matching cabinet cutter by Furnima Industrial Carbide. This bit cuts both mating profiles of the rail and stile. Illus. 104 (above right). These miniature router bits by Byrom International have ⅛-inch shanks. Note the collet bushings above, which are available in many sizes.

Part II
Safety

My earlier book, *Router Handbook*, establishes and describes the essential safety rules for basic and standard routing operations. In this section, I discuss and illustrate tool-testing techniques (Chapter 5) and devices (Chapter 6) that can improve safety-related working conditions. Those using the new, larger, shaper-type router bits and the larger and heavier routers now available should be aware of the particular safety concerns with these tools, which are also addressed.

5

Matching Bits and Routers

Most of the newer specialty bits now available are generally considered to be on the large side for nonproduction woodworkers. These bigger bits require well-built routers that are the appropriate size in horsepower and have reduced spindle speeds. There is growing concern among bit and router manufacturers that these big bits will be carelessly mismatched with light-weight, high-speed, low-horsepower routers. (See Illus. 105–107.)

There can also be problems with larger, heavy-duty routers in certain situations. The weight and increased horsepower of these large routers, coupled with the use of big bits, may actually be too much for some woodworkers to handle. It's possible to actually lose control of some of the bigger, powerful hand-held routers available today. That's why, wherever possible, it is usually best to run the bits and router in well-built, sturdy router tables. (Refer to Chapters 28 and 29.)

One major power-tool manufacturer at one time produced a 5 horsepower, 18,000 RPM hand-held router, an extremely powerful tool. I'm not sure if this particular router is still in production. There are however, a number of routers available with 3 horsepower motors, and some rated at 3½ horsepower. Bosch Power Tools lists in its catalogue two routers with over 3 horsepower. If you take a deeper cut than

is practical with a big, powerful router, you may find it a physical challenge to control feeding.

As a note of interest, there is now available a German-made 3½ horsepower, 3-phase hand-held plunge router. The major advantages of this router are cheaper operating costs and the fact that there are no brushes and problems associated with them, such as burned armatures, as there are with conventional single-phase motors. The router itself costs over $1,000, and a special frequency changer that's priced at nearly $2,000 by itself is required to run it.

To use most of the big specialty bits, you need at least a 2 horsepower router. Any router you use, with or without big bits, must be in good operating condition. It must have near-perfect spindle and collet accuracy, with practically no indication of runout. You'll want the smoothest possible operating mechanism that doesn't have any bit-whipping tendencies or vibrations.

Even if you have a new router, it is wise to inspect and check the collet and bit trueness. You may find problems.

It is really very easy to inspect and check your router or router machine for runout. Two items are needed: A dial indicator and an approximately 3-inch length of very accurately

Illus. 105. My standard 1½ horsepower 23,000 RPM router is definitely undersized and too fast to safely carry this large panel-raising bit, especially as shown, since the bit is fully exposed because the subbase hole is too small to permit the usual reduction in the vertical depth of cut.

Illus. 106.   Even in this case, with the subbase removed so that the bit can be raised with the motor unit adjustment to reduce the vertical depth of cut, there is too little base support. The RPM is still too high, and the horsepower is still not sufficient.

Illus. 107. Here's another dangerous situation—a bit that's too big for the opening of the cast-metal base on this plunge router. This is especially dangerous because if the depth-of-cut clamp is released the motor unit will retract, pulling the bit directly into contact with the metal-base housing surrounding the small opening.

machined steel rod (such as a piece of clean drill rod or a machinist's dowel pin) of a diameter that matches the collet size. These items occasionally appear in advertisements in woodworking magazines, and sometimes show up in some of the woodworking mail-order catalogues. If you have difficulty purchasing them, try borrowing what you need from a machinist friend or from the local machine shop.

The major problem in checking a hand-held router for runout is holding or clamping the measuring instrument steady as the metal dowel or drill rod is rotated by hand against the point of the "feeler" of the dial indicator. (See Illus. 108–109.) Sometimes the dial-indicator base can be securely clamped directly to the router base with small C-clamps. If the motor unit is removable, its spindle and collet can be checked when mounted in a pin router, if such circumstances permit. Otherwise, use a dial indicator with a magnetic base that works with a switch or lever that can be turned on or off. Since most router bases are made of nonmagnetic aluminum and plastic, you will have to clamp something like a steel rule to it so that the magnetic base of the dial in-

dicator will be anchored steadily to it. (See Illus. 108.)

Essentially, the same technique can be applied when checking routers mounted in self-made wooden router tables or in the commercially made aluminum and plastic router tables. Illus. 110 shows a setup that uses a steel framing square to provide the "attraction" for the magnetic base of the dial indicator.

Make sure that the power is disconnected, and take a reading. Then carefully rotate the router spindle by hand and note the dial reading. It should not exceed a total of .002 inches, with a reading of .001, or less, preferred. A dirty collet—one impacted with dust, pitch, and sap—can alone throw off collet accuracy by .002 or .003 inches.

Check new routers and their collets, as well as replacement collets on used routers. You may be surprised to discover differences in the quality and workmanship of various router manufacturers.

The longer the drill rod or metal dowel used in the test, the more pronounced the actual runout will be. But, that's exactly what happens when long bits are used.

When comparing one router or collet to

Illus. 108 (left). The setup for checking a hand-held router for runout with a dial indicator. A metal rule clamped to the router base provides contact for the magnetic base of the dial indicator. Illus. 109 (above). Checking the runout of a pin router spindle.

Illus. 110. Checking the runout of a mounted router in a wooden table. A steel framing square is used as the "contact" for the magnetic base of the dial indicator in this setup. Plans for the router table are given in Chapters 28 and 29.

another one, always check them with the feeler point at the same distance from the end of the collet, to get comparable readings. Also, use the dial indicator to check for any vertical up-and-down movement of the router spindle. A vertical-thrusting problem will cause vibration, even under light loads, and affect tool life and finish-cut surface quality.

Remove the collet and check the inside taper of the spindle itself for runout. (See Illus. 111.) If anything, the runout should be less than the reading taken with the collet and testing rod in place. A runout exceeding .002 inches is dangerous, and repair by the router manufacturer is strongly suggested.

The use of bushings to reduce collet sizes increases run-out tendencies. A dial-indicator check will point out to you the need to use bushings sparingly and only for short-run jobs.

Another test can be made with an inserted bit. Use a new, clean or freshly resharpened bit. Clamp it up as usual with the power disconnected. Check the cutter or bit for runout. (See Illus. 112.) If the bit has any wobble of more than .002 inches, it is dangerous at high speeds and needs to be corrected or replaced.

It's a good idea to check your bits as they come back from the tool sharpening service. Reconditioned and/or resharpened bits should be every bit as good in balance, sharpness, and cutting capability as new bits.

The use of a dial indicator and the testing techniques discussed may appear to be overly precautionary, but they are basic industry safety standards. Incidentally, a dial indicator is a good preventive-maintenance purchase for your shop. Shop around. Prices vary considerably, but you don't need an expensive one. You will find uses for it in your woodworking shop, like, for example, checking radial arm- and table-saw blades, fence alignments, and arbor trueness, and setting and adjusting planer and jointer knives.

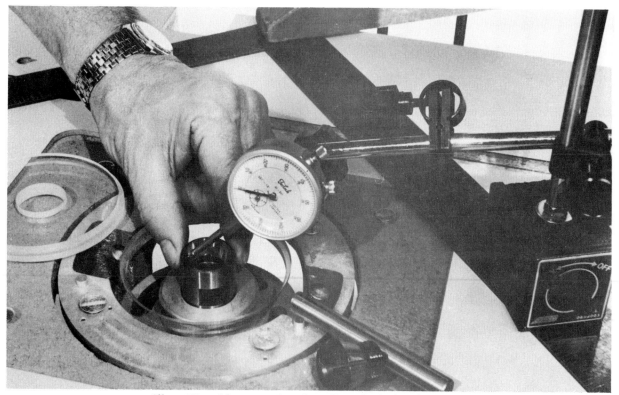

Illus. 111. After removing the collet, check the inside taper of the spindle for runout.

6

Safety Devices

There are a number of new devices that have become available recently that will definitely improve safety conditions when routing.

Light-Weight Hearing Protectors These devices effectively block out the high-pitched "whine" of routers provide the same suitable protection given by the larger, ear-muff types. Illus. 113 shows two of the newer versions, each of which only weighs slightly over one ounce. One such type is available from Shopsmith, Inc.

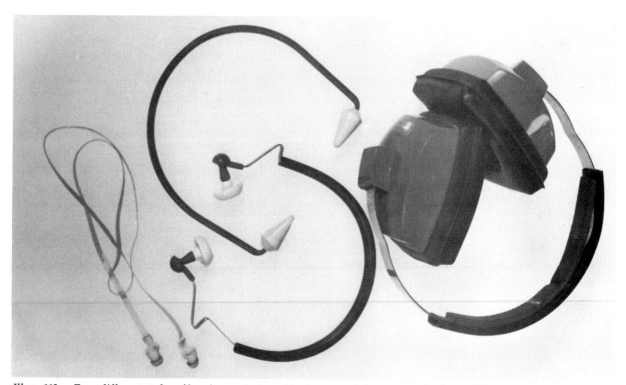

Illus. 113. *Four different styles of hearing protectors. The two new light versions in the middle are effective for routing, and weigh just over one ounce.*

Dust-Collection Vacuum Attachments These devices, which attach directly to hand-held routers, are now available from two major router manufacturing companies: Bosch Power Tool Corp. and the Porter-Cable Corp. Each attachment was developed to fit the routers of that particular manufacturer, but they could be adapted to fit some other makes of routers without too much effort.

Both vacuum attachments look similar, and there are no major differences. (See Illus. 114 and 115.) They protect your eyes from flying chips and suck away much of the irritating and often dangerous dust particles that contaminate the workshop air you breathe.

Bosch calls their attachment the Air-Sweep Router Vacuum system. Porter-Cable calls theirs simply Routo-Vac. Both link to regular shop vacuum-cleaners via a 1½-inch-diameter flexible hose.

Both the Bosch and Porter-Cable models are designed to attach directly to the base of the router after the standard subbase is removed. (See Illus. 116.) Likewise, these units can be used when surface-routing. (See Illus. 117.) Both have add-on attachments. What Porter-

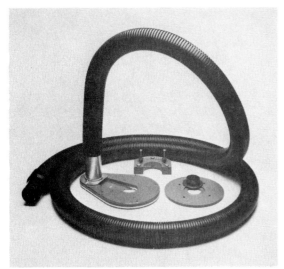

Illus. 114. *The Bosch Air-Sweep Router Vacuum System fits most Bosch routers.*

Illus. 116. *Here the Bosch Air-Sweep is attached to the router with the standard subbase removed.*

Illus. 115. *Components of Porter-Cable's Routo-Vac attachment.*

Illus. 117. *Routing over flat surfaces with the Bosch Air-Sweep.*

Cable calls the "air dam" creates the proper air flow to pick up chips when you are performing edge-forming jobs like those shown in Illus. 118 and 119. Even template-routing can be performed with the addition of special template-guide mounting subbases attached to the undersides of the dust-collecting attachments. In this operation especially, dust and chip removal adds to routing accuracy and improves routing pleasure immensely. (Illus. 120 and 121.)

Illus. 118.   The Porter-Cable dust collection attachment set up for edge-routing.

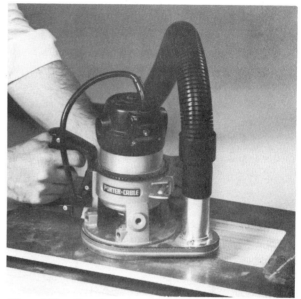

Illus. 120.   Routing a recess using a template-guided router base in conjunction with the Porter-Cable dust-collecting attachment.

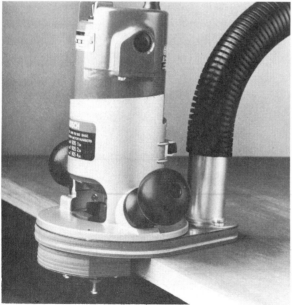

Illus. 119.   The Bosch edging attachment in use.

Illus. 121.   A closeup look at the Bosch template-guided subbase that attaches below the dust-collecting unit. Here you can see the guide following the edge of a template, thus making a dust-free guided cut.

Foot Switches If you have ever observed industrial production machinery, you may have noticed that most have foot-powered feed controls and on-and-off foot switches. These types of controls and switches give the operator more freedom to use both hands to their fullest capacities.

I like to use foot switching whenever I use routers that have flip-type switches or routers with switches that require me to reach for them, leaving my grip on the knob or handle. I prefer the faster-operating and convenient trigger-switches, but not all routers have that feature.

A foot switch is a useful safety feature that is worthy of consideration. The one shown in Illus. 122 is simply an extension cord with a foot-activated switch on the end. Simply plug your router into it and you're ready to use the router. Be sure to match the switch capacity to the amperage of your router.

Use a foot-activated switch whenever the operation requires more than one hand to control the tool or when you have to use two hands to handle or hold down the work piece. It's comforting to know that you are fully prepared should an emergency develop. Incidentally, I occasionally use the same foot switch for drill-press and scroll-saw work.

Hold-Downs and Hold-Ins Not only are these helpful devices for some router-table and pin-routing jobs, they also eliminate the need to place hands and fingers in danger zones. There are several different types available. You can make your own wooden feather-board types that are similar in function to the plastic ones available from Shopsmith Inc., which are shown in Illus. 123 and 124. These plastic versions are very versatile and can be used for both right-to-left and left-to-right stock-feeding directions. They also have a unique self-clamping system that fits into mitre-gauge slots of machine tables. A bar located under the feather piece expands as the adjustment knob is tightened. Refer to pages 158–180 for more information regarding the use of this accessory, and page 335 for another version of the device.

Anti-Kickback Device The wheel-type anti-kickback device shown in Illus. 125 is being used more and more for various wood-machining operations. It has a more sophisticated design concept and is more expensive than other hold-down, hold-in devices. However, the versatility and performance of this type of production-safety device often more than justifies the purchase price—particularly when you consider the price you would pay by losing your fingers.

The wheels are made of a special non-marring rubber-like material. They are spring-loaded and fully adjustable to accommodate stock as thin and narrow as ¼ inch in size. (See

Illus. 122. A foot switch can be regarded as a specific safety asset.

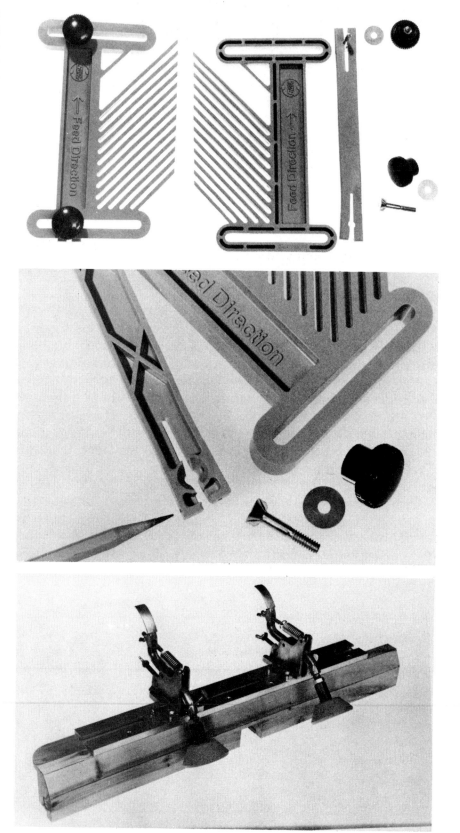

Illus. 123. These plastic feather boards can be used as hold-ins and hold-downs for certain router table and pin router operations. At left is an assembled unit. At right are the unassembled parts. Note that they can be adapted to two different feeding directions as desired when you simply flip the fingers over.

Illus. 124. A closeup look at the components of the plastic feather board. The bar at left fits into a ⅜ × ¾-inch-mitre-gauge table slot, and expands to lock its position firmly. The wedge head of the adjustment and locking screw develops outward clamping pressure as the screw is tightened.

Illus. 125. This wheel-type hold-down and hold-in is adjustable, and is an effective anti-kickback device suitable for table-routing; used with other special wheels, it can be used with overarm-mounted pin-routing machines.

78

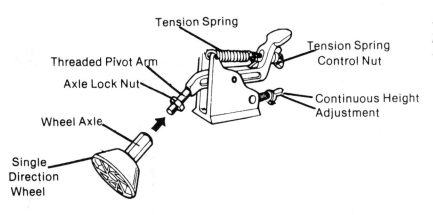

Tension Spring

Threaded Pivot Arm

Axle Lock Nut

Wheel Axle

Single Direction Wheel

Tension Spring Control Nut

Continuous Height Adjustment

Illus. 126. The functioning parts of the Shophelper anti-kickback stock feeder.

Illus. 126.) They operate on nonreversible ratchet-type bearings and thus permit rotation only in one direction.

When properly adjusted, this device is one of the most effective anti-kickback devices available. The infeed wheel is set to steady and hold in the stock as the cut starts. The outfeed wheel continues to control the workpiece until it exits from the bit or saw and is clear of the cutting area.

When an opposite or other-than-normal feed direction is required, you can buy special wheels from Western Commercial Products, of Tulare, California. Let me explain what I mean by "opposite" feed direction. The feed directions of table saws, jointers, and table routers are generally all the same. However, the feed direction for standard, overarm pin-routing fence-guided jobs, for example, is just the opposite. Turn to pages 336 and 337 for information on how to make the wooden auxiliary fence and an illustration showing this device in use.

Variable Speed Control This is an electronic device that you plug your power tool into and then dial-control your RPM speeds on. Illus. 127 shows the Speedial®, a device manufactured by the Lutron Co., of Coopersburg, Pennsylvania. It is sold through electrical contractors and distributors. It is also sold by some woodworking mail-order catalogues, such as Woodworker's Supply Co., of Albuquerque, New Mexico. *A note of caution:* This accessory should only be used on either Universal (AC–DC) brush-type motors or DC motors. If

Illus. 127. The Lutron Speedial in the 10-amp size. When it is used with a router, you can decrease router spindle speeds to safer levels for special jobs such as panel raising with large bits.

it is used with AC motors, the high-starting currents will destroy the unit.

This speed control is really an advantage when you use "special"-type bits like large panel raiser bits because then you can slow down your router speed, which makes the operation safer and allows you to get a more smoothly cut surface. If you use a speed control when cutting tough materials, your tools will also stay sharper longer, because a slower RPM increases the chip load per cutting edge. Slowing the RPM is essentially the same thing as increasing the feed rate, which is not always easy to do—especially when cutting around inside corners and curved edges with a sharp radius.

To use the Speedial, simply plug it into an outlet and, with the tool switch off, plug the router (or other tool) into the unit. Set the Speedial switch to the variable position. Turn on the router and set the control knob at the desired speed. When full RPM is desired, simply flip the switch to the "full" position. The numbers on the dial are for reference to a specific point of adjustment only and should not be considered the specific speeds.

It should be noted that as a motor slows down, its fanning and cooling action decreases. Consequently, motors should not run for extended periods at very slow speeds. Totally enclosed motors, however, do not depend on outside air for cooling and, therefore can usually be run at slow speeds for longer time periods.

The Speedial is fused to protect it from overload. (See Illus. 128.) It has a handy clip on the back (Illus. 129) so that it can either be attached to your belt for complete portability or mounted on or near your workbench. This is another device that has multiple uses in the woodworking shop. Turn to pages 322 and 323 to read how I incorporated the Speedial into the design of the Ultimate Router Table.

The plunge-type routers would make ideal portable boring devices if it weren't for one problem: Because of their high speeds, it is

Illus. 129. When you hook the clip on the Speedial onto your belt, the Speedial becomes a portable device that you can use with hand-held tools.

dangerous to use standard boring tools and bits with them. The high speeds would cut too aggressively, and might even pull the bit right out of the collet or snap the spindle. However, if you use a great deal of caution, you can use conventional boring tools, with shanks that fit the collet, for boring as long as the correct RPM speed is regulated appropriately with a speed control. (See Illus. 130.)

There are router bits designed specifically for plunge entry that can be used to bore holes. In fact, some bases and jigs for plunge-boring operations are included on pages 201 and 202 and 256–267.

When buying a Speedial, select a unit with the most appropriate amperage capacity. Check the amps specified on the nameplate on the motors you intend to use with the Speedial. (See Illus. 127.) Speedials are available in several models: those with 5-amp, 10-amp, and 15-amp capacities.

Illus. 128. A view showing the 3-prong receptacle and line fuse.

Illus. 130. With judicious caution, you can use a plunge router with a speed-control set to slow the RPMs, which permits the use of conventional boring tools.

Part III
Commercial Aids and Devices

*I*n this section, I discuss and illustrate a number of router accessory devices currently available that may help satisfy certain individual routing requirements. Just as there has been a proliferation of many new router bits on the market recently, there has also been a surge in router devices. Some of those included here are manufactured by reputable, established companies with a long-standing reputation for customer service. Others are only available from small "one-man" mail-order companies. (As you know, small companies occasionally change names or locations, or just "go under." Consequently, though the names and addresses of the companies discussed here and the specific product descriptions are now accurate, they may not be in the future. Please do not hold me responsible if you have some difficulty in correspondence or service matters. When dealing with mail-order companies, it is best to first write for current catalogues and product pricing, while simultaneously verifying the actual availability of the product and the existence of the company.)

In Chapters 7–10, you'll find some unique timesaving devices. There are also descriptions and illustrations of some special-purpose routers, and many commercially manufactured jigs and templates, including devices used to make mortises, tenons, dovetails, and even a jig that, when used with your router, cuts dowels from scraps.

7
Routing Aids

Router Depth Gauge This gauge (Illus. 131 and 132) is calibrated for 15 different cutting depths, each marked in 16ths of an inch from $1/8$ inch through 1 inch. It is made of aluminum, and can be purchased through the Leichtung Inc. Catalogue, at 4944 Commerce Way, Cleveland, Ohio 44128.

Double-Faced Tape It would be an exaggeration to call double-faced tape one of the greatest inventions of all time, but it does have so many uses in the woodworking shop. It can be used for all sorts of temporary work-holding jobs, such as securing workpieces to templates. It also holds small workpieces for routing, temporarily attaches guides and other jigs to router bases, and has other routing uses.

One major advantage of double-sided tape is that none of the adhesive on the tape penetrates into the pores of the wood. Even small pieces of this tape have good holding power. Cover larger areas with proportionately more tape, but don't use more than is necessary—it may become difficult to pry the pieces apart if too much tape is used. If this happens, use a putty knife to pry them apart.

Two kinds of double-sided tape are available in most hardware stores: the thin vinyl type that works adequately on smooth surfaces like plastic, and, for heavy-duty holding, the cloth-type designed for putting down carpeting, which you should use.

Illus. 131.   *Router bit depth gauge from the Leichtung catalogue.*

Illus. 132.   *Checking the bit projection for depth of cut.*

Illus. 133. A roll of double-faced tape has unlimited uses in the wood shop.

Router-Master Pad This product, from Kencraft Company, 5212 Tractor Road, Toledo, Ohio 43612, resembles foam-carpet underlay material. According to the company's brochure, Router Master is a "high-density bonded urethane with urethane adhesives added for strength." It's a pad that permits very small workpieces to be routed without clamping. (See Illus. 134–136.) The standard size pad is 2 feet × 3 feet and costs approximately $10.

Quick-Release Clamps These workshop aids are available from several mail-order houses. Those shown in Illus. 137 come from Woodworker's Supply Company, 5604 Alameda Place, N.E., Albuquerque, New Mexico 87113. These special clamps are ideal to use when making custom work-holding jigs and fixtures. Use them to hold templates to workpieces and to secure irregular and/or small pieces for production-routing operations.

There are two basic styles of quick-release clamps: those that provide a vertical clamping pressure and those that provide horizontal clamping pressure. All have adjustable rubber

Illus. 134. To rout the inside and outside edges, hold the workpiece in a stationary position without any clamps or double-faced tape. The special urethane foam called Router Master keeps the workpiece from slipping.

Illus. 135 (above). *Very small workpieces are safely held for routing with the Kencraft Company's Router Master padding. Illus. 136 (right). The standard Router Master pad is 2 × 3 feet, big enough to handle larger workpieces without clamps or special fixtures.*

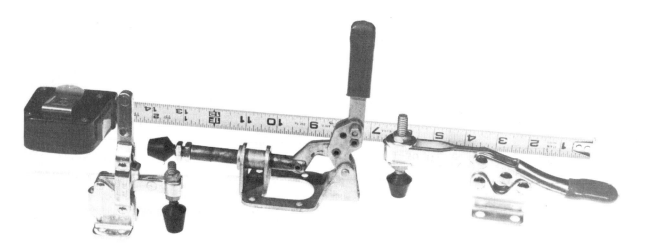

Illus. 137. *Quick-release toggle clamps are ideal for making custom jigs and fixturing. There are two types of toggle clamps: the ones at the left and right provide vertical pressure, and the center example produces a horizontal clamping force.*

pressure tips. They are available in different sizes, with working-force pressures that range from 190 to 575 pounds. Prices range from approximately $12 to $25.

Clamping Straightedges These aids are especially handy for the active router craftsman. The ones shown in Illus. 138–141 are called the Clamp 'N Tool Guide; these handy tools are manufactured by Griset Industries, 1521-F E. McFadden Avenue, Santa Ana, California 92705. These perfect straightedges are made of aluminum and feature a low-profile design with a built-in clamp. They are ideal for guiding a hand-held router while making straight-line cuts. These straightedges hold a few advantages over homemade straightedges. A homemade straightedge cannot always be depended on to be true and has to be secured to the work surface with C-clamps or hand screws. Also, sometimes the job is such that conventional clamps obstruct the routing or are otherwise impossible to use.

The Clamp 'N Tool Guide is instantly adjustable to any position along any board or assembly with two reasonably parallel edges. (See Illus. 139.) However, when it is clamped to the work, there is some slight sideways play in the jaws when the tool is pressed against the guide. Consequently, to precisely locate and make a cut, always take this play into consideration and compensate for it when securing the clamp straightedge to the workpiece.

A doubled-up version of the Clamp 'N Tool Guide is shown in Illus. 140 and 141. This version has bottom jaws on one side that clamp to a workbench, while the upper clamp jaws hold the workpiece.

Clamp 'N Tool Guide clamps are available in various sizes, with gripping capacities that range from 18 to 50 inches. An 8 foot-long-model of the Clamp 'N Tool Guide should be on the market soon.

Illus. 138. *A clamp within a low-profile aluminum straightedge is used to guide the router for straight-line cuts. The guide must be offset the distance from the bit to the edge of the router base.*

Illus. 139. This straightedge is instantly adjustable along surfaces with parallel edges.

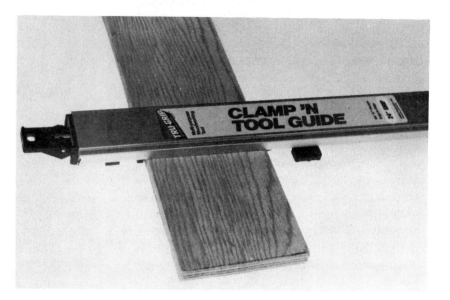

Illus. 140. Above is a back-to-back clamping device which is actually a doubled-up version of the Clamp 'N Tool Guide, and has the same jaw mechanism.

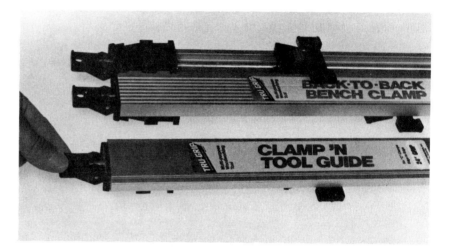

Illus. 141. Here the back-to-back clamp holds the workpiece, creating an obstruction-free access to the working surface. The bottom jaws will attach the unit to any workbench or tabletop.

Router–Shaper Guide Black & Decker's Router–Shaper Guide (Illus. 142) is an accessory item designed primarily for use with the company's "Workmate" workbenches, shown in Illus. 143. This device makes many routine routing jobs easier because it allows the woodworker to move the workpiece, rather than the router, over the work. The router is held rigidly in position above the workpiece, and the work is guided against the fence. The unit is easily adjustable for dadoing and grooving. (See Illus. 144.) The reach of the router–shaping guide is somewhat limited; it can only handle stock that is less than 1⅝ inch in thickness, and only bits up to a maximum cutting-edge diameter of 1 inch can be used.

Router Bracket This device consists of two pieces of cast aluminum that cradle the router motor unit for mounting in a radial arm saw. It is available from The Router Bracket Company, P.O. Box 533, Richmond, Virginia 23204, at a cost of approximately $35, plus shipping.

Illus. 143.   Black & Decker's Workmate Workbench is adjustable to either a 32 or 23½-inch height. It has vise jaws and pegs to hold workpieces for routing, and folds up when not in use.

Illus. 142.   Black & Decker's Workmate Router and Shaper Guide is an accessory for straight-line routing on the Black & Decker portable workbench, shown in Illus. 143.

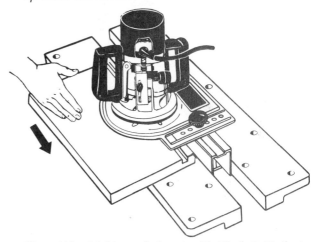

Illus. 144.   Making a dado cut with Black & Decker's Router and Shaper Guide.

The Router Bracket is essentially developed for use with Sears radial arm saws, but might also be adaptable with other radial arm saws. This should be verified before you order one.

The Router Bracket, shown in Illus. 145 and 146, actually requires the complete removal of the radial-arm saw motor from the saw yolk,

Illus. 145. *The Router Bracket consists of two cast-aluminum cradles that hold the router motor.*

Illus. 146. *The bracket is attached in place of the radial arm saw motor, which must be removed with its electrical system disconnected.*

and the disconnection of the wiring. The idea of combining the high-speed, smooth-cutting capabilities of the router with the versatile carriage movement and arm positions of the radial saw has been a concept I've favored for many years.

Inca Radial-Arm-Saw Router Carriage This new accessory has been specifically made for use with the Inca Model 810 Radial Arm Saw. (See Illus. 147 and 148.) The entire sawing motor unit quickly slides off of the arm and can be replaced with the router carriage in just seconds. Thus, a quick conversion turns this sawing machine into a radial-arm router. Dadoes, grooving, etc., can be accomplished in any 90-degree straight cut or angular direction, as facilitated by the design of the saw.

With the Inca Radial-Arm-Saw Router Carriage you can easily make sliding dovetails. You can also make stopped dadoes, grooves and various decorative cuts with it by clamping a stop to the appropriate location on the arm. (See Illus. 149.) This controls the distance of carriage travel. The carriage can also be fixed to one location on the arm. (See Illus. 150.)

Illus. 147. *The router carriage accessory for the Inca Model 810 Radial Arm Saw.*

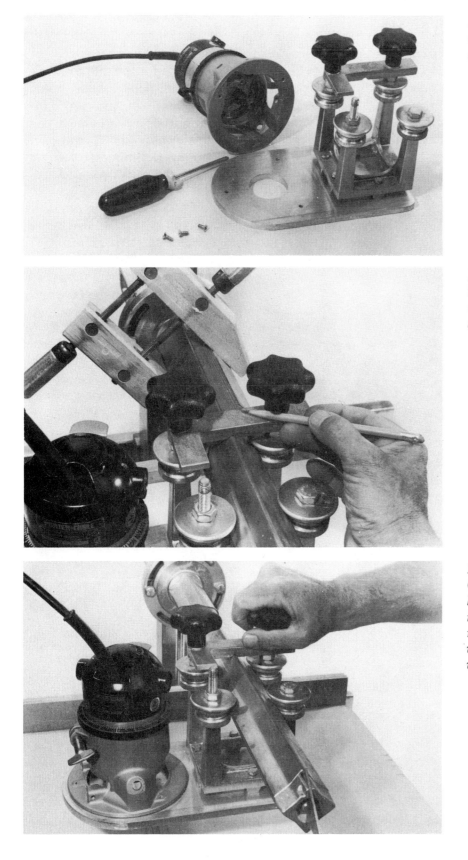

Illus. 148. The Inca Router Carriage removed from the saw arm.

Illus. 149. Clamping a stop block to the arm limits carriage travel for making stopped dadoes and similar cuts.

Illus. 150. The Inca Router Carriage can be clamped at any location along the arm. When it is rigid, pin and plunging routing techniques are possible with vertical movement provided by the elevation crank.

With this setup you can make pin-routing type of operations. Vertical router motion is provided by the elevation crank, which permits you to perform some pattern and pin-routing techniques.

When you mount the router carriage to the saw arm in an inverted position, you have a router table arrangement. (See Illus. 151 and 152.) The heavy aluminum plate measures ³⁄₈ × 6 × 10½ inches. When you clamp a straightedge to it, as shown in Illus. 152, you can do some straight-line work.

Illus. 597 gives details for making a radial-arm-saw router bracket. This version holds router motors of various sizes, and can be installed on the motor arbor as easily as a saw blade. Also turn to pages 286–288 for more on radial-arm-saw routing techniques.

Illus. 151. The Inca Router Carriage inverted and locked on the arm to serve as a router table.

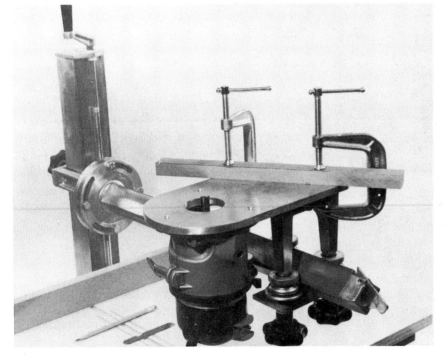

Illus. 152. Though a small table (6 × 10½ inches), a wood fence can be utilized, as shown, for some straight-line work.

Router Support Arm This is a balanced extension arm onto which a router is mounted. (See Illus. 153 and 154.) Through a system of brass pivoting bushings and a gas-cylinder spring action, the router support arm relieves the weight of the hand-held router—the router virtually floats on air—and greatly reduces operator fatigue, especially in production-like situations. This device is ideal when you are doing any repetitive surface-routing, such as that done when sign-carving or making template-guided cuts for extended periods of time. The physical task of lifting and setting down the router between cuts is eliminated—thus saving time as well as energy.

The router support arm—called the Rout Arm by the manufacturer, Woodmachine Com-

Illus. 154. When the Rout Arm is used with the Omnijig dovetailing device, it speeds the operation and makes it less tiring in production applications.

pany, Route 2, Box 227, Mebane, North Carolina 27302—will carry the router through any side-to-side or up-and-down motion while keeping the router base in a constant horizontal plane so that the router bit itself is always rotating in a true vertical axis. The Rout Arm was originally developed to carry Milwaukee routers and some of the Bosch routers. Contact the Woodmachine Company; indicate your brand and model of router. The company has indicated that this product is being continually improved in design and versatility, which soon should prove advantageous to owners of other router brands.

Dry wall and Panelling Cutout Router This router utilizes a special bit that quickly does jobs that can often take considerable time, like making cutouts for electrical duplex boxes,

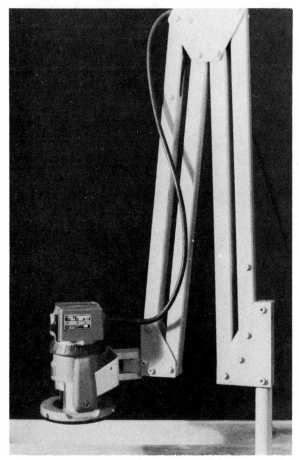

Illus. 153. Used with the Woodmachine Company's router counterbalance Rout Arm, the router virtually becomes free-floating, which reduces physical fatigue in many hand-routing operations.

Illus. 155. This 28,000 RPM, 3½-pound drywall and panelling cutout unit from Porter-Cable is designed to cut openings for electrical outlets, etc.

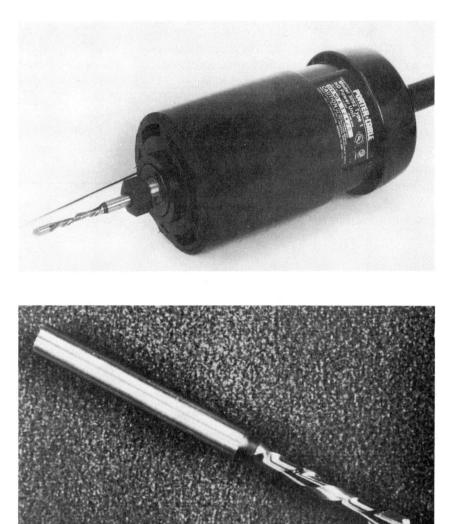

Illus. 156. This ³⁄₁₆-inch down-spiral self-drilling bit with an end pilot is used with the panelling and drywall cutout router unit.

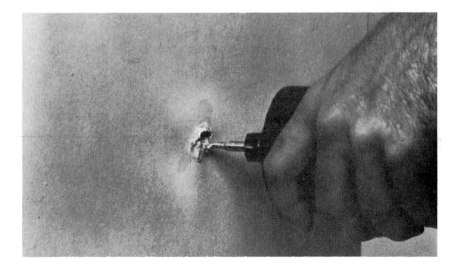

Illus. 157. The bit penetrates the approximate center of the outlet box or opening.

Illus. 158. The bit is moved to the right until the pilot contacts the inside wall of the box. Then, the bit is lifted slightly over the lip of the box to its outside wall.

Illus. 159. The pilot rides smartly around the outside of the box with the operator feeding in a counter-clockwise direction, as shown.

window openings, etc. (See Illus. 155 and 156.) The unit weighs about 3½ pounds and is only 3 inches in diameter, and can be controlled with one hand if desired. The 28,000 RPM motor and collet takes a special ³⁄₁₆-inch-diameter down-cutting spiral bit that will not tear the dry wall paper or splinter thin wood panelling. The self-drilling bit (Illus. 156) has an end pilot that follows along the outlet box. The dry wall or panelling cutouts are made all at once after the sheets are put up and tacked in place.

To use this tool, simply mark the approximate center of the opening or outlet box and make a penetration cut. (See Illus. 157.) Then cut to the right until the pilot contacts the inside of the box. (See Illus. 158.) Next, lift the bit slightly over the lip of the box to the outside. The pilot of the bit will ride smartly around the outside of the box with a counter-clockwise feed direction. (See Illus. 159.) The result will be clean and perfect cutouts, each requiring only a few seconds to complete.

Large Router Bases These bases, made of phenolic plastic, can be used to install your router into a home-made table. They are available from Oak Park Enterprises, Ltd., Box 13, Stn. A, Winnipeg, Manitoba, Canada R3K-129. (See Illus. 160.) Oak Park Enterprises offers a set of solid-brass template guides in various sizes that fit the phenolic bases, as well as various ready-made jigs and accessories.

Inlay Bushings These bushings, which fit over template guides, make the art of inlaying various designs extremely easy. (See Illus. 161–163.) Inlays can be cut into solid wood, veneered panels, decorative laminates, and other overlay materials.

Inlay bushings with companion template guides are manufactured by several companies, including Oak Park Enterprises Ltd. (Illus. 161), the Robert Bosch Power Tool Corporation (Illus. 162), and the Porter-Cable Corporation (Illus. 163).

Oak Park Enterprises offers two different-size bushings: one with a ¼-inch-wall thickness and one with a ⅛-inch-wall thickness. The Bosch and Porter-Cable bushings have a wall thickness of ⅛ inch. The router bit used must equal precisely the wall thickness of the bushing. (See Illus. 164.) Thus, when one part is routed with the bushing on, it will be offset exactly the correct distance after the mating cut to the second part is made with the bushing off.

The design must not be too intricate or highly detailed. Make a suitable template from ¼-inch hardboard or plywood. (See Illus. 165.)

Make the inlay by securing the template to

the workpiece that you want to inlay with double-faced tape. If the template is larger, it can be clamped. With the bushing over the template guide, rout around the inside of the template. (See Illus. 164 and 166.) Clean out the waste of the recess as needed. If the inlay is to be made into a surface covered with decorative laminate, you can remove the inside waste with solvent or with a heat gun, which softens the adhesive.

Next, using the same template, but with the bushing removed, rout the inlay profile. (See Illus. 167.) This is somewhat tricky to do, especially if you attempt it without a plunge-type router. The guide must be positioned against the template, and the router lowered carefully with the bit entering the work at precisely the right location. Once the bit is entered into the work, feed the router in a clockwise direction to make the inlay insert. The fit should be perfect. (See Illus. 168.)

Plunge routers and/or routers fitted with clear plastic bases make the entire process of inlaying so much easier. You can see more closely where you are with the router as you follow along the edge of the template. "Outside templates," as shown in Illus. 169, are easier to make than inside templates (Illus. 165), but are definitely more difficult to use. (See Illus. 170.) The choice is yours. The advantages and disadvantages of each type should be evaluated with regard to the job at hand and the type of router you are using.

Illus. 160. These phenolic router bases are suitable for mounting your router in a router table. A solid-brass template set, inlay bushing, other jig accessories, and templates are available from Oak Park Enterprises, Ltd.

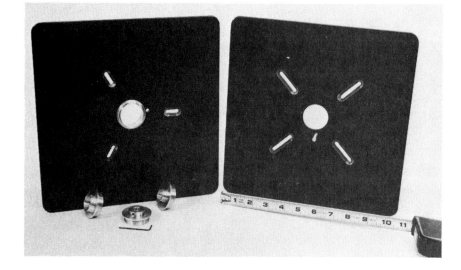

Illus. 161. The inlay template guide and bushing (with a ¼-inch wall thickness) from Oak Park Enterprises is made of solid brass. This system requires a ¼-inch bit and a router base (Illus. 160) that accepts the special-size template guide.

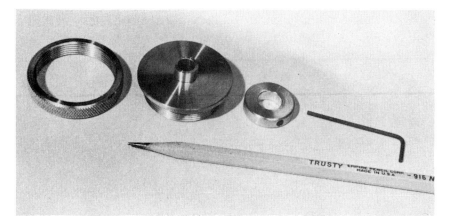

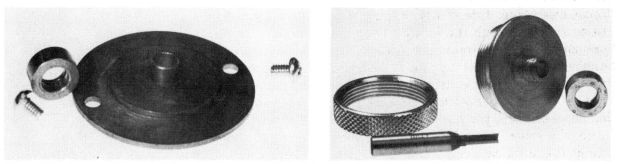

Illus. 162 (above left). Bosch template guide and ⅛-inch inlay bushing. *Illus. 163 (above right).* The Porter-Cable inlay template guide, ⅛-inch bushing, and ⅛-inch solid carbide bit.

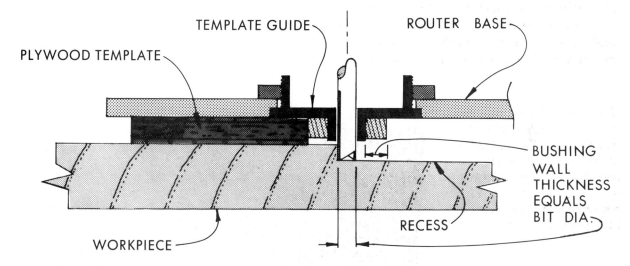

PLYWOOD TEMPLATE
TEMPLATE GUIDE
ROUTER BASE
BUSHING WALL THICKNESS EQUALS BIT DIA.
RECESS
WORKPIECE

Illus. 164. Making the recess cut in the workpiece that will receive the inlay. Note that when the inlay collar is added to the template guide the size of the pattern being cut is offset a distance that exactly equals the diameter of the bit.

Illus. 165. An inside template for an inlay. Note that the sharpest curve cannot be less than that of the bushing diameter. In this case, the bushing is ⁹⁄₁₆ inch in diameter, which means that the sharpest radius must not be less than ⁹⁄₃₂ inch.

Illus. 166. Routing the work-piece that will receive the inlay. The bushing offsets the cutting path of the bit, so the recess is ⅛ inch smaller all around.

Illus. 167. The inlay itself is routed with the same template, but with the bushing removed from the template guide. The line of cut will be offset a distance equal to the diameter of the bit, making a perfect, matching fit.

Illus. 168. Router-cut inlays. The one at the left was made with a plunge router and an outside template. The inlay at the right was made with a conventional router and inside template.

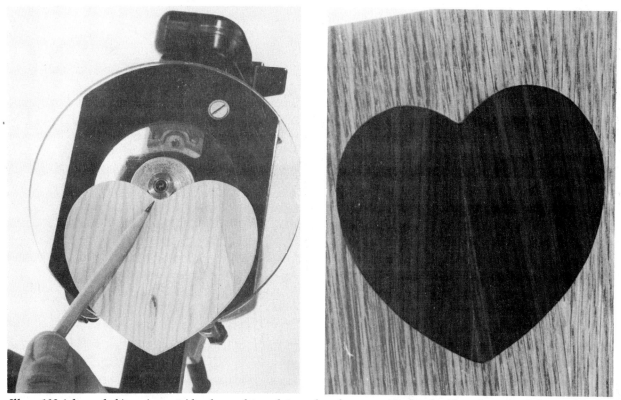

Illus. 169 (above left). An outside plywood template and a plunge router fitted with a clear plastic base with the template guide and bushing. Illus. 170 (above right). A closeup of a finished inlay.

Betterley Underscribe This ingenious device, which is developed, manufactured, and marketed by Art Betterley, of Art Betterley Enterprises, Inc., 11160 Central Avenue, N.E., Blane, Minnesota 55434, makes cutting joints in plastic laminates unbelievably fast, easy, and accurate. (See Illus. 171 and 172.) A typical project appropriately suited to this tool is shown in Illus. 173 and 174. However, it is most commonly used in cabinetry to joint laminate-covered facings of stile and rails.

The Underscribe works equally well on V-32 (vertical) or $1/16$-inch (standard) laminate material. Cut the joint after gluing or laying the pieces down, one piece slightly overlapping the other. The design of the base is such that only a minimal amount of dust from the routing finds its way under the joint. Illus. 175 depicts all of the components involved and shows how the Underscribe makes the joint. Illus. 176–180 illustrate the step-by-step procedures for making a typical rail-to-stile butt joint on a cabinet-facing using a decorative laminate. The same procedures can be applied to other similar cutting situations.

The tool utilizes a $1/8$-inch solid carbide bit, and is built to be used with either Bosch or Porter-Cable trimming routers. The Underscribe can be used to make tight laminate butt joints on cylindrical forms, circular edge bands, and even mitre or framed joints with 45-degree corners. An eccentric cam built into the lower aluminum plate ensures precise adjustment of the tool. Rotating the eccentric cam (with an accessory wrench that comes with the unit) one way leads to a tighter-fitting joint; turning it the other way leads to a looser-fitting joint. (See Illus. 181.)

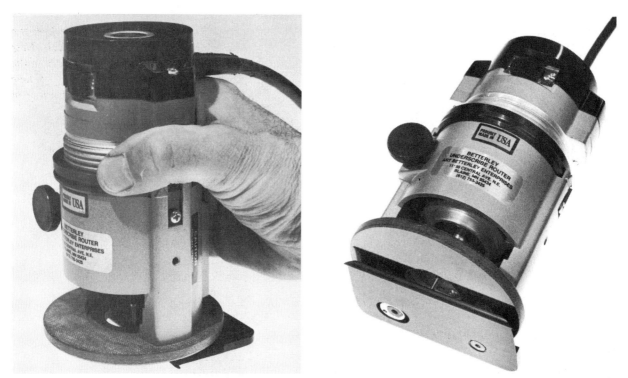

Illus. 171 (above left).   The Betterley Underscribe is used in many cabinet shops or by anyone substantially involved with decorative laminates. Illus. 172 (above right). The Betterley Underscribe consists of a small trim router, a special base, guide, and a ⅛-inch solid carbide bit.

Illus. 173.   A typical job for the Betterley Underscribe. All of the joints in this decorative-laminate table can be cut more quickly and accurately than by any other process. (Photo courtesy of Nevamar Corporation.)

Illus. 174. A closeup look at a kaleidoscope custom table. Note the precisely sharp joints of the many laminate pieces. (Photo by Blakeslee-Lane, courtesy of Nevamar Corp.)

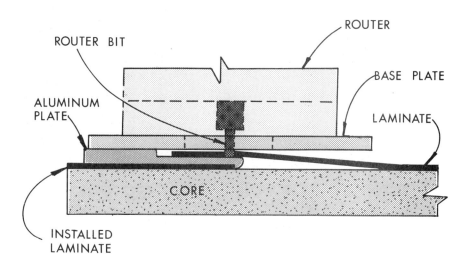

Illus. 175. This representation of Underscribe's components shows how a perfect joint results.

ROUTER

ROUTER BIT

BASE PLATE

ALUMINUM PLATE

LAMINATE

CORE

INSTALLED LAMINATE

Illus. 176 (above left). *Demonstration of typical rail-to-stile butt joint of decorative-laminate cabinet facing. For the first step, apply contact cement to all surfaces of the face and laminate components. "Put down" the vertical stile pieces first.* Illus. 177 (above right). *Next, apply horizontal rail pieces, allowing for a slight overlap (½ inch) over the previously applied stile laminate.*

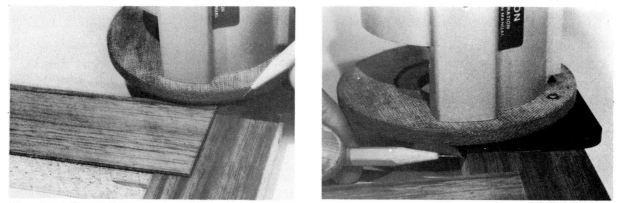

Illus. 178 (above left). *Now, use the Underscribe to make the joint cut. The bevelled edge of the router base shown here picks up the end of the rail laminate.* Illus. 179 (above right). *The "hook" on the lower aluminum plate is the straight-line guide; it follows along the inside edge of the stile laminate.*

Illus. 180. *The cut has been completed, and the rail fits perfectly butted to the stile laminate.*

Illus. 181. Bottom view of router shows a cam eccentric that is used to adjust the lower plate to a precise relationship with the bit, facilitating extreme accuracy and resulting in joints cut without any gaps at all.

Betterley Seaming Router This device, which is also used for making joints (seams) in plastic laminates, is somewhat different than the Underscribe in that it functions somewhat like a mini-jointer. Illus. 183 compares the base of the Seaming Router to the base of the Underscribe. A straightedge placed against the following edge of the Seaming Router base shows it to be, within a few thousandths of an inch, tangent to the cutting circle of the small ⅛-inch solid carbide bit. (See Illus. 184.)

Illus. 185 shows how the base of the Seaming Router is designed to trim the two matching edges in unison as the tool is passed along the seam. With the Seaming Router, only one member of the joint may be glued in place prior to machining. When using the Seaming Router, place the second sheet over the first, overlapping it by ⅛ to ⅞ inch, and then clamp it. The edge of the bottom sheet must be reasonably straight. Once the cutting pass is made, the top sheet must move ⅛ inch, to take up the space of the resulting cutting path made by the bit, before bonding it to the substrate.

Like Betterley's Underscribe, the base of the seaming router is fitted with an eccentric cam for making precise adjustments. (See Illus. 186.)

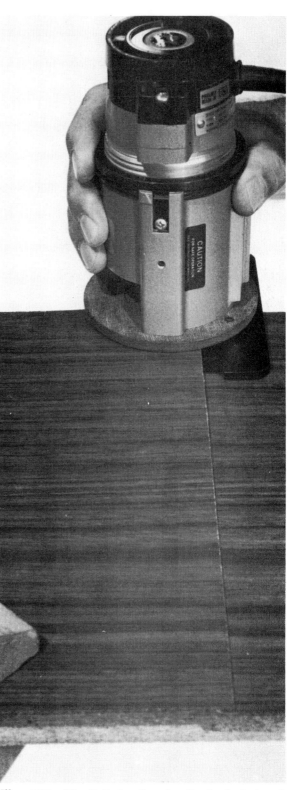

Illus. 182. The Betterley Seaming Router is designed to make perfect seams in large sheets of decorative laminates.

Illus. 183. Bottom view of the Betterley Underscribe on the left compared to the base of a Seaming Router on the right. The hole receives a ⅛-inch solid carbide bit.

Illus. 184. A straightedge against the "following edge" of the base illustrates its jointer-like relationship to the cutting circle of the bit.

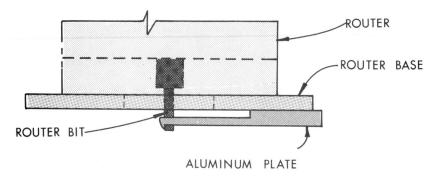

ROUTER

ROUTER BASE

ROUTER BIT

ALUMINUM PLATE

Illus. 185. A schematic showing how the Seaming Router works.

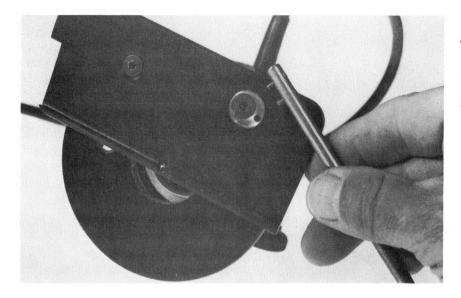

Illus. 186. You can adjust the Seaming Router with this special wrench. It rotates an eccentric cam that moves the base into the correct relationship with the bit.

Mitre-Fold Router This is still another remarkable tool from Art Betterley's parade of devices that facilitate fabricating with decorative laminates. (See Illus. 187 and 188.) The Mitre-Fold Router comes in three different models. Each one is designed specifically for one of the three different thicknesses of plastic laminates: the V-32, or vertical-type laminates; the post-forming laminates; and the more standard, 1/16-inch thickness laminates. This tool is especially helpful whenever you don't want to show the unsightly dark line that's typical of most conventional laminate work.

The Betterley Mitre-Fold Router mitres all pieces of the laminate so precisely that it is sometimes hard to tell if there is, in fact, a joint; this is a very effective technique when you are using laminates that are patterned, such as those with marble or wood-grain patterns. Illus. 189 and 190 show marble-pattern laminate applied so effectively over a particle-board core that it looks like a solid piece of marble. Illus. 191 shows how much more natural wood-grain patterns look when applied with the mitre-fold system.

The mitre fold is a worthwhile approach to making self-edge cabinet doors, drawer fronts, display fixtures, case goods, and many kinds of household furniture.

A six-tooth circular cutter, shown in Illus. 192, which makes a V-cut into the laminate as it is fed along it, rides tightly against the edge of the core. (See Illus. 193.)

To make a mitre-folded panel, block, or cube, first bond a single piece of laminate to the face of the core. Make sure sufficient extra material covers the edges or other remaining surfaces.

Illus. 187. The Betterley Mitre-Fold Router is operated horizontally, with a rear support attached to the end opposite the cutter.

Illus. 188. *Making a cut with the Mitre-Fold Router. The face of the corestock has been previously bonded, leaving enough extra overhang to cover the vertical edges. After the cuts are made, the laminate will fold up to cover the edges.*

Illus. 189 (above left). *A completed mitre-fold job with marble-patterned laminate makes perfect, undetectable joints.*
Illus. 190 (above right). *Above, another look at the marble pattern and excellent joints that result after bonding to the particle-board core. Below is another piece with the mitre cuts completed, ready for folding and bonding.*

Illus. 191.   A mitre fold with a wood-grain pattern creates a more realistic look than when it is done conventionally.

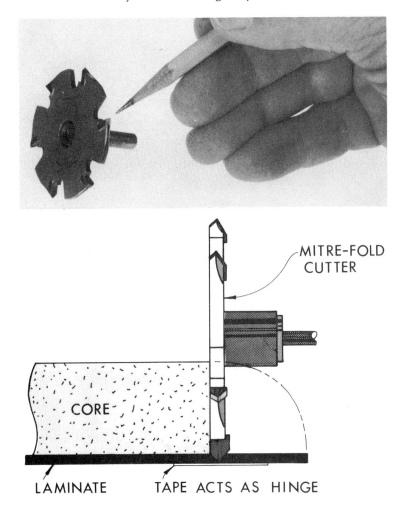

Illus. 192.   The mitre-fold cutter has 90-degree carbide V cutting edge.

MITRE-FOLD
CUTTER

Illus. 193.   The cutter follows tightly against the core edge, and cuts to a precise depth that equals the thickness of the type of decorative laminate being used.

CORE

LAMINATE   TAPE ACTS AS HINGE

105

This material can be pretrimmed to the specific dimension necessary, if desired, before you make the mitre-fold cuts, or you can trim it after the folds are made and bonded. Betterley has yet another special tool for this trimming job called the Sizing Router. However, you can devise your own trimming system.

Apply masking tape to the face side of the laminate directly opposite where the V-cuts will be made. (See Illus. 194.) (When working with metallic laminates, taping is not necessary. Set the cutter to cut just to the metal face, and the metal will then act as the hinge.) Make the V-cuts with the Mitre-Fold Router, as shown in Illus. 188. To rout the V-cuts, place the face of the laminate down on any smooth, flat surface. Once they are cut, the corners will come loose, and can be discarded. (See Illus. 195.) If any adhesive curls up along the sides of the V-cuts, it can be removed very easily with a sharp chisel.

Before applying the adhesive to the remaining surfaces to be bonded, make sure the folding cuts are crisp and clean. (See Illus. 196.) Then you'll be assured that no chips or sawdust particles remain to cause problems. The whole process is exceptionally precise, very fast, and uncomplicated.

Illus. 194. Masking tape is applied to the face side directly opposite the line of cut.

Illus. 195 (above left). Once cut, the corners will come loose, and can be discarded. Illus. 196 (above right). A closeup look at a corner ready to fold.

8
Commercial Mortising and Tenoning Jigs

Porter-Cable Morten Jig Porter-Cable offers woodworkers a jig with which you can easily make matching mortise-and-tenon joint cuts (Illus. 197); when these clean and crisp cuts are glued properly, they make this joint very strong. To make the cut, all you need, beside the jig, are a router, bench vise, and C-clamp or hand-screw clamp. The creative craftsman will have fun devising various adaptations of the basic mortise-and-tenon joint with this device—called the Morten jig. Illus. 198 shows a number of different joint applications.

The Morten jig is essentially a basic template-routing technique. A ¼-inch router bit fitted with a ball bearing on top cuts (with the guidance of the slot in the template) a ⅜-inch mortise that's 1¼ inches wide and ¾ inch deep. The dual-purpose template is made of steel. It has a machined slot opening for making the full mortise in one setup, and a machined tongue-shaped opening that's directly aligned with the mortising slot. (See Illus. 199.)

Tenons, however, cannot be cut in one setup. One half of the tenon has to be cut, and then the template remove from the frame, flipped over, and repositioned on appropriate alignment pins. (See Illus. 200.) Cutting mortises is a little more difficult. (See Illus. 201.)

Illus. 197. The components of the Porter-Cable Morten Jig, which is essentially based on a template-routing technique. Note the steel template in the foreground that guides the bit, making a complete mortise slot at one setting. Cutting the tenon requires two setups.

The perfect joint for volutes, newels, table and chair legs.

Haunched mortise and tenon for better quality frames.

Bareface tenon, off-set with perfect interference fit — clamping is not necessary.

Panel side, blind draw pin.

Floating tenon with precision fit — clamping is not necessary.

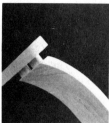
Chair back tandem tenons.

Chair side apron tenons at angle.

Mortise and tenon mitre at any angle.

Up to three in a row without moving workpiece. Plenty of long grain to long grain glue surface.

Blind haunched with perfect interference fit — clamping is not necessary.

Illus. 198.   With a little imagination, these examples of unusual adaptations of the mortise-and-tenon joint can be made with Porter-Cable's Morten Jig.

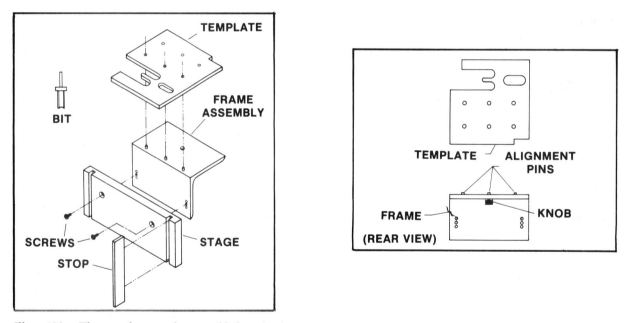

Illus. 199.   The template can be assembled to the frame in various positions, thus permitting specific operations.

When you are making mortise-and-tenon cuts, hold the workpiece together with the jig in the vise. (See Illus. 200.) When you are working on a larger piece hold it in the vise, and simply clamp the jig to it. Joints can be cut singularly, as multiples in tandem, side by side, or all in a row. (See Illus. 200–202.)

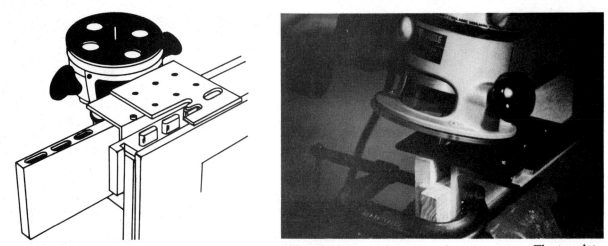

Illus. 200 (above left). *Cutting tenons in tandem. Note that only ½ of the tenon is cut per setup. The template must be removed from the aluminum frame, flipped over, positioned on alignment pins, and resecured before you can rout the second half of the tenon. Illus. 201 (above right).* *Making a simple mortising slot cut is a little tricky when you lower the router to reach full cutting depth. You must be careful not to nick the template. Note that the router is tipped and held securely as it is pivoted on the edge and pressed carefully downwards.*

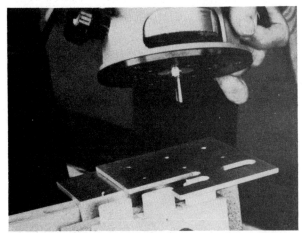

Illus. 202. *It is somewhat easier to make the tenon cuts because the router can be set flat on the template at the start of the cut as long as the bit clears the work when the router starts up. Always allow the bit to come to a dead stop before lifting the router from the template as shown.*

Woodhaven Mortising Router Base The Woodhaven Company, Inc., of 5352 West Kimberly Road, Davenport, Iowa 52806, sells a clear-acrylic plastic base for portable hand-held plunge routers that is adjustable and simplifies the mortising of stock of almost any thickness. (See Illus. 203.) You could even cut a mortise in the center of a 4½-inch timber with this jig.

The concept behind the router base is very basic, and the device itself is easy to use. It has an overall size of $7\frac{3}{4} \times 10\frac{1}{4}$ inch, and actually consists of two bases, each $\frac{3}{8}$ inch thick. The upper base attaches to the plunge router. It comes undrilled, so you have to mark, drill, and countersink the holes yourself according to your own size and spacing needs. This is not a critical step, and once it is done you will have a heavy, clear base that can be used for many other jobs.

Remove the existing subbase and use it as a pattern for locating the holes. The "under base" is split into two adjustable pairs, each with a guide fence. (See Illus. 203–205.)

To make a mortise, install a bit that's the appropriate size. Depending on the way the cut is going to be made and the required width of the mortise, the bit can be smaller in diameter than the width of the mortise. Unless the width is extremely critical, the easiest way to make the mortise is as follows:

1. Adjust both fences to the thickness of the material; they should cradle the work snugly, and be located so that the bit is at the approximate center of the stock thickness. You can determine this by "eyeballing" the setup.

2. Cut the mortise to the length desired.
3. Rotate the router, along with the mortising jig, 180 degrees. Recut the same mortise; the result will be a perfectly centered mortise. Then, cut the tenon to fit this mortise using a table saw or router.
4. If you're cutting many mortises in straight pieces on a production basis, and all of them are of uniform thickness, then adjust the jig carefully by trial and error and by checking the exact measurements. When the jig is adjusted, centered mortises can be cut in one pass.

Turn to pages 243–248 for details on making a tenoning jig, and Illus. 736–738 for more information on cutting mortises with the router.

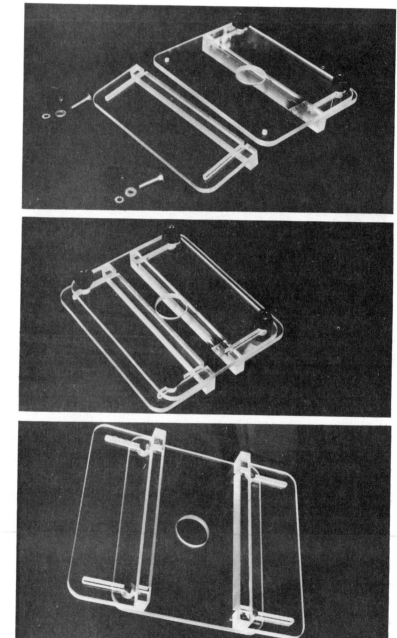

Illus. 203. Woodhaven's Mortising Router Base is designed for use with plunge routers.

Illus. 204. The lower base has two adjustable halves with support fences.

Illus. 205. The Woodhaven mortising attachment is adjustable and can be used to cut centered or off-centered mortises in stock from 5/16 to 4½ inches thick. Here it is shown at the largest setting.

9

The Precision Dowel Maker

With the Precision Dowel Maker, you can use your router to spin out an endless number of dowels in all popular sizes by utilizing scrap from wood of any species. This noteworthy device (Illus. 206 and 207) is a commercial adaptation of my wooden dowelling jig, which first appeared in the *Router Handbook*, and has essentially the same design.

Manufactured and distributed by S/J Fine Woodworks, E. 18913 Jackson Drive, Otis Orchards, Washington 99027, this refined model has many advantages over my earlier wooden one. My homemade wood jig, with which I made hundreds of dowels, worked well as long as there were no changes in atmospheric moisture conditions, which cause wood parts to expand, shrink, and distort. The Precision Dowel Maker is made entirely of steel and is

Illus. 206.   The Precision Dowel Maker is made of thick machined steel. When used with a router and electric drill, it will make smooth dowels in ¼-, ⅜-, ½-, ¾-, or 1-inch diameters from scrap wood.

Illus. 207. Make dowels from any species of wood in the size and quantity you want. Begin by ripping your scraps into blanks, as shown at the left. Note the homemade subbase for the router.

far more dimensionally stable and, thus, more accurate and precise, than my old wooden version. The Dowel Maker works the same every day, regardless of changes in shop humidity.

The Precision Dowel Maker is made of heavy industrial steel plates that are ³/₈ inch thick and have precisely milled and aligned holes. It has an overall size of approximately 2¹/₂ × 3 × 9 inches.

To produce your own dowels, you need the jig, of course, your router, a ³/₄-inch round-nose or core-box bit (a good HSS bit will make a lot of dowels before it dulls) and a ¹/₄ or ³/₈-inch electric hand drill, which you use to feed and spin the wood through the jig. (See Illus. 208.)

The setup is very simple. Clamp the jig and the router together at the edge of the workbench with two small bar clamps, as shown in Illus. 208. Position the router so that the bit is approximately centered vertically over the hole for your selected dowel size. Also position the bit front to back so that the bit center axis is aligned with the front of a wood insert that's premounted inside the jig. The front-to-back positioning will be easier to do if you make a special router base that has two strips of wood attached to it that cradle the outside of the jig. (See Illus. 209.)

Once the router-positioning step is completed, set the bit depth so that the bottom of the bit is cutting exactly tangent to the smaller exit hole. A slight adjustment in depth of cut

with the router can make your dowels slightly undersize if desired. When the final vertical adjustment has been established, you can move the router to any other dowel-size cutting position without further adjustment.

You can chuck the wood square blanks in the electric drill in two different ways. Either round by knife or file or sand the smaller dowel blanks to a diameter that fits directly into the drill chuck (Illus. 210 and 211), or use hanger bolts to drive the larger-size blanks. Make sure that the hanger bolts are inserted straight, and in line with the center axis of the wood blank to prevent and minimize wobble when feeding.

The size of the rough blanks is not very important, but they should be just slightly oversize so that the outer corners get knocked off during the feeding of the wood. Oversize blanks have some support while they are being cut and are actually easier to feed straight than blanks that are cut undersize. (See Illus. 212.) It's helpful to sand or cut off a little of the corners at the entry end of the blank. (See Illus. 213.) This will make it easier to place the blank into the entry hole.

It is surprising how easy it is to make perfect dowels once you have tried this device. The cut-surface quality is very smooth with either hard wood or soft wood, and only requires minimal sanding, if any. Illus. 214 and 215 look at some dowels cut from different kinds of wood with the Precision Dowel Maker.

Illus. 208. Completing a ¼-inch dowel. Note the setup and hand drill that provides the rotation for the wood blank that exits the jig as a perfect dowel.

Illus. 209. A closer look at the router bit and the router subbase recommended for use with the Precision Dowel Maker.

Illus. 210. Drill-chucking methods. Above shows a blank with a sanded round end. The lower portion of the illustration shows hanger bolts used to drive larger-size blanks.

Illus. 211. Driving a ⅜ × ⅜-inch blank with the drill through the jig produces a ¼-inch-diameter dowel.

Illus. 212. A closeup look at the blank going through the entry side of the jig. Note that the dowel blank is slightly oversized so that the corners get knocked off.

Illus. 213. Taking the corners off the end, as shown, makes the initial entry into the jig easier.

114

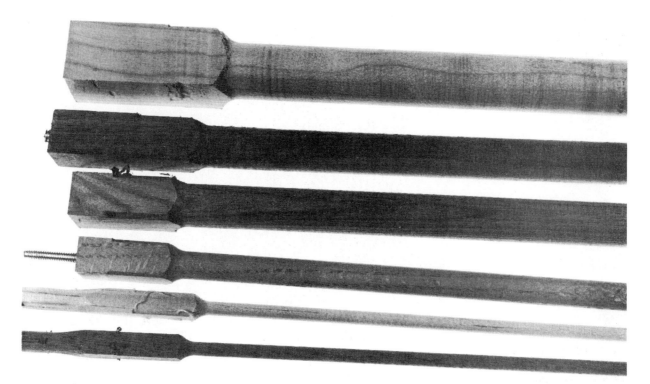

Illus. 214.   Some dowels exactly as they come from the jig. From top to bottom: cherry, walnut, butternut, oak, pine, and walnut.

Illus. 215.   This closeup shows that hard wood (walnut, below) cuts as smoothly as soft wood (pine, above).

115

10
Dovetail Jigs

Leigh Dovetail Jigs Leigh is a well-known company that's associated with dovetail jigs. Its products were introduced in my *Router Handbook*, and have since been improved. The manufacturer, Leigh Industries Ltd., P.O. Box 4646, Quesnel, British Columbia, Canada, now has available four different jigs. (See Illus. 216 and 217.) Their first models, the TD 514's, are still available in the 12- and 24-inch sizes. They were discussed and illustrated in the *Router Handbook*, and will not be repeated here.

The newest Leigh dovetail jigs are the model D-1258's which, like Leigh's earlier ones, are available in 12- and 24-inch sizes. They are

Illus. 216. The new Leigh dovetail jigs are available in 12- and 24-inch sizes that handle stock up to 1¼ inch thick.

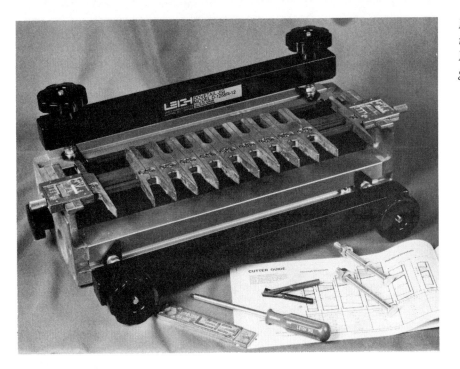

Illus. 217. A closer look at the new 12-inch Leigh dovetail jig. Note the complete instruction guide in the foreground.

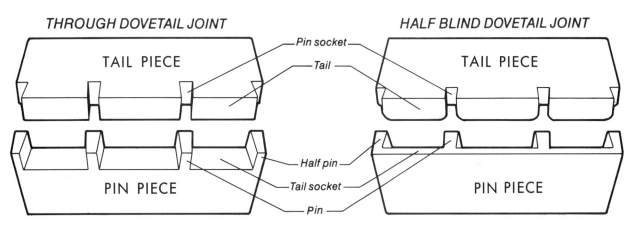

THROUGH DOVETAIL JOINT

TAIL PIECE

Pin socket

Tail

PIN PIECE

Half pin

Tail socket

Pin

HALF BLIND DOVETAIL JOINT

TAIL PIECE

PIN PIECE

Illus. 218. Basic types of dovetail joints made with the new Leigh dovetail jigs.

used in essentially the same way as the first jigs. However, in addition to through dovetails, they can also be used to make half-blind dovetails. (See Illus. 218.)

All of the Leigh jigs function around the concept of the individually adjustable router-guiding fingers, which permit the operator to adjust the size and spacing of the pin and tail cuts as he desires. The cutting is done with a template guide mounted in the router base; the template guide controls the cutting with the straight and dovetail bits. The straight bit

is used to cut the pins, and the dovetail bit cuts the tail pieces. (See Illus. 220 and 222.)

The key component in the new Leigh jigs is the "four-position" finger assembly. (See Illus. 219.) Rotating the finger assembly 180° on its lengthwise axis changes the position from pin fingers to tail fingers, or vice versa. The fingers to the front of the jig are the "active" ones.

Illus. 217 and 220 show the pin ends of the fingers forward on the "active" side. Illus. 220 and 221 show the setup for routing pins. Illus. 222 and 223 show the fingers flipped over so

Illus. 219. The heart of the new Leigh jigs is the finger assembly. Depending upon the kind of joint or cut, you can rout with it in any of four different positions which are achieved by flipping it end for end or rotating it 180 degrees on its axis.

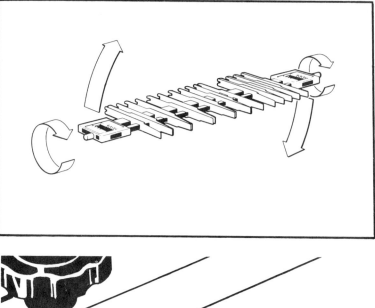

Illus. 220. Routing the pins with a straight-cutting bit.

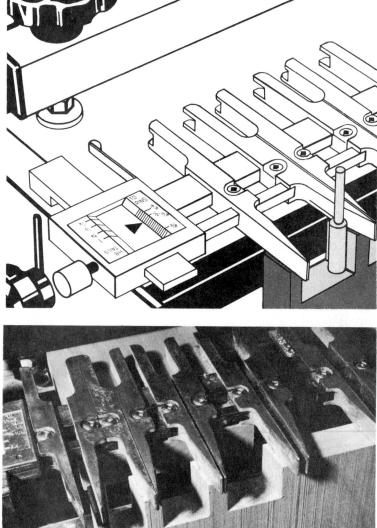

Illus. 221. A look at the pins that have been cut with the router guided by the angled ends of the fingers. Note that the spacing between the pins can be variable.

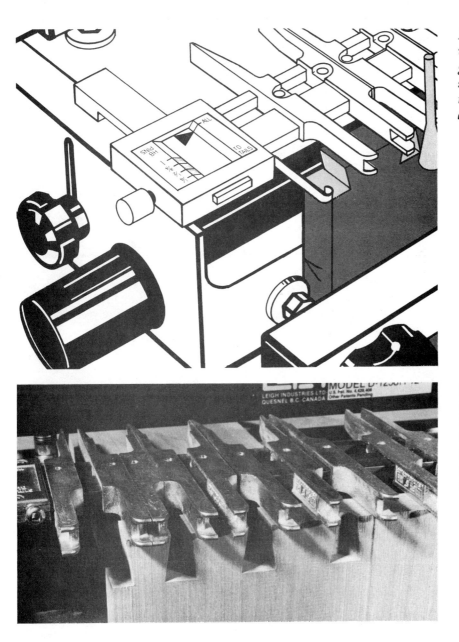

Illus. 222. The tails are routed with a dovetail bit. A template guide mounted to the router subbase controls the cut along the straight ends of the fingers, as shown here.

Illus. 223. Making the tail cuts. Here the finger assembly has been flipped over so that the tails are cut with the aid of the straight ends of the fingers. The spacings of pins and tails will, thus, correspond.

that the finger-assembly position setup can be changed to make the tail cuts.

When switching from the through dovetail setup to the position for routing half-blind dovetails, flip the finger assembly end for end. When you are routing through dovetails, all of the workpieces are clamped into the front of the jig in a vertical position. This is *not* the case when making half-blind dovetail joints. The half-blind pin piece should be routed while in a horizontal position secured under the rear clamp bar. (See Illus. 224 and 225.)

Both the pin and tail for the half-blind dovetail should be made with just a single dovetail bit.

Make the tail cuts for half-blind dovetails with the stock clamped vertically. (See Illus. 226 and 227.) This operation must be done with two setup steps if you are using the manufacturer's "first-cut bar," as shown in the insert in Illus. 226. It can be done as a one-step operation if you make up $1/4 \times 1/2$-inch hard wood bridging pieces and insert them into the fingers. (See Illus. 227.)

These new Leigh jigs are so versatile they can

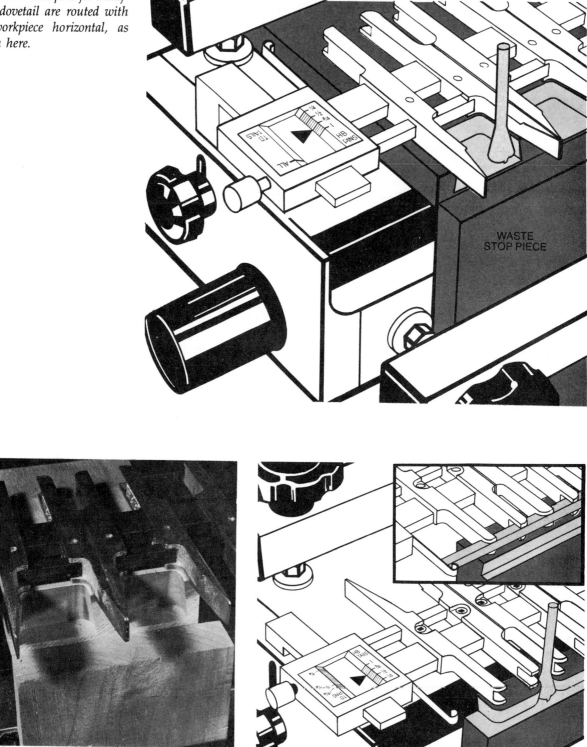

Illus. 224. The pins for a half-blind dovetail are routed with the workpiece horizontal, as shown here.

WASTE
STOP PIECE

Illus. 225 (above left).   The pins as cut for a half-blind dovetail joint on the new Leigh jig. Illus. 226 (above right). Making the tail cuts for a half-blind dovetail joint. The insert shows the Leigh "first cut bar," which is used to cut the shoulder along all of the tails, as shown. Once that is cut, the bar is removed and the bit cuts in and out appropriately between the fingers, as shown, to complete the half-blind tail cuts.

120

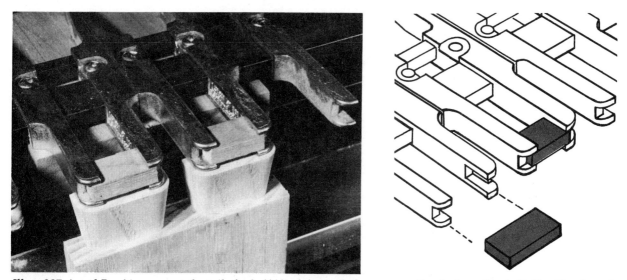

Illus. 227 A and B.   You can cut the tails for half-blind dovetails in one operation by inserting individual hardwood bridging pieces, shown, instead of using the "first cut bar" shown in Illus. 226.

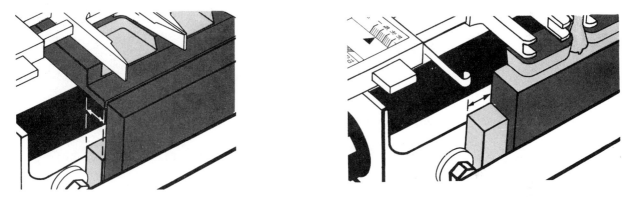

Illus. 228.   Setups for routing rabbeted half-blind dovetails on the Leigh dovetail jig. At left: A spacer piece the same dimensions as the depth of the rabbet brings the workpieces farther out from the jig body for the-pin routing operation. At right: A spacer that's the same size as the depth of the rabbet moves the workpiece away from the side stop for the routing of the tail member.

be used to make a rabbeted version of the half-blind dovetail, a type of joint that is widely used in drawer construction. Illus. 228 shows the setups for routing the two members of the joint.

If you use a plunge router with the Leigh dovetail jig setup, as shown in Illus. 229, you can make individual or multiple, through or blind, mortise cuts. If you clamp the work vertically in the jig you can also make tenon cuts. (See Illus. 230.) The mortise-and-tenon joinery

cut on the Leigh jigs is of the carcass type, not the typical frame-and-rail or leg-and-rail mortise-and-tenon joints.

Leigh also makes a special attachment, an optional accessory, for making variable-spaced carcass mortise-and-tenon joints. With this accessory and a plunge router, you can cut mortises from $5/_{16} \times 5/_{8}''$ up to $1\frac{1}{2}$ inch $\times$ any variable length. When used, the mortise-and-tenon unit replaces the four-position finger assembly, which must be removed entirely.

121

Illus. 229. Carcass mortises cut on the Leigh jig with the workpiece in a horizontal position.

Illus. 230. Tenons are cut with the stock in the vertical position.

Incidentally, Leigh Industries has published a dovetailing guide, written by Bill Stankus, which deals with the techniques used for many unusual dovetailing jobs and special joints.

Keller Dovetail Templates These templates are used to make basic through dovetails with fixed pin spacings. (See Illus. 231–233.) Manufactured by Keller and Company, 31 Terrace Avenue, Bolinas, California 94924, they are made from accurately milled aluminum that is ½ inch thick. When clamped to the work, they guide the router bits with shank-mounted bearings. (See Illus. 232 and 233.)

Keller now has available three models of dovetail template sets. Each model includes two templates, one for the tails and one for the pins. Also included are the two router bits, with mounted bearings, and the necessary instructions.

Keller's first model, the 3600, is the largest

Illus. 231. Keller dovetail templates come in pairs: one for making the tails (above), and one for routing the pins (below). The set includes two bits with shank-mounted bearings.

Illus. 232. The parallel-slotted template is used with the dovetail bit to cut the tail members of a through dovetail joint.

Illus. 233. Here you can see how the straight bit with the fitted top bearing follows the pin template.

123

(36 inches long); it handles stock from $\frac{5}{8}$ inch to $1\frac{1}{4}$ inches in thickness. In 1985, Keller came out with the 2400 model; it is a template 24 inches long that can cut through dovetails in stock from $\frac{3}{8}$ to 1 inch thick. The most recent model, the 1600, is a 16-inch-long template that is used to dovetail stock from $\frac{3}{16}$ to $\frac{5}{8}$ inch thick.

The pin spacings are all established and nonadjustable because the templates are solid, one-piece construction without moveable fingers. The center-to-center pin spacings produced are different with each model; they range from $1\frac{1}{8}$ inches on the small 1600 model to $1\frac{3}{4}$ inches on the 2400 to 3 inches on the 3600.

To use the templates, you have to mount each one to a flat wood blocking that you must provide yourself. (See Illus. 234 and 235.) The pin templates have oblong screw slots that you should adjust slightly in and out until the fit between the cut tail and pin members of a test joint is just right. If you move the pin template one way in relation to the face of the wood backing board, you will produce slightly smaller pins; if you move it the opposite direction, you will slightly increase the pin size. The workpieces should be held vertically on end in a vise for routing. Clamp the appropriate template to the end of the workpiece, as shown in Illus. 234 and 237.

The tails are usually routed first. (See Illus. 234 and 235.) Once the cut(s) are made, mark the pin board using a tail insert as a pattern. (See Illus. 236.) Use the reference lines marked on the end grain of the pin member to accurately position and clamp the pin template to this workpiece. Then rout the pins, as shown in Illus. 237 and 238.

With all template dovetail routing systems, it is important to always be on guard against nicking the template with the bit, which is usually caused by inadvertently lifting the router vertically from the template when completing a cut. If such an incident should happen, you can restore the damaged area of the aluminum with an aluminum-epoxy filler and by careful filing.

Illus. 234. Here the Keller dovetail template is used to cut the tail member of a through joint. The template is screwed to a flat backing block. The workpiece is held vertically in a vise, with the Keller template clamped to the end of the workpiece.

Illus. 235. Another view of the routing of the tail member.

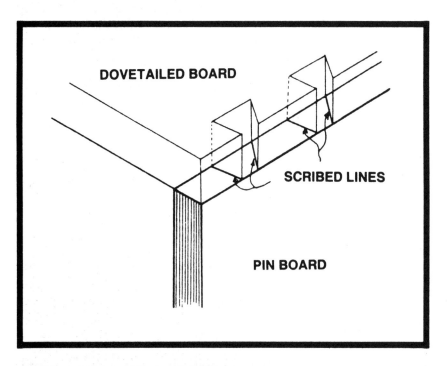

Illus. 236.   Marking. With the tails previously cut and positioned in place, mark one dovetail socket on the end grain of the pin board. Then clamp the pin template to the workpiece relative to the scribed lines.

Illus. 237.   Cutting the pins. Note how the templates are screwed to the wood-backing blocks. The workpiece is held vertically in a vise with the Keller jig clamped to it.

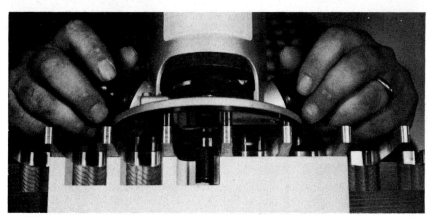

Illus. 238.   Another view showing the pins being routed.

The Omnijig   This is a relative newcomer to the market. (See Illus. 239 and 240.) This jig was developed by Don Thomas, who also holds some of the patents for it; he introduced it to the woodworking market in 1984. The manufacturer is the Woodmachine Company, Route 2, Box 227, Mebane, North Carolina 27302.

The Omnijig makes the popular half-blind dovetails used in drawer construction, and many other joints, some of which are shown in Illus. 241. It is based on the same design principle as those light-duty fixtures, such as the Sears, Porter-Cable, Black and Decker, and Bosch fixtures, that all have the plastic template fingers.(See *Router Handbook*, pages 153–156, for a look at these jigs.) However, you can do more with the Omnijig, which has a much better construction and is of better overall quality. (See Illus. 242.) It is also more expensive.

The Omnijig comes in two different sizes: a 16-inch model and a 24-inch model; 16 inches and 24-inches are the maximum width of board that can be clamped in the jigs.

The best indicator of the heavy-duty construction of the Omni jigs is their weight. The 16-inch model weighs 55 pounds and the 24-inch one a robust 65 pounds. In comparison, the biggest Sears dovetail-fixture set weighs less than 2½ pounds.

The Omnijig's primary function is to make various sizes and styles of the popular half-blind drawer dovetails. Both the tails and pins can be made in one pass, just as they are with the cheaper, light-duty versions. Clamp the workpieces into the jig in the same way, i.e., one vertically and one horizontally, with both pieces cut simultaneously in one pass. Clamp the pin piece vertically to the front, and the tail member of the joint horizontally on the top of the jig.

The cam-action clamps of the Omnijig are made of 1¼-inch-diameter steel. They operate with a single, quick lever action and are so hefty they will actually press cupped boards flat, tightly against the cast-aluminum base. The base is ⅝ inch thick and precisely machined to a 90-degree top-to-front work surface.

The manufacturer has interchangeable templates for making approximately six other kinds of joints (Illus. 241), including the sliding or tapered dovetail (used to join shelves to carcass sides, as in book cases and cabinetry), box joints (Illus. 244) and, variably spaced through dovetails, the latter underscoring the tool's versatility.

Illus. 239.   The Omnijig with the new variable, adjusting through dovetail template installed. Note the router set up in back.

Illus. 240. *The Omnijig, ready to be used with the optional router arm accessory by the same manufacturer, carries the router's weight and functions like a counterweight.*

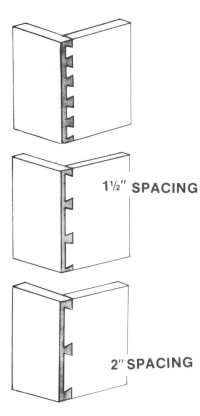

1½″ SPACING

2″ SPACING

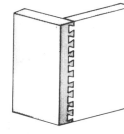

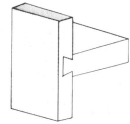

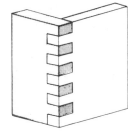

Illus. 241. *In addition to through dovetails, here are some of the other joints that can be made with the Omnijig. See Illus. 251.*

Illus. 242. Here is the basic Omnijig, stripped down without any template installed. Note the front (vertical) working surface and the top (horizontal) surface, to which the workpieces are clamped. Also note the heavy-duty, adjustable stops at both sides of both surfaces.

Illus. 243. Here are some of the templates available for the Omnijig. Note that some are in pairs and most are machined from ¼-inch aluminum, except the adjustable through dovetail template which has fingers (guide forks) of solid ½-inch aluminum extrusions.

Illus. 244. Omnijig's template for making box joints.

Illus. 245. With this heavy-aluminum template, you can make tapered sliding dovetails on the Omnijig.

Illus. 246. A look at the adjustable through dovetail template accessory for the Omnijig.

Illus. 247. The guide forks (fingers) are easily adjustable. They slide on the steel rods with thumbscrews and can be secured in any position for the spacing of through dovetails, as desired.

The template used to make variably spaced through dovetails combines some of the features of the Keller templates and some of the features of the Leigh dovetail fingers. (See Illus. 246–248.) However, unlike the Keller and Leigh models, it has dual-purpose fingers (also called "guide forks").

To determine which part or area of the fingers should be used to cut the pin or the tail, install the adjustable template assembly towards or away from the vertical, front working surface of the base with a simple system of spacers. (See Illus. 249–250.)

Through dovetail corner joints, as shown in Illus. 246 and 251, are made with each member routed in a vertical position. One pass is made to cut the tails; another pass, and another bit (straight cutter), is necessary, as it is on the other jigs, to make the pins. (See Illus. 250.)

Some interesting joints can be made by interlocking tail cuts to tail cuts. Illus. 251 shows an end-grain-to-end-grain application and a dovetailed flat mitre joint. The adjustable fingers (or "guide forks") for this operation should be positioned closely together, side by side, as shown in Illus. 252. Clamp the workpieces vertically, and make the cuts with a dovetail bit.

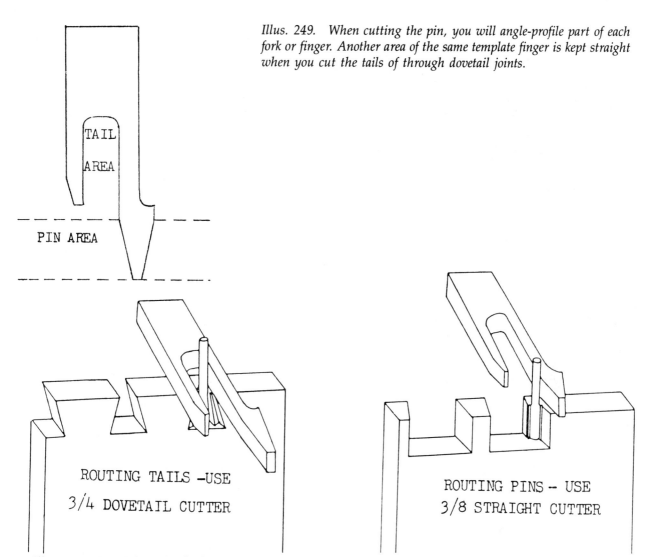

Illus. 249. When cutting the pin, you will angle-profile part of each fork or finger. Another area of the same template finger is kept straight when you cut the tails of through dovetail joints.

TAIL AREA

PIN AREA

ROUTING TAILS —USE 3/4 DOVETAIL CUTTER

ROUTING PINS -- USE 3/8 STRAIGHT CUTTER

Illus. 250. Here's how the dual-purpose adjustable guide forks or fingers are positioned to cut both the tails (left) and the pins (right) when you are making through dovetail joints. Note: A dovetail bit makes the tail cuts, and a straight bit produces the pins; both members of the joint are cut in a vertical position.

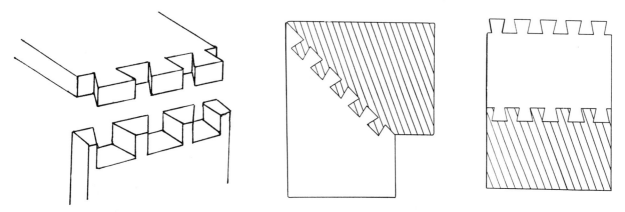

Illus. 251. Some of the joints you can make with the Omnijig with the optional through dovetail, variable-spacing template.

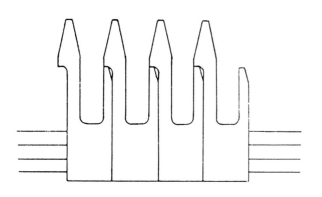

Illus. 252. The adjustable guide forks (fingers) are positioned flush against each other, as shown, when you are making joints with interlocking tails, such as the end-to-end and dovetailed mitre joint shown in Illus. 251.

Part IV
Commercial Router Machines

*T*his section deals with some of the multipurpose machines available that incorporate the motor units of the hand-held router. Also discussed are the new pin routers and router tables. Understanding the structural and mechanical features of these devices should prove helpful when you try to develop your own approaches to specific jobs. Included with some of the descriptions of these devices are machining techniques that can be applied to other machines discussed in this section or to devices and machines that you may have purchased or made yourself.

11
The Joint-Matic

The Joint-Matic (Illus. 253 and 254) is a heavy-duty machine that can perform a multitude of operations with the router positioned horizontally on a vertical, adjustable slide. The workpiece is supported on a small, but adequate, horizontal table. The Joint-Matic, which weighs

Illus. 253. *The basic Joint-Matic machine has to be supported on two blocks for normal workbench-top usage. A standard mitre gauge fits the ³⁄₈ × ³⁄₄-inch slot milled into the workbench.*

Illus. 254. *The Joint-Matic machine on an optional stand accessory.*

approximately 75 pounds, is a product of Strong Tool Design, 20425 Beatrice Street, Livonia, Michigan 48152.

The vertical slide (Illus. 255) is made of ribbed cast iron. It will, with adapters, accept most standard routers, but it was essentially designed to accommodate the Bosch and Stanley routers. The 10 × 16¾-inch slide has a total vertical travel of 8½ inches, which is one reason the Joint-Matic is able to make many different joints in stock of good size.

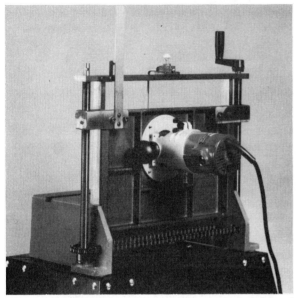

Illus. 255. A rear side look at the vertical slide and router mounting.

The vertical-adjustment mechanism (Illus. 256) is a chain-and-sprocket system that rotates two heavy (¾-inch diameter) vertical screws with a thread pitch of 16 per inch. Thus, one full turn of the screws with the adjusting handle moves the router ¹/₁₆ inch. (See Illus. 257.) Eight full turns move the bit exactly ½ inch without any need for measuring. If you are making box joints with a ½-inch bit, simply count the turns, make the cut, count again, etc., until all the cuts are completed.

Fine adjustments of less than ¹/₁₆ inch can be made by a partial turn of the crank handle. (See Illus. 258.) A ½ turn changes the adjustment ¹/₃₂ inch, and a ¼ turn moves the cut ¹/₆₄ inch, etc.

The 7½ × 18-inch worktable (Illus. 259) is part of a cast-aluminum base. A ³/₈ × ³/₄-inch milled slot accommodates a standard mitre gauge or an accessory called a "bevel mitre" which is also available from the manufacturer. (See Illus. 260 and 261.) The bevel mitre is made of cast aluminum and has an adjustment range with which you can make a wide variety of angular joints.

The horizontal depth of cut is controlled or established by the router's own depth-of-cut adjustment. Sometimes it's important to have a reference system for various depth settings. This is easy to accomplish with pencil markings on the base, as shown in Illus. 262. When the indicator mark on the motor unit lines up with your mark on the base, you know you are at the predetermined horizontal depth of cut.

Illus. 256. A close look at the adjustment mechanism shows a chain-and-sprocket drive with lift screws pitched at 16 threads per inch.

Illus. 257 (left). A scale provides readings for vertical adjustments to 1/16 inch. Illus. 258 (above). Very accurate tolerances of less than 1/16 inch can be established simply with a turn or a partial turn of the crank handle. One full turn equals 1/16 inch, a half turn raises or lowers the slide or cut 1/32 inch, a quarter turn moves it 1/64 inch, and so on. When the arm of the handle and the cross bar are parallel, as shown, they make a good reference or starting point for counting full turns or partial turns.

Illus. 259. The worktable to slide is fixed at 90 degrees and is nonadjustable.

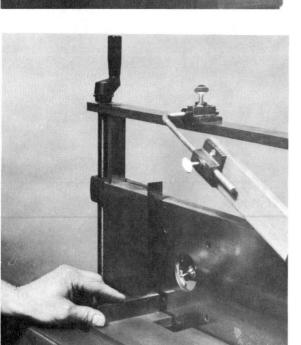

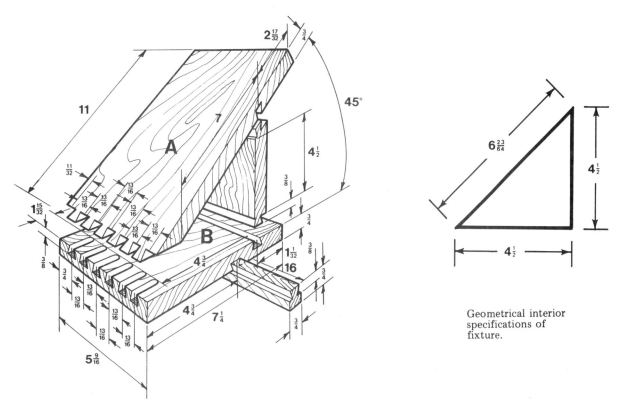

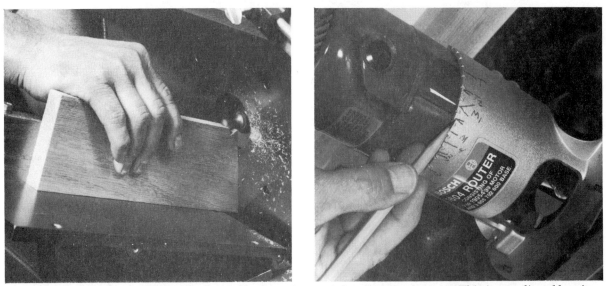

Geometrical interior
specifications of
fixture.

Illus. 260. Here's a challenging project to make as an accessory for the Strong Joint-Matic. This fixture supports stock for making a variety of bevel-joint cuts at 45 degrees. Measurements given here and in rest of book are in inches. To convert to metric, see Metric Equivalency Chart on page 377.

Illus. 261 (above left). Work supported on the manufacturer's bevel mitre accessory. This is an adjustable mitre gauge that carries the work into the bit at any angle desired. Illus. 262 (above right). Precise horizontal depth of cuts can be referenced with pencil markings, as shown. The marks on the base indicate final depths for various mortises and tenons to be cut with the same bit.

The vast majority of joints are all made using straight-cutting bits. When using these bits, it takes a little while to get used to the left-to-right feed direction. Also, you should always grip the workpiece tightly when feeding and be aware that the bit can kick the work away from you grip. Heavy cuts can be a problem if attempted in one pass.

Making mortise-and-tenon frame joints is one of the easiest and best applications of the Joint-Matic machine. Illus. 263 shows the technique for making the mortise. The final depth is best and most safely achieved if you make several passes, cutting less per pass. (See Illus. 262.) After the mortise is completed, cut the tenon cut to fit, as shown in Illus. 264.

A dado–rabbet corner joint is another joint that's very easy to set up and complete because of the precision-bit positioning possible with the Joint-Matic. (See Illus. 265 and 266.) So is the box joint. To make the box joint, remove a cut equal to the diameter of the bit from the bottom edge, as shown in Illus. 267. Then raise the bit a distance equal to the diameter of the bit for the next cut. Repeat the process until all cuts are finished, as shown in Illus. 268.

Housed dovetail cuts would be very difficult

Illus. 265.   A dado–rabbet or housed joint.

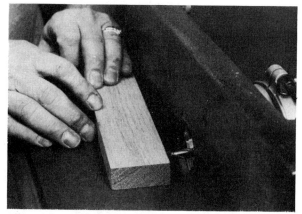

Illus. 263.   The Joint-Matic is great for cutting frame-type mortise-and-tenon joints. Here the final pass is about to be made to complete a mortise.

Illus. 266.   The dado is cut with the stock in a vertical position, as shown.

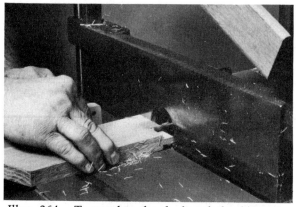

Illus. 264.   To complete the cheek and shoulder cuts, make the second cut of the tenon in one pass.

Illus. 267.   The start of the box joint. A cut equal to the diameter of the bit is removed from the bottom edge, as shown.

Illus. 268.   Making the box-joint cuts. Each successive cut or pass is made by raising the bit a distance equal to its diameter. If using a ¼-inch bit, you will have to make four full turns of the handle between cuts.

to make with just a hand-held router; with the Joint-Matic, they can be completed in just three passes. (See Illus. 269.) This housed dovetail is very strong; it is used in the assembly of framework and in the leg-and-rail construction of furniture. (See Illus. 270 and 271.) Illus. 272 shows how to make a flat mitre dovetail, which is a challenging technique.

The Joint-Matic comes complete with a well-illustrated operator manual that gives instruc-

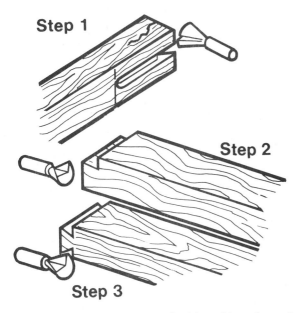

Illus. 269.   The three steps involved in making a housed dovetail.

Illus. 270.   Leg-to-rail jointery with a corner bracing—all involving dovetailing cuts made on Strong's Joint-Matic machine.

Illus. 271.   Cutting a dovetail tenon on a 45-degree corner brace. The workpiece is supported on Strong's bevel mitre accessory.

Illus. 272.   Cutting dovetails on flat mitre joints.

tions for making many joints in addition to those just discussed. One joint it gives instructions on how to make is the through dovetail. Making the tail cuts is relatively easy with the dovetail bit. Cutting the pins is much more difficult and requires much care and, eventually, some hand work.

Cutting mouldings and sliding dovetails, as well as rabbeting, slotting, and grooving, are some of the operations that can be performed with the Joint-Matic. This versatile machine has unlimited potential when it is used with the many special-purpose bits now available and a ½-inch-collet router.

One characteristic of the machine that I especially like is the ease with which it can be converted into a mini-jointer. To do this, simply attach a strip of 1/16-inch decorative laminate to the exit (right) side of the bit opening in the table, as shown in Illus. 273. Then raise or lower a straight or spiral bit so that the top of its cutting circle is tangent to a line extending from the surface of the laminate. This is exactly how a jointer functions.

If you are using a carbide bit, you can even joint the edges of tough materials such as the abrasive glue lines in plywood and the resins in particle board. (See Illus. 274.) Jointing such material with a hand plane or on a regular jointer will dull even the best tool-steel knives very quickly.

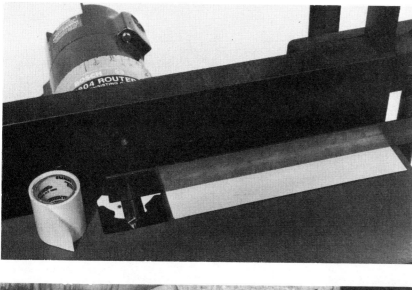

Illus. 273. To convert the Joint-Matic into a mini-jointer, position a strip of 1/16-inch decorative laminate, as shown, with double-sided tape.

Illus. 274. You can joint particle board with Strong's Joint-Matic with a carbide-tipped router bit and this jointer-like setup. Note that the feed direction is left to right, and should be quite fast.

12

Universal Joint Maker

The Universal Joint Maker is actually a routing attachment that mounts to your table saw. (See Illus. 275 and 276.) It is a product of G & F Precision, Inc., R.R. 1, Box 173, South Parliman Road, LaGrangeville, New York 12540.

The Universal Joint Maker consists of two major parts: A router plate and an extension plate that replaces the left tabletop extension on your table saw. Illus. 277 shows the principal parts. The design concept is based on all the operations that can be performed with a router when it is mounted horizontally, with a provision for its vertical adjustment. The vertical movement is obtained by a pivoting action of the router plate on one shoulder screw. (See Illus. 277.) The bit can be raised or lowered in relation to the table saw's surface with a crank handle. The horizontal depth-of-cut adjustment is provided by the router itself.

The router plate is made of ½-inch anodized

Illus. 275. The Universal Joint Maker is actually an attachment for your table saw. Here it is shown with a plunge-type router horizontally mounted to the router plate.

Illus. 276. The Joint Maker in its retracted (out-of-the-way) position permits normal table saw operations without interference.

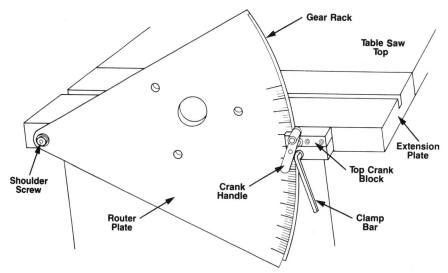

Illus. 277. The essential functioning parts of the Universal Joint Maker as supplied by the manufacturer include an extension plate that replaces the left table wing of your table saw.

Gear Rack

Table Saw Top

Extension Plate

Top Crank Block

Clamp Bar

Crank Handle

Router Plate

Shoulder Screw

aluminum with a vertical-adjustment range of seven inches. The table-extension plate is made of cast alloy-aluminum construction. The overall size is 18 × 27 inches, with a shipping weight of approximately 22 pounds. The router plate is custom-drilled to accommodate your own router. Standard or plunge routers can be mounted, with a range of 1 to 3 horsepower recommended by the manufacturer. A broad range of joints can be cut if you use the basic

Universal Joint Maker in conjunction with a regular table-saw mitre gauge. The joints shown in Illus. 278 include those that require that you feed the work into the bit at a 45-degree or other angle of support to make the cut. You can either make your own angular mitre-gauge work-supporting block or purchase another special accessory from the manufacturer that does the job.

The Universal Angle Plate is an accessory

item that multiplies the capabilities of the Universal Joint Maker tenfold. Illus. 279 and 280 show this unique version of a mitre gauge in use. The angle plate is adjustable 45 degrees

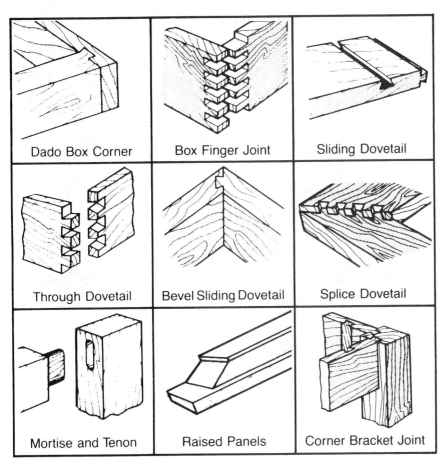

Illus. 278. Some of the basic joints produced with the Universal Joint Maker.

Dado Box Corner	Box Finger Joint	Sliding Dovetail
Through Dovetail	Bevel Sliding Dovetail	Splice Dovetail
Mortise and Tenon	Raised Panels	Corner Bracket Joint

Illus. 279 (above left). The Universal Angle Plate feeds the work, supporting it vertically at 45 degrees. Illus. 280 (above right). Here the workpiece is tilted backwards against the angle-plate mitre gauge so the pin cuts of through dovetails can be made.

143

horizontally right and left, as is a regular table-saw-type mitre gauge. It also permits a forward or backward vertical support tilt so that a wide variety of standard angular cuts can be made on either the routing accessory or for table-saw feeding.

The Universal Angle Plate comes as an assemble-it-yourself kit. (See Illus. 281.) The angle plate base has bevelled edges, as do large and small plates that are fixed to it with screws in the desired configuration to get the proper stock feeding or work-support angle. Angles of 9, 14, 22½, 45, and 90 degrees can be set up quickly and without difficulty.

Some of the stock-feeding positions permitted with the angle plate are shown in Illus. 282–286. These illustrations do not depict all setups, angles and combinations that are possible with this tool.

The Universal Joint Maker retails for approximately $500, and the Universal Angle Plate for approximately $130.

Illus. 281. The parts of the Universal Angle Plate as supplied by the manufacturer are complete and even come with a ball-type screwdriver. Note the degree markings and bevelled edges machined into the plates.

Illus. 282 (above left). The Universal Angle Plate in a 90-degree vertical and 90-degree horizontal position. Illus. 283 (above right). The angle plate assembled at a 90-degree horizontal and 14-degree vertical position.

144

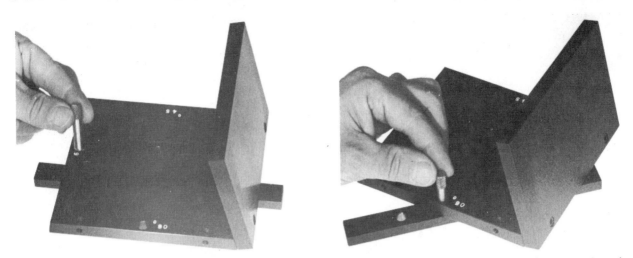

Illus. 284 (above left). With the index pin, you can quickly change the Universal Angle Plate from a setting of 90 degrees horizontal to 45 degrees left or right. Note that the vertical plate tilt is at 14 degrees. Illus. 285 (above right). The Universal Angle Plate is now at 45 degrees right, and has a 14-degree vertical tilt.

Illus. 286. The setup of the Universal Angle Plate at 45 degrees vertical and 90 degrees horizontal.

13

The Multi-Router

The Multi-Router floats vertically, on its side, and has a mechanism with which it can be used to make a multitude of different cuts to the workpiece as it is moved to any position or direction on a flat or tilting table, with a fence, an array of stops, work-locating pins, etc. And, it still incorporates all of the advantages of precise template-routing; it can even use templates that are designed to compensate for bits that are ground less than accurately.

The Multi-Router (Illus. 287–290) is one of the most recent joint-making routers to hit the market. This machine was originally developed by manufacturer John Ducate, Sr., to simply do a few jobs for his own weekend woodworking projects. However, with encouragement from his friends, Ducate refined the machine and added features to it. It is now made of heavy-cast aluminum by the JDS Company, 800 Dutch Square Boulevard, Columbia, South Carolina 29210. Illus. 291–297 show only a few of the many different joints this machine is capable of producing.

The essential functions of this machine are based upon a work-supporting table with a X–Y axis motion (8 inches each way) on linear bearings and hardened steel rods. (See Illus. 298–299.) The free-moving table is used in conjunction with the router unit that travels vertically (on the Z axis), thus providing a

multitude of combinations in work positions and routing directions. A system of stops can be set to either control the distance of travel or lock steady any one or all of the XYZ movements.

The table also tilts up to 45 degrees, which

Illus. 287. The Multi-Router and operator showing a tenon cut made with a template guide.

Illus. 288.   A closer look at the Multi-Router.

Illus. 289 (above left).   The Multi-Router on the floor stand. Illus. 290 (above right). Work-holding air-cylinder clamps are an optional timesaving accessory recommended for production work.

Illus. 291.   Mitre joint with a stub tenon.

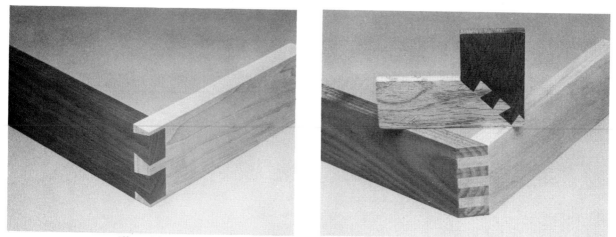

Illus. 292 (above left). *Double mortise and tenon. Illus. 293* (above right). *Round tenons.*

Illus. 294 (above left). *Angled tenon. Illus. 295* (above right). *Box joint.*

Illus. 296 (above left). *Through dovetail joint. Illus. 297* (above right). *Decorative joints.*

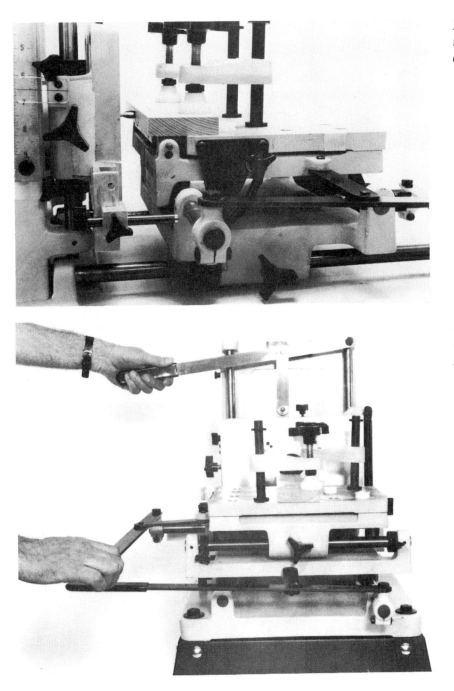

Illus. 299.   Here the operator's left hand (above) holds the lever for the vertical router movement while the right hand is on the table Y-axis movement handle. The combination of router and the work movements controlled by the stylus on a template makes the desired cut.

adds to the versatility of the machine. (See Illus. 300.) It has a narrow-edge fence that can be raised for use and lowered out of the way when not needed, or you can use an auxiliary wooden fence with an adjustable stop. (See Illus. 301 and 302.) A series of holes in the table, when used with removable locater pins, will orientate the workpiece to any of three dif- ferent angles to the bit—either 15, 22½, or 45 degrees. (See Illus. 303 and 304.)

The router and the Z axis (vertical) movement of six inches are essentially controlled through a feather-touch system because of a gas-cylinder counterbalance that offsets the physical weight of the router. The counter- balance cylinder is calibrated to work effective-

Illus. 300. The worktable tilts to 45 degrees, which adds still another dimension to the X–Y–Z features of the Multi-Router machine.

Illus. 301. Setting one of the stops to limit a cut or to locate workpieces when making duplicate cuts.

Illus. 302. A closeup look at the air clamps and an auxiliary wooden fence attached to the table with a stop block to locate identical pieces.

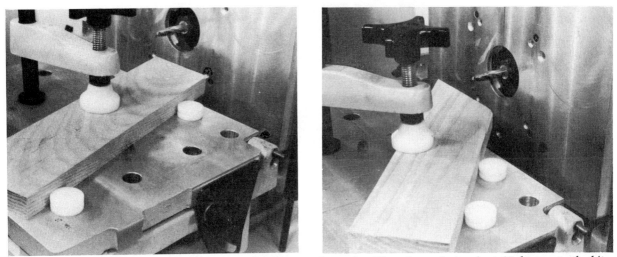

Illus. 303 (above left). *Table-locating pins establish specific angles. Here the workpiece is at 45 degrees to the bit.*
Illus. 304 (above right). *Here the locating pins are set to position the work at 15 degrees to the bit.*

ly with most average-to-heavier routers on the market, so the router will, if anything, automatically move safely to an upward position when released by the operator. Other features include a chip deflector and height scale on the Z-axis components.

The template system incorporated in the machine is one of its most distinct and interesting features. The key to template joint work is the template-following device, which is simply a round-rod stylus with a ball-bearing mounted to the end of it, as shown in Illus. 305. This stylus is held by a bracket attached to the vertically moving slide (of the Z axis). The templates are heavy milled aluminum, and are attached to the Y axis part of the Multi-Router with an Allen wrench and two shoulder screws. (See Illus. 306.) Either of two different kinds of template systems can be used for tenoning. The one shown in Illus. 306 is the "standard" type that is used when the bit being used is precisely ground. Sometimes even new bits are not ground to an exact cutting-edge diameter, or a used one may be slightly undersized because of resharpening. For questionable bits, the manufacturer provides a "variable"-size template set that consists of three inserts, each sized slightly different. (See Illus. 307.) Tenon templates are

available to cut tenons $\frac{1}{4}$, $\frac{3}{8}$, or $\frac{1}{2}$ inch in thickness, and from 1 inches to 3 inches in width in $\frac{1}{2}$-inch increments.

To operate the Multi-Router, mount the workpiece to the table and adjust the work or

Illus. 305. *The ball-bearing on the end of the stylus traces the template pattern from interchangeable templates while simultaneously controlling the movement of the workpiece into the cutting bit.*

Illus. 306. This type of standard template for tenoning is used with a bit that is ground to a dimensionally accurate cutting diameter.

Illus. 307. A variable-sized type of template is used when some compensation is required because the cutting diameter of the bit may not be precisely accurate. One of the inserts for the size tenon required will do the job regardless of bit inaccuracies.

stylus probe appropriately so that the ball-bearing follower is either engaged in a groove or following along a raised portion of the template. Turn the router on and move the stylus against the template, with one hand controlling the Z-axis movement lever and the other hand working the Y-axis movement lever, as shown in Illus. 299.

In addition to templates for various-sized standard oval tenons, the manufacturer can provide templates for making round tenons, through dovetails, and box joints. (See Illus. 293 and 308.)

Illus. 309 shows the template used to make the tail cuts of a through dovetail joint that is being installed. Illus. 310 shows a dovetail joint with the tail cuts completed. Another template is required to make the pin cuts, and you must change the router bit from the dovetail to a ³⁄₈-inch straight cutter. (See Illus. 311.)

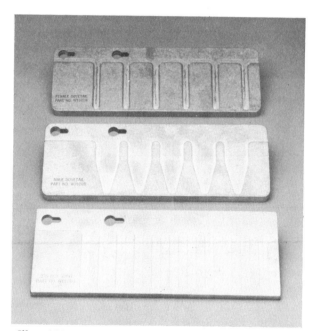

Illus. 308. Templates for making through dovetail tails, above, for dovetail pins, center, and for box joints, below.

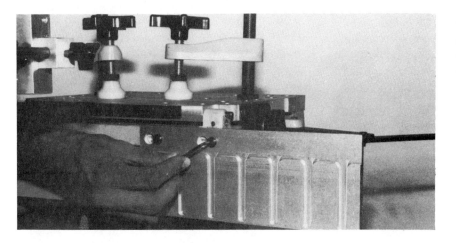

Illus. 309. Dovetail cuts are guided with templates that can be installed quickly, as shown here.

Illus. 310. The tail member of a dovetail joint is cut with the bit shown.

Illus. 311. Installing the template used to machine the pins of a dovetail joint.

On the Multi-Router, only one template is required to make both members of the box joint. (See Illus. 312.) Use a ⅜-inch straight bit. A simple system of layout markings orientate the top and outsides of the joint. (See Illus. 313.)

With some creative innovations, the Multi-Router can be employed to do much more than make the few joints that have been illustrated and described. John Economaki, at the Bridge City Tool Works, for example, has made wooden gears that utilize a custom-ground router bit and a shop-made indexing table.

The Multi-Router comes with a fairly complete and well-illustrated instruction guide.

The machine weighs about 100 pounds and costs approximately $1,300 (plus freight), and over $1,500 if you include the air-clamping system and other options, such as templates, bits, and stand. An instructional video is also available from the manufacturer.

Illus. 312. Installing the template used to make box joints.

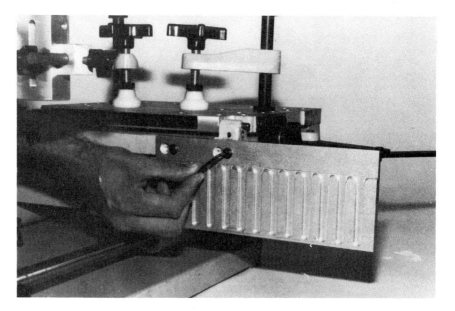

Illus. 313. A box with box joints in progress. Marks indicate the length of fingers, and the X indicates the top and outside of the joint.

14

Ryobi Radial-Arm-Saw/Router

This portable, benchtop 8¼-inch radial arm-saw, Model RA 200, was introduced by Ryobi in late 1986 and is rapidly becoming a popular home-shop tool. Surprisingly, Ryobi does not mention in its advertising the unique feature of this saw: its capabilities as a multipurpose routing machine. In fact, this unusual machine is truly a tough, dual-purpose tool. Perhaps it should be renamed, because it was designed to, and does, rout very well with minimal limitations for the home-shop do-it-yourselfer. (See Illus. 314 and 315.)

Illus. 314. Ryobi's 8¼-inch portable benchtop radial arm saw doubles very well as a multipurpose routing machine because of its 2 horsepower, 18,500 RPM spindle accessory that is part of the machine.

Illus. 315. The "saw" set up in one of its routing modes. Though not necessary, I added an auxiliary table over the existing saw table.

Though this tool weighs only 53 pounds, the adjustments and locking-in stops are very rigid and sturdy. The routing spindle (Illus. 316) is geared to rotate from 5,000 RPM on the sawing end up to 18,500 RPM on the router spindle, which is ideal for almost all routing jobs that can be performed within the capabilities of the machine. The double-insulated motor unit is rated at 11 amps, or approximately 2 horsepower, which is certainly sufficient power for routing, even when using many of the larger, $\frac{1}{2}$-inch-shank bits. However, the manufacturer wisely designed the unit for just a $\frac{1}{4}$-inch router collet. (See Illus. 317 and 318.) The machine would not be able to handle the larger, more aggressive, cutting bits.

Some operations that can be performed on this machine require more aggressive cutting bits and techniques than other operations. You'll soon learn which cuts have to be handled in multiple passes of shallower depths. This requires extra patience, but remember that this tool should not be considered, by any stretch of the imagination, a production machine.

The range of routing jobs that can be performed on this product is surprisingly more extensive than those that can be performed on some of the expensive rigid-arm, production pin routers. I've always liked the concept of a

Illus. 316. A small cap covering the end of the spindle protects a $\frac{1}{4}$-inch router collet.

Illus. 317. Any router bit with $\frac{1}{4}$-inch shank can be used.

156

Illus. 318. A shaft lock button located on the saw side of the motor makes blade and bit changing easy.

router system that, used within the design mechanics of the radial arm saw, can be operated in many different positions.

This tool is capable of an array of routing techniques, and I simply do not have the space here to describe each and every one. A multitude of routing jobs can be performed with the motor positioned so that the spindle is vertical. (See Illus. 315 and 319.) When the tool is used with a simple board fence (Illus. 315) and the router is used in a movement mode like crosscutting or mitring, you can cut quite easily any number of singular or multiple parallel and angular dadoes by simply using the carriage travel of the arm to guide the router movement. Stopped dadoes and grooves can be made easily by clamping wooden stop(s) to the arm which, incidentally, is easy to clamp to. (See Illus. 320.) The elevation crank permits vertical plunge entry for many jobs.

When you clamp the yoke rigidly to the arm, you will have an overarm routing setup. Now you can advance the work into the bit, rather than moving the router and bit through the work. In this setup, all sorts of rabbeting (Illus. 321), grooving, slotting, and edge-forming operations can be performed. Special mouldings (Illus. 322) are easy to produce. Standard bit profiles will create innumerable new or different shapes with a simple slant or tilt of the routing axis, as shown in Illus. 323.

With a pin router, you can perform an array of routing operations. Here I'll give you a few ideas to show you some of the possibilities.

You can drill pin holes ¼ inch in diameter into the table with the unit itself simply by making a plunge cut by using the elevation crank to feed the bit downward. It is best to locate the pin holes as close to the rear vertical column as possible. The farther out or away from the column the carriage, motor, and bit is, the less rigid the entire setup becomes. Different-size pins can be made, as dictated by the bit diameters or other needs. Refer to pages 248–250 and 366 for some ideas about making interchangeable pins.

You can use pins set into the table either to guide templates against to produce various

Illus. 319. Here the motor unit is set up in a vertical pin routing mode. The pins are simply ¼-inch dowels that can be removed.

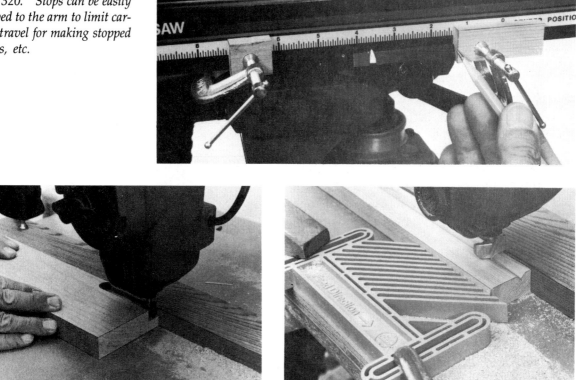

Illus. 321 (above left).   Rabbeting involves feeding the stock along the guide fence into the fixed router. Here a ¾-inch-wide cut must be made in several shallower passes. Note that the feed direction is left to right. Illus. 322 (above right). A point-cutting ogee bit is used to make the first pass for a custom moulding. Note that the motor unit is fixed vertically and a plastic feather board is used as a hold-in.

Illus. 323.   This cove-cutting bit, angularly positioned to approach the workpiece, will produce a moulding with a specific profile.

designs, or as pivot points for rotating workpieces to make circular cuts and form round discs such as wheels. It's often essential that the cutting area be guarded. Illus. 324–326 show two shop-made guards designed for pin-routing. If you are working thicker stock, it can be shimmed with scrap so that it clears the work.

To make circular cuts such as cuts used to make wooden wheels, dishes, round trays, etc., simply pivot the workpiece so that the feed is against the bit rotation. Successive cuts of shallow depth can be made to handle even some of the toughest jobs. The wheel shown in Illus. 327 is a good example. The stock is 1¼-inch-thick pine with a ¼-inch center hole. The initial circular cut is a roughing cut done on the scroll saw, band saw, or by hand. (See Illus. 328.) Move the arm to a suitable angle of approximately 15 degrees. With the blank in position on the pin, move the carriage towards the workpiece until the bit reaches the point where it will cut at the appropriate radius. Clamp it securely.

With the power on, lower the bit to about a ⅛-inch depth and rotate the workpiece against the rotation of the bit. Continue with ⅛- to ¼-inch-depth-of-cut increments until the circular form is perfectly sized, true, and round. (Illus. 329.)

You can make surface cuts that give the wheel a suitable contour in essentially the same manner. (See Illus. 300.)

Pin-routing techniques that produce various cutout shapes can also be employed on the Ryobi Radial-Arm-Saw/Router. The process is basically the same as that used on other pin routers except that additional passes of less cutting depths are required to cut thick materials.

The objective in pin-routing is always to produce a perfect one:to:one ratio copy of the pattern. When using the Radial-Arm-Saw–Router for pin-routing you must reach a compromise between practical results and time needed to achieve perfect results. The machine does have a certain amount of "play" at the yoke, carriage and arm. When all three assembly areas are combined, the amount of total play involved can become a problem if you are cutting too deeply or hitting hard areas such as knots during cutting.

This problem, however, can be resolved. In a typical pin-routing application, the bit-cutting diameter is normally equal to the diameter of the table pins. A little deviation from normal procedure is suggested here. Make the first cuts so that the resulting piece will be slightly larger than the final shape desired. This can be accomplished in one of two ways: (1) Using a bit that is slightly smaller

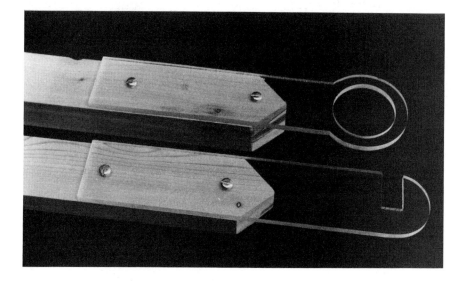

Illus. 324. Here are two guards that work essentially the same. The one above is made for routing thicker stock with larger bits.

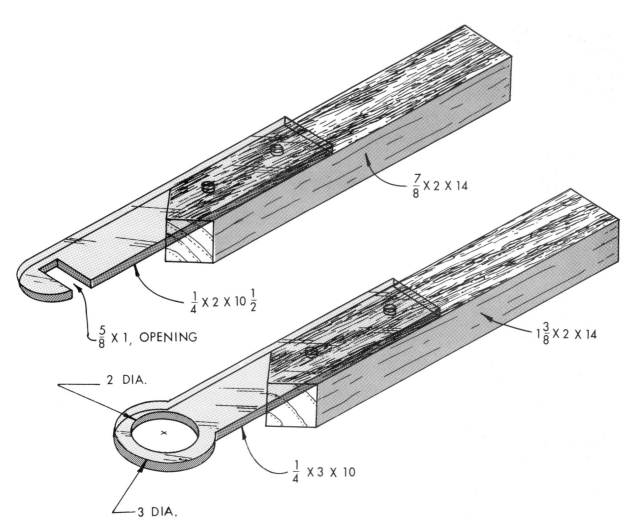

$\frac{7}{8}$ X 2 X 14

$\frac{1}{4}$ X 2 X 10 $\frac{1}{2}$

$\frac{5}{8}$ X 1, OPENING

1 $\frac{3}{8}$ X 2 X 14

2 DIA.

$\frac{1}{4}$ X 3 X 10

3 DIA.

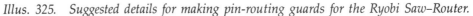

Illus. 325.   Suggested details for making pin-routing guards for the Ryobi Saw–Router.

Illus. 326. When used, the guard should be securely clamped to the table.

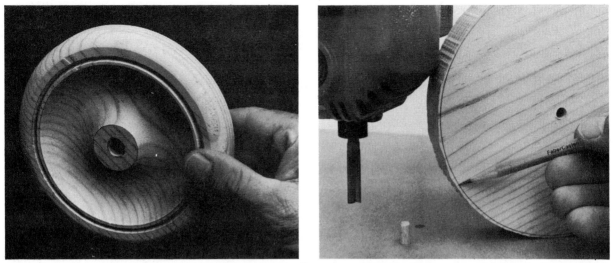

Illus. 327 (above left).   A wooden wheel, 6 inches in diameter × 1¼ inch thick, was made with the Ryobi Radial Saw–Router. Illus. 328 (above right). You can use a band saw, scroll saw, or hand saw to produce the initial rough shape, but remember to cut safely away from the layout line.

Illus. 329.   Truing the sawn edge to produce a perfectly round shape.

Illus. 330.   Surface-contouring using Sears' 1-inch radius end-cove bit that has an overall cutting-edge diameter of 1½ inch.

in its diameter than the table pin, or (2) simply enlarging the size of the existing pin so that it is larger than the cutting edge of the bit.

When the part has been completely cut out, either change the bit to a slightly larger size or reduce the diameter of the pin so that the diameter of the pin and bit are exactly equal. Then take one final pass at full depth; this slight shaving cut along the entire edge will result in a perfect one:to:one template copy. The entire process just described is depicted in Illus. 331–336.

With an easy-to-build box-like, shop-made

accessory, the Ryobi Radial-Arm-Saw/Router can be converted into a unique joint-making machine. Here you work with a vertically slotted fence and a horizontal worktable grooved for a mitre gauge. (See Illus. 337–340.) The router unit is rotated towards the front, and clamped in a horizontal position so that the bit projects through the slot in the vertical fence. (See Illus. 340, which shows a basic tenoning operation.)

A wide variety of routed joints can be made with this arrangement, in which the bit is projected through on a horizontal axis. If

Illus. 331. Preparing to produce this key-shaped cutout of ¾-inch stock employing pin-routing techniques. Note the plywood template ready to be secured to the workpiece with double-faced tape. First, saw the blank to a rough shape as indicated by the white chalk markings.

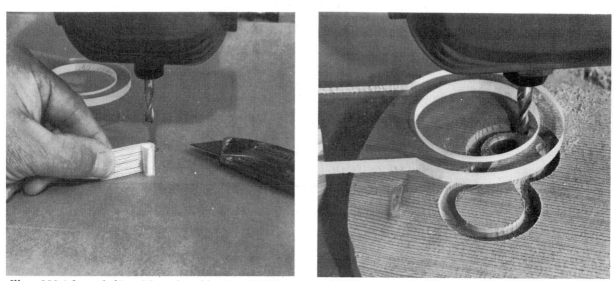

Illus. 332 (above left).   Wrap the table pin with tape to temporarily increase its diameter. Illus. 333 (above right). Make all inside and outside cuts in successive passes of shallow depths, ⅛ inch or less.

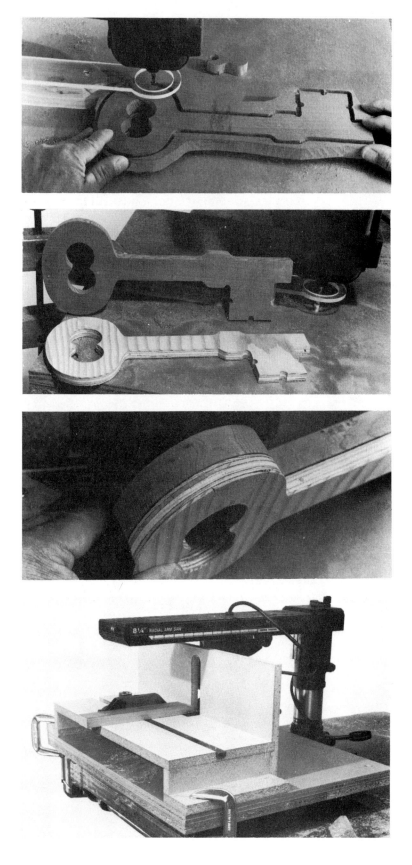

Illus. 334.   Continuing the pin-routing operation with the pattern (under the work) bearing against the table pin.

Illus. 335.   Remove the tape from the table pin and make one final pass all around at full depth to trim-out the entire edge to the size of the template.

Illus. 336.   The completed shape and the pattern.

Illus. 337.   A simple box-like attachment converts the Ryobi Radial Arm Saw–Router into a unique joint-making machine.

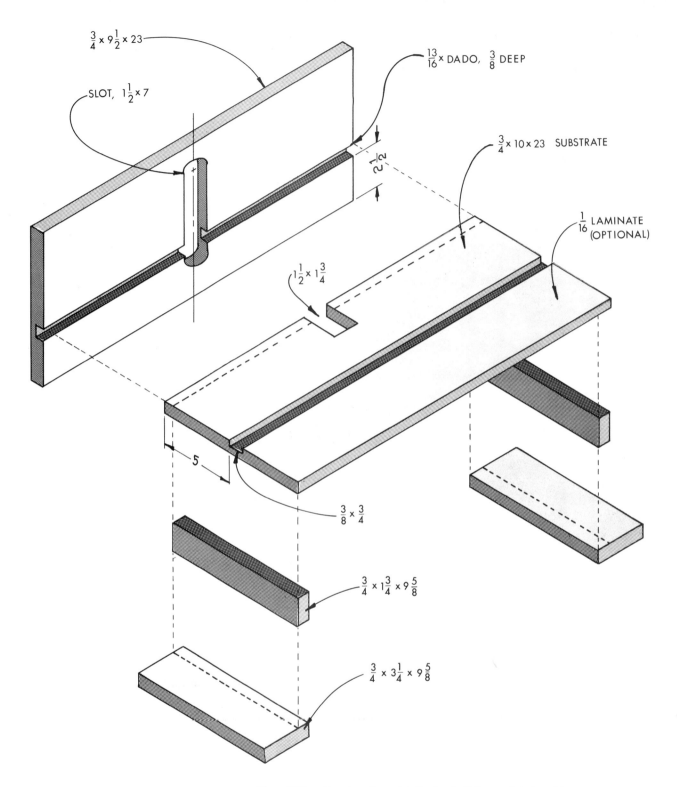

$\frac{3}{4} \times 9\frac{1}{2} \times 23$

SLOT, $1\frac{1}{2} \times 7$

$\frac{13}{16} \times$ DADO, $\frac{3}{8}$ DEEP

$2\frac{1}{2}$

$\frac{3}{4} \times 10 \times 23$ SUBSTRATE

$\frac{1}{16}$ LAMINATE (OPTIONAL)

$1\frac{1}{2} \times 1\frac{3}{4}$

5

$\frac{3}{8} \times \frac{3}{4}$

$\frac{3}{4} \times 1\frac{3}{4} \times 9\frac{5}{8}$

$\frac{3}{4} \times 3\frac{1}{4} \times 9\frac{5}{8}$

Illus. 338. Construction details for building a joint-making accessory.

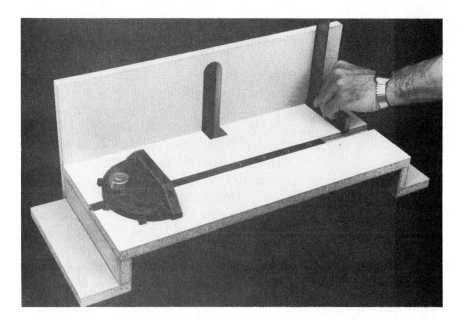

Illus. 339. *A closeup look at the joint-making accessory. The fence must be vertical to a table grooved for a standard mitre gauge. The table surface is covered with decorative laminate, and all surfaces were paste-waxed.*

Illus. 340. *A tenoning operation being performed on the Ryobi Radial Arm Saw–Router with the shop-made accessory supporting the work.*

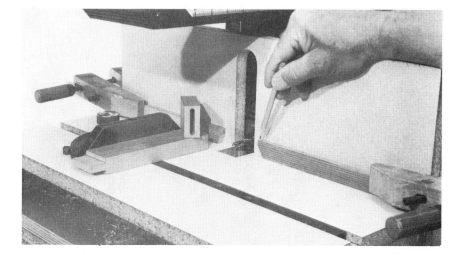

Illus. 341. *Wood stops can be clamped to control cutting distances such as needed when mortising. Here an end mortise has just been completed with the setup shown.*

necessary, you can make multiple passes as required until the desired horizontal depth is attained. The bit can also be raised or lowered, as desired, with the elevation crank. One full turn elevates or lowers the bit $\frac{1}{16}$ inch. Cutting box and dovetail joints, slotting, grooving, and a multitude of straightedge-forming operations will work with this setup.

To further expand the capabilities of this setup, reposition the motor unit so that the bit is rotating on an angular axis from the true horizontal position. (See Illus. 342.) Certain angular cuts, such as the one shown in Illus. 342, must be made in just one pass. This is not always possible because the size of cut, type of wood, and bit performance must all be favorable to the job at hand. Note that the slotted angle cut cannot be made in multiple passes by advancing the bit horizontally; nor can it be done by raising it vertically between cuts.

There are some interesting cuts you can make with the setup just discussed. Angular tenons are one possibility. However, they are much trickier than you might think. Almost all cuts should be tested on scrap stock before you use the workpiece. Illus. 343–347 show the steps involved in making angular tenons.

Interesting mouldings, angular splines, slots and grooves, and fake mitred dovetails are all examples of work that can be done with the joint-making attachment.

The ideas just discussed are included to spark your inspiration; you are sure to invent other personally customized cuts and joints to satisfy certain project needs.

Illus. 342. This 15-degree angled end slot cut in redwood was made in one pass.

Illus. 343. The first cut involved in making a 15-degree angular tenon.

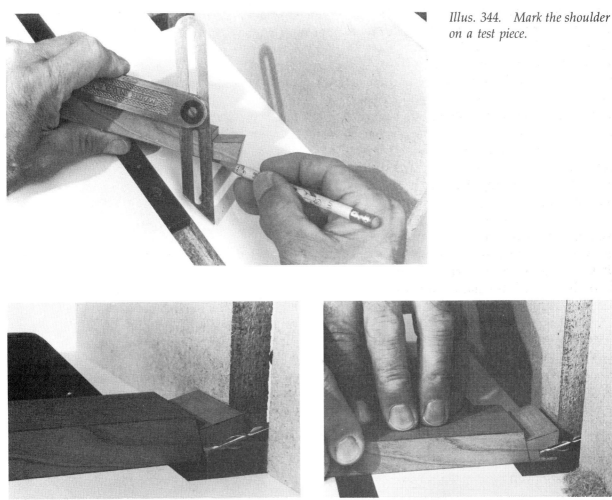

Illus. 344.   Mark the shoulder on a test piece.

Illus. 345 (above left).   Adjust the bit vertically and horizontally to the finished cheek- and shoulder-cutting position, as shown. Illus. 346 (above right). With the stock supported against the mitre gauge and away from the fence, take multiple cuts and shift the stock closer towards the fence with each succeeding pass until the end of the work strikes the fence. Your final pass will cut the shoulder and cheek to final size.

Illus. 347. The completed 15-degree angular tenons. The tenon ends can be squared (if desired), as shown on the lower piece.

167

15

The Mill–Route Machine

The Mill-Route Machine (Illus. 348 and 349) is a hobby woodworking device that duplicates patterns. It is manufactured by Progressive Technology, P.O Box 98, Stafford, Texas 77477. When you attach your own router to the unit you can do furniture work, make toys, models, and wood signs, make relief and incised carvings, rout plastics and light metals, and do other projects. (See Illus. 350–352.)

Any router can be attached to the machine's carriage, which moves smoothly in a combination of or any one of three different directions: 24-inch-side-to-side travel (X axis), 20-inch front-to-back travel (Y axis), and 3-inch vertical travel (Z axis). Originals, templates, and paper-pattern designs can be copied precisely in their actual size or reduced, if desired, within the capacities of the machine.

The Mill–Route's major parts are made of plated and painted stamp-formed sheet metal

Illus. 348. The Mill-Route Machine provides router movement vertically, side to side, and front to back through a system of rollers and triangular rails.

Illus. 349. The Mill-Route requires a 44 × 44-inch mounting surface. Here it is shown on an accessory worktable.

Illus. 350. Some of the carvings produced on the Mill-Route Machine.

Illus. 351 (far left). An eagle plaque design created from a line drawing. Illus. 352 (left). A picture frame with some relief carving cut with the Mill-Route Machine.

and hollow, triangular aluminum rails. (See Illus. 353–355.) The router carriage (Illus. 353) tracks side to side, forward and back. The vertical-lift action is provided by an adjustable-spring counterbalance system that maintains a vertical bit-axis position through the full 3-inch range of movement. (See Illus. 356 and 357.) The carriage can be locked in one position, which permits straight-line grooving and dadoing, rabbeting, and moulding cuts.

A number of interchangeable stylus points come with the machine. (See Illus. 358.) The total shipping weight is approximately 32 pounds. There is a considerable amount of assembly required, but the instructions are clear and easy to follow.

The unit requires a work space of 44 × 44 inches, which takes up a good deal of room in a crowded shop. The work-area capacity is 24 × 20 inches, which is adequate for most cabinet doors, smaller signs, and wall plaques.

The stylus, 19 inches from the bit, follows various 3-D or paper patterns in a one:to:one copy ratio. The manufacturer also has attachment that will reduce the X and Y axis movements to 75, 62½, 50, 37½ and 25 percent

Illus. 353. A bottom view of the main carriage assembly.

of the original pattern or template. (See Illus. 357 and 358.) Several alphabet templates (Illus. 359), as well as some other carving-design templates, are available that can be used with or without the carving reducer attachment.

Other accessories are available from the manufacturer, including an adjustable circle-cutting guide that can cut perfect circles of any size up to 19 inches in diameter.

Illus. 354.   An underneath look at the side carriage rollers, side rail, and center rails.

Illus. 355.   A closeup look at two of the 16 V-groove ball-bearing rollers and the triangular rails that provide the linear tracking of the Mill-Route Machine.

Illus. 356.   When the operator removes his hands from the front stylus control, the router automatically retracts to an up position. Here he follows a paper pattern to make a carving on a 1:1 size ratio.

Illus. 357.   Carving on a 1:1 copy ratio. Insert at left show the Mill-Route reducer attachment, which reduces the X and Y axis to 75, 62½, 50, 37½, and 25 percent of their original size.

Illus. 358.   Using the tracing stylus with the reducer attachment converts a paper pattern to a carving of smaller size. Note the tray in the carriage holding interchangeable stylus points, various bits, and tools.

Illus. 359.   One to one copying of letters. Individual plastic templates are assembled, as shown at right, to make engraved letters in wood, as shown on the left.

16

Mini-Max Mitre-Joining System

The Milton W. Bosley & Company, Inc., P.O. Box 576, Glen Burnie, Maryland 21061, manufactures machinery for production-joining of mitred mouldings. Picture-framing producers and fabricators are obviously primary users of this special equipment, which is also used to fabricate doors, windows, cabinets, furniture components, and anywhere mitre joints are used. All of this company's machines utilize router motors and specialty ground bits.

The Mini-Max (Illus. 360) is a smaller version of the large production counterparts. It cuts matching round-bottomed slots into the rear faces of both members of the joint. (See Illus. 361 and 362.) Special, plastic ball-end insert connectors fit into the routed slots cut by the special bit shown in Illus. 361. These plastic inserts are tapered at the end so that when driven in, they draw both members of the joint tightly together. The advantage of this system

Illus. 360. The Mini-Max Mitred Frame-Joint System utilizes a router motor unit, a special ground bit, and this device, which incorporates a system of clamps and stops.

Illus. 361. A drawing of the assembled joint, plastic insert, and the special solid carbide bit used to cut the slots for the plastic connector.

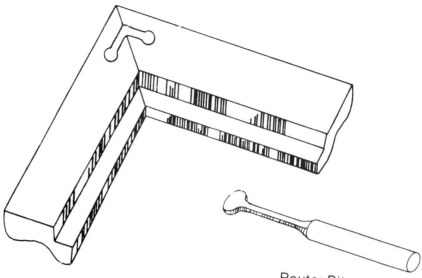

Router Bit

Illus. 362. A look at the joint cuts and the plastic insert that fits into the round-bottomed slots that draw the mitre tightly together.

is that strong, tight joints can be achieved without any nails, staples, or visible holes that require drilling and wood fillers.

The Mini-Max portable machine lists at over $1,000. It measures 18 inches in overall length, plugs into any shop vacuum outlet, and will adjust to any moulding between ½ and 3 inches in width, and of unlimited length.

17

Overarm Pin Routers

Since the publication of my *Router Handbook* in 1983 several manufacturers have come out with new or improved overarm routing machines. The Bosch, Router-Mate, Shopsmith, and Delta machines are American-made, and the Leader machine is by a Canadian manufacturer.

Bosch and Router–Mate Machines These machines are essentially the same. (See Illus. 363 and 364.) The specifications for both are so close that for our purposes they will be considered identical.

The basic machine specifications include a gross weight of about 95 pounds, an 18-inch

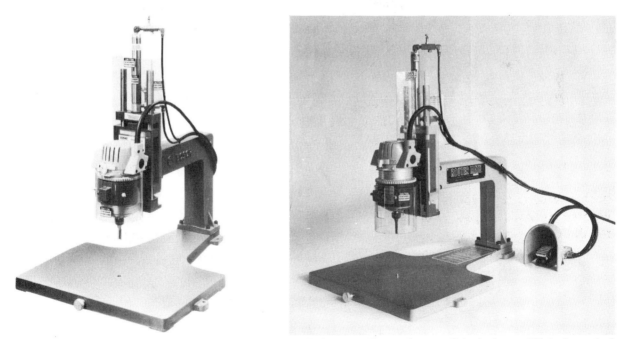

Illus. 363 (above left). The Bosch Model 93950 Bench Overarm Router has an 18-inch throat, 7¼-inch vertical clearance, and a 5⅛-inch variable stroke with pneumatic plunge and retract features. Illus. 364 (above right). The Bench Router-Mate has the same specifications as the Bosch Overarm unit. Note the foot-activated air control.

throat capacity, 7¼-inch vertical clearance, and a 5-inch stroke activated by a pneumatic foot-controlled air cylinder. Fifty to ninety PSI (pounds per square inch) of compressed air pressure are required to operate the machine. Any-size router motor unit up to 4½ inches in diameter can be fitted to the mounting bracket. (See Illus. 366–368.) The machines are designed to carry heavy-duty routers up to 3½ horsepower, which permits deep, continuous cutting in production situations.

You can adjust the stroke for travel distance with two threaded stops (Illus. 369), and regulate the speed of the router plunge-and-retraction action with an air-flow control on the cylinder (Illus. 370). To activate the vertical plunge movement, depress the foot control.

Illus. 366.   The motor mounting bracket for the Bosch and the Router-Mate routers is shown at the left. At center is a typical plastic-insert sleeve to facilitate the holding of motor units of smaller sizes.

Illus. 367.   Plastic sleeves of various sizes are available that slip over the router motor so that any size router can be mounted in the motor holder.

Illus. 365.   The floor stand accessory for the Bosch router overarm measures 36 × 24 inches and is 35½ inches high. Note the foot-pedal air control.

Illus. 368.   Installing the motor unit with the correct-size plastic ring into the clamping ring of the machine.

Illus. 369 (above left). *The vertical-depth-of-cut stops are set on this threaded rod to limit the stroke travel of the motor and bit. Illus. 370 (above right).* *The speed of the up-and-down motion can be controlled by this air-flow control located at the top of the air cylinder.*

The router retracts vertically when foot pressure is released. (See Illus. 371.)

The foot control is not only a convenience, it is also a safety feature. The operator always has the use of both hands to hold down and control the work when feeding and, especially, when starting and ending a cut.

These machines are very heavy because they have machined-cast bases and rigid cast-iron overarms. You can clamp a straightedge to the base for straight-line routing operations; this allows you to make rabbeting, grooving, dadoing, slotting and mortising cuts as well as edge-profile moulding, and do similar jobs.

The machines come with various guide pins ($\frac{1}{2}$, $\frac{3}{8}$, $\frac{5}{16}$, and $\frac{1}{4}$ inch), which can be quickly inserted and clamped with a convenient front knob. (See Illus. 372.)

The best work application for these machines is standard template routing of light or heavy material following a table pin. (See Illus. 373–375.) With any shape pattern, you can make accurate repetitive cuts that produce

Illus. 371. *Depressing the foot-controlled air valve plunges the router into the work. When it is released, it will retract the bit out of the work.*

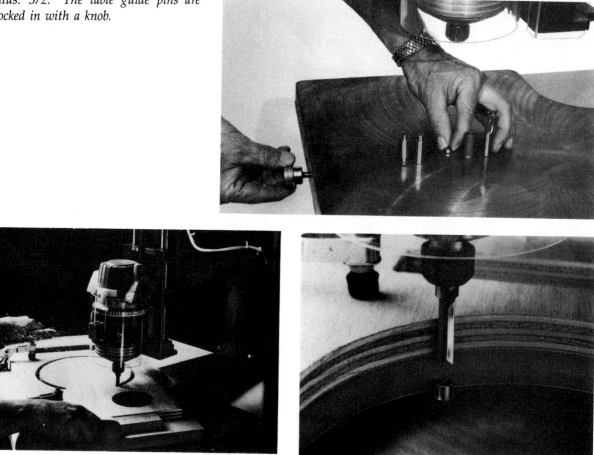

Illus. 373 (above left). Cutting the workpiece mounted on top of the template. (Photo courtesy of Bosch Power Tool Corporation.) Illus. 374 (above right). A view showing the relationship of the table pin, bit, template (below), and the plywood workpiece above it. (Photo courtesy of Bosch Power Tool Corporation.)

Illus. 375. The plunging and retraction of the motor unit by air foot control is ideal for repetitive work. It's also a safety feature because the operator can use both hands to hold and control the work. (Photo courtesy of Bosch Power Tool Corporation.)

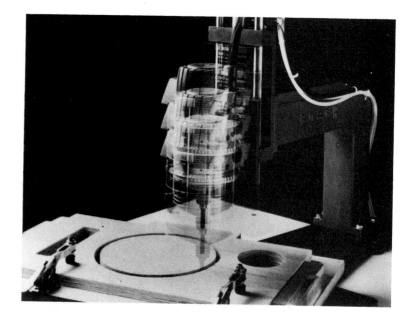

identical parts. The air-activated plunge-and-retraction features are ideal when the job requires the cutting-out of many inside openings, such as the job shown in Illus. 375. Refer to pages 301–310 for information about pin-routing techniques using vacuum chucks and vacuum templates.

The Bosch machine is manufactured by the Bosch Power Tool Corporation, 3701 Neuse Boulevard, New Bern, North Carolina 28560. The Router-Mate is manufactured by Porta-Nails, Inc., P.O. Box 1257, Wilmington, North Carolina 28402, in association with Ring Master Inc., P.O. Box 8527, Orlando, Florida 32856.

Leader Pneumatic Pin Router This router is manufactured by Pointras Machinerie, 70, 5e Avenue, P.O. Box 128, L'Isletville, Quebec, Canada G0R 2C0. This machine looks and functions very much like the Bosch and Router-Mate pin routers.

The essential specifications listed include a 18-inch throat, 7¼-inch clearance, 5⅞-inch vertical stroke, and a bulk weight of 95 pounds.

Illus. 376. *The Leader Pneumatic Pin Router is a Canadian machine. Note the turret-head stop system at the right, which the operator can use to quickly employ any one of three preset adjustments to control cutting depths.*

The machine comes with ¼-, ⁵⁄₁₆-, ⅜-, and ½-inch guide pins, and it has a foot-activated pneumatic stroke drive similar to that on the Bosch and Router-Mate models. Eighty to one hundred pounds of air pressure is required. The router-mounting bracket will receive motor units of up to 4⅛ inches in diameter.

There is one primary feature the Leader model has that the Bosch and Router-Mate machines do not have: a turret-head depth-of-cut stop system that is especially convenient for presetting three different cutting depths. The concept is the same as the turret stops found on the bases of hand-held plunging routers. Thus, when deep cuts are required, as many as three separate passes can be made at progressively greater depths as preset by the turret stops.

A chip-blower accessory is also available from the manufacturer. This accessory uses air from the line feeding the air cylinder to blow the work area close to the cutting bit clean.

Notice that all of the three air pin-routers discussed have adjustable clear-plastic circular guards to keep the operator's fingers from the cutting area.

Delta Overarm Router This is a big-capacity, heavy-duty, pneumatically controlled spindle-rising-and-lowering machine. (See Illus. 377.) Its net weight of almost 450 pounds is considerable when compared to the three 95-pound pin routers discussed.

The power unit is driven by a 2 or 3 horsepower motor through a belt drive to the spindle on a two-step pulley. This permits a choice of 9,000 or 18,000 RPM, for optimum efficiency in various routing jobs.

Some of the other features include a 21-inch throat capacity, 8⅛-inch vertical clearance, and a six-position turret depth stop. The 17⅝ × 23⅝-inch table tilts up to 45 degrees for angle-routing. The routing head has a vertical-stroke travel of 2¾ inches, and the table can be raised or lowered another 4½ inches with a hand wheel.

The Delta router also has a chip blower that can be adjusted for position and for the specific

Illus. 377. Delta's new two-speed (9,000 or 18,000 RPM) Model RU-50 Overarm Router has a ½-inch spindle capacity, pneumatic spindle plunge-and-retract control, a tilting and vertically adjustable table, and other features appropriate for heavy work.

amount of air volume. Ninety pounds of air pressure is required for the spindle-raising-and-lowering mechanics.

One feature that this machine suprisingly lacks is a slotted table so that a mitre gauge could be used to increase the machine's overall versatility. An accessory split fence is available for doing straight-line shaper-type work, and so is a vacuum connection attachment that attaches near the cutting area to draw chips and dust away from it. The list price of the basic

machine with a two horsepower single-phase system is over $2,500.

Shopsmith Router Arm This is an improved version of the tool that Shopsmith has been selling for a number of years. Refer to my *Router Handbook*, which describes how to use this basic piece of equipment.

The Shopsmith Router Arm is not an air or pneumatic vertical-entry-and-retract machine, as those previously described. It is designed for serious woodworkers, and light-production shops. The 3½-inch vertical-travel feed system is a hand-operated rack-and-pinion gear mechanism that has essentially remained unchanged since Shopsmith's earlier models.

The major new features include a stand and a wooden worktable with a mitre gauge slot. The new model now comes with a plastic featherboard (see page 78), a shaping fence, a built-in dust-collection hookup that can be connected to any workshop vacuum with a 2½-inch hose, and a comprehensive user's manual. Shopsmith has also produced a training video to help Router Arm owners learn all of the techniques and capabilities this machine offers. For more information, write Shopsmith Inc., 3931 Image Drive, Dayton, Ohio 45414.

Illus. 378. The improved Shopsmith Router Arm features a new table, stand, vacuum connection, and other accessories.

18

Router Tables

Here I will take a look at four different commercially produced router tables. Two are bench-top, self-standing units, one is simply a table work surface with several accessories, and the last is a special accessory unit designed to be used in conjunction with any table saw that has 27-inch table-leaf extension wings.

Commercially manufactured router tables available today are not much better than those that were available ten years ago. Tables suitable for light work have some unique design innovations, but there isn't anything manufactured commercially that could be sincerely recommended for medium-to-heavy-duty routing jobs.

Most router tables are not designed for the new, larger routers in the 1½ to 3 horsepower, ½-inch collet range. The router tables today are best limited for use with smaller routers carrying spindles with less than ½-inch capacities. For these reasons, I have included in Section VI (Chapter 28), plans and construction details for building the ultimate heavy-duty router table.

Before purchasing any commercial router table, determine if the shop-made version is a viable choice for your individual routing needs. If heavy-duty, limited production routing is not a high priority, consider using one of the router tables that I am about to describe for light work.

Sears Router Tables The new, and better, Sears router tables now feature what is called a "full-function, unitized fence" with retractable guards and a dust-collection connection. (See Illus. 379.) The fence has several design concepts exclusive to Sears models that revolve around unique devices for holding, supporting, and guiding different kinds of work across the cutting bit. The 4-inch-high fence is made of an injection-moulded structural foam-plastic that's very durable, true, and warp-resistant. This higher-than-usual fence provides good support when machining pieces on edge as, for example, when grooving, slotting, tenoning, etc. A special push-block clamp that rides on the top edge of the fence helps when cutting end grains, a technique that is used when making regular and dovetailed rail tenons. Illus. 380–382 depict these particular features and the setups involved in making regular tenons.

Another component of the unitized fence is a little plate, called the jointing fence, that can be set out tangent to the cutting circle of the bit or cutter; this plate functions like the out-feed table of a jointer. (See Illus. 383.) The joint-

Illus. 379. A Sears router table with a new "full-function, unitized fence."

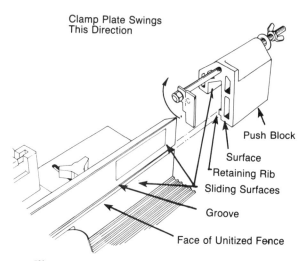

Clamp Plate Swings This Direction

Push Block
Surface
Retaining Rib
Sliding Surfaces
Groove
Face of Unitized Fence

Illus. 380. The push-block clamp plate assembly ready for vertical feeding, and its relationship to the Sears fence.

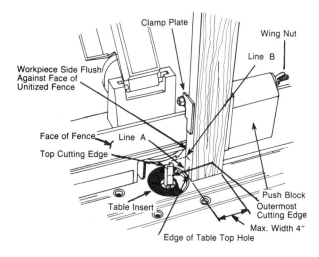

Clamp Plate
Wing Nut
Line B
Workpiece Side Flush Against Face of Unitized Fence
Face of Fence
Line A
Top Cutting Edge
Table Insert
Push Block
Outermost Cutting Edge
Max. Width 4"
Edge of Table Top Hole

Illus. 381. A typical tenoning operation on the new Sears fence. Note the workpiece clamped against the push block. Layout lines A and B indicate full width and length of the tenon.

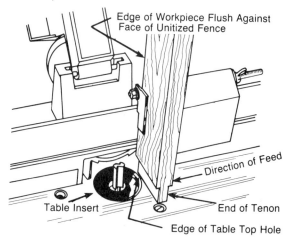

Edge of Workpiece Flush Against Face of Unitized Fence
Direction of Feed
Table Insert
End of Tenon
Edge of Table Top Hole

Illus. 382. To complete the tenon, feed with the piece in a second, vertical position.

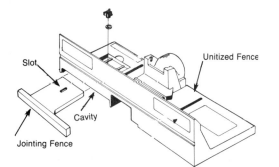

Slot
Unitized Fence
Cavity
Jointing Fence

Illus. 383. The jointing fence fits neatly back into its pocket cavity when not needed.

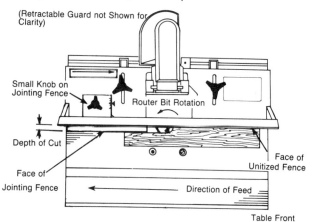

(Retractable Guard not Shown for Clarity)
Small Knob on Jointing Fence
Router Bit Rotation
Depth of Cut
Face of Jointing Fence
Face of Unitized Fence
Direction of Feed
Table Front

Illus. 384. Top view illustrating the jointer fence in its out position to support the work for full edge-cutting.

182

ing fence provides needed support as the workpiece is fed beyond the cutter. It compensates for the gap created on the exit side when some of the entire edge thickness is cut away by the bit. (See Illus. 384.)

As already mentioned, the Sears unitized fence has two guards. One, made of clear plastic, is called the "retractable guard"; it covers the cutting area somewhat like the pivoting "leg-of-mutton"-type guard on a jointer. The retractable guard is spring-loaded and pivots out of the way when the work is advanced into the bit and against the guard itself. As the cut is completed and the trailing end exits the bit, the guard automatically moves back into position, protecting the cutting area.

The other guard, as shown in Illus. 385, is on the back side of the unitized fence, and is

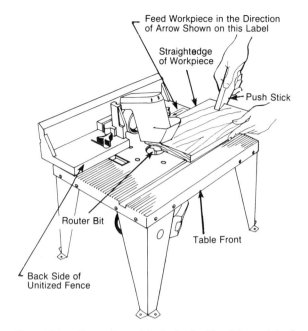

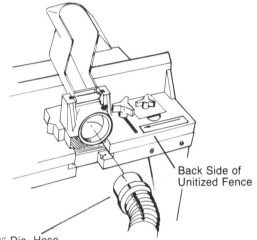

Illus. 385. View showing the vacuum connection, which can be fitted with a 1¼-inch reducer if necessary. Note the guard in its out-of-the-way position.

used when the entire fence assembly is removed from the table, turned around, and remounted to the table. When this happens, the vacuum hose must be removed because it's in the way of the normal guard operation. (See Illus. 386.) The unitized fence can then be used in a mode that permits guarded surface-routing jobs that are done away from the edge of the workpiece, such as dadoing, grooving, fluting, veining, and making face moulding cuts.

Illus. 386. Operating with the back side of the unitized fence positioned on the table to face the bit. This setup permits use of the second guard, as shown, for face-routing operations as, also shown. Note that the vacuum hose must be removed.

Porter-Cable Router and Shaper Table This table comes in two models that essentially look alike. (See Illus. 387.) One model comes with a 1½ horsepower router as standard equipment; the other comes without any router or router-mounting bracket, which means that the table can be custom-drilled to support any router. When the larger-size routers are used with the second model, riser blocks must be placed beneath the legs to provide sufficient space for the router under the table.

The tables have 16 × 18-inch work surfaces and a table height of approximately 10 inches. A special stand is an optional accessory available for permanent mounting of the router/shaper table unit at a comfortable working height. When using larger-size routers in the table, use the floor-stand accessory instead of elevating the worktable on riser blocks on top of the workbench; this way you'll be working at a convenient and safe worktable height. The tables have mitre gauge slots that are ¾ × ⅜ inch deep.

Illus. 387. Porter-Cable's router table is available in two models. One comes complete with a 1½ horsepower router; the other comes without any router or motor mounting bracket, so the table can be drilled to accept any brand of router.

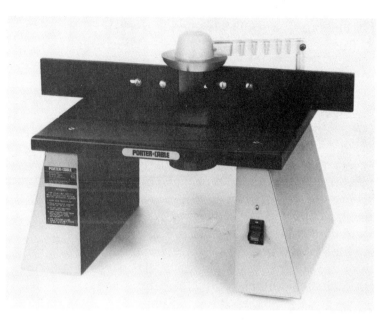

Illus. 388. The Porter-Cable Router/ Shaper Table Fence comes in two parts, with each half adjustable in and out.

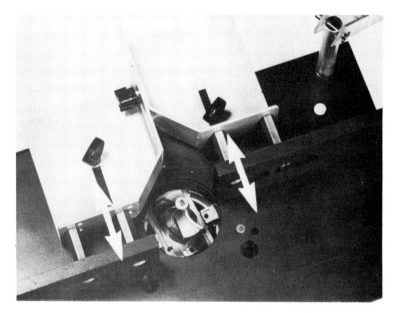

Illus. 389. Both halves aligned to a straightedge.

The fence is a split-shaper type, with each half independently adjustable in and out, as shown in Illus. 388. Ideally, both halves should either be in parallel planes or adjusted to a straight-face alignment, as shown in Illus. 389. Because of the stamped-sheet steel construction backing the fence, the alignment might be slightly off; it can be easily and simply checked with a straightedge, as shown in Illus. 389. However, should the assembly need adjustment, place a folded paper shim between the adjoining contact area of the fences, as shown in Illus. 390; this will correct the situation. Always check off-set adjustments as well, to ensure that the faces of the fences are parallel. (See Illus. 391.)

Both Porter-Cable Router/Shaper Tables come with a 20 amp prewired double-pole switch that is conveniently located in one of the supporting legs. Both models also come with starting pins (Illus. 392) for edge-forming work, an overhead cutter guard, and a set of table-opening inserts that permit $1\frac{1}{4}$-, 2-, and 3-inch-diameter-hole bit openings in the table.

Illus. 390. A folded paper shim inserted between the back structures of the fences, as shown, may be necessary to align the surfaces to each other.

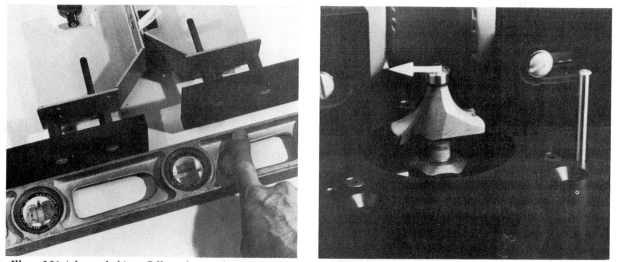

Illus. 391 (above left). Off-set fence adjustments to ensure that the faces are exactly parallel to each other. Illus. 392 (above right). A pin in the Porter-Cable router table fits either of two predrilled holes. Usually it is used, as shown, to the right as the work is fed (with the arrow) against the rotation of the bit.

Woodhaven Router Table and Wonderbase
This unit, as shown in Illus. 393–396, takes all of the work (and some of the fun) out of making your own custom router table. Manufactured by Woodhaven Company, 5323 West Kimberly Road, Davenport, Iowa 52806, the Router Table is a large (24 × 32 inches) flat top with an applied decorative-laminate surface, and is made of medium-density fibreboard; it also has a premachined recess that accepts a

Illus. 393. *The Woodhaven table panel with plastic Wonderbase takes all of the work out of making your own customized router table. Note the premachined opening in the top.*

Illus. 394. *Use your own router base as a guide for drilling mounting holes in the Wonderbase.*

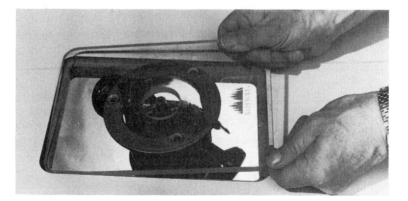

Illus. 395. *Shown is a router with the Wonderbase simply being set into the rabbeted opening; the Wonderbase is gravity-held in position, which means it can be easily moved in and out for various other uses.*

$^3/_8 \times 7^3/_4 \times 10^1/_4$-inch clear-plastic drop-in insert. You design and make your own legs or stand as dictated by your individual needs.

The plastic base comes with a $1^1/_4$-inch-diameter-bit hole opening, or you can buy a blank without a hole if you wish. In either case, you'll have to drill holes to match those of your base. To do this, simply remove the existing plastic subbase from your router and center it with tape or clamps over the Wonderbase; then use your subbase as a drilling guide, as shown in Illus 394. Once you attach the Wonderbase to your router, it can be dropped in or out of the table at will in just a couple of seconds. Gravity holds the assembly in position; no threaded fasteners are required to secure or anchor the router.

Woodhaven also manufactures some router table accessories. One accessory is a one-piece straight-line fence (Illus. 397 and 398) machined from a $^1/_4 \times 3 \times 3$-inch-stock aluminum angle. It is faced with a piece of oak, and has a plastic bit guard and a square-end plastic elbow. You can use either a $2^1/_2$-inch-diameter shop vacuum hose, which will fit inside the square end, or a 3-inch dust-collector hose, which will fit around its outside.

A combination safety starting-block-and-bit-guard (Illus. 399), used like a shaper starting pin, is another Woodhaven router-table ac-cessory. To use it, simply clamp each leg to the table. You can also attach the dust pick-up connection for a shop vacuum hose as shown in Illus. 399.

Woodhaven also has a circle-cutting attach-ment. This plastic-fabricated jig, shown in Illus. 400 and 401, is used to trim or machine circles that range from 3 up to 37 inches in diameter. The jig consists of a lower plate (Wonderbase

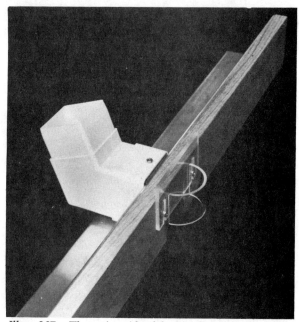

Illus. 397.   The action side of the Woodhaven router table fence.

187

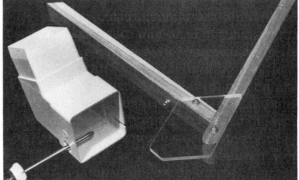

Illus. 398 (left). The back side of the Woodhaven fence. Note the bit opening and the wood-mounting block for the vacuum-hose connection. Illus. 399 (above). A safety starting block (used like a shaper starting pin) with plastic bit guard is clamped to the router table. A vacuum-hose connection can also be incorporated, if desired.

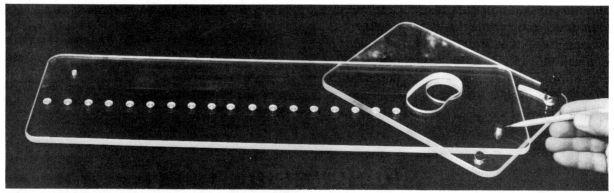

Illus. 400. The Woodhaven circle-cutting jig accessory fits into the rectangular opening of their router table. Note the pivot point at the pencil.

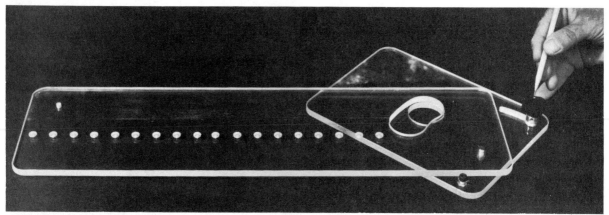

Illus. 401. An adjustable stop on the Wonderbase (below, at right) limits the pivoting travel of the workpiece when it is mounted on the circle-cutting assembly (the upper piece).

size) that fits into the top recess of the Woodhaven Router Table, and a longer, rectangular upper circle-cutting assembly, onto which the work is mounted. This system, which employs an adjustable stop to establish the precise radius and pivots to advance the work to the starting point, will produce perfect circular cuts to an exact radius. Usually, the workpiece is band-sawn to a prior rough circular shape. If not, multiple passes at shallower depths will be required. Illus. 402 and 403 show and explain how the workpiece pivots on a pin in the upper plate.

Bosch Table-Saw Router Table This accessory is designed for use on table saws with 27-inch leaf extensions. (See Illus. 404 and 405.) This unit replaces the saw table's standard extension leaf. The component parts make it easy to mount any router to the underside of the leaf (Illus. 406), which means that you can utilize the saw-table's surface, fence control,

and lock to good advantage. This creates a substantial router-table setup without sacrificing additional floor space. Other essential component parts include a swing-away guard and an auxiliary wood fence with a bit opening. (See Illus. 407 and 408.)

Inca Table-Saw Router Table Also new on the market, but not illustrated here, is a router table made specifically for Inca Table Saws—Models 250, 249, and 259—that is made of $3/8$-inch clear plastic and comes undrilled. With this router table, you drill your own mounting holes to match the base of the router. When installed in place of a typical 4-inch table extension, this plastic router table measures $8\frac{1}{2}$ inches wide, which increases the table surface considerably. The router table is, obviously, used in conjunction with the mitre guide, saw fence, and Inca hold-down accessories. For more information, contact the Garrett Wade Company, 161 Avenue of the Americas, New York, New York 10013.

Illus. 402. A closeup look at a pivot pin, which is driven into the underside of the wood workpiece.

Illus. 403. Set the rough-sawn circular blank with the pivot pin in its underside into the pivot-pin hole that is nearest to the desired radius. With the router on, the entire upper plate (Illus. 401 and 402) with the workpiece will pivot into the bit until it hits the stop adjusted for the precise radius. Rotate the workpiece clockwise, against the bit rotation, to complete the cut.

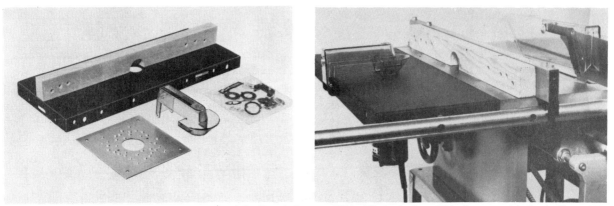

Illus. 404 (above left).   *The components of the Bosch Router Table Kit include a 27-inch extension leaf. Illus. 405 (above right). The Bosch router table mounted on a table saw utilizes the fence adjustment provided by the saw.*

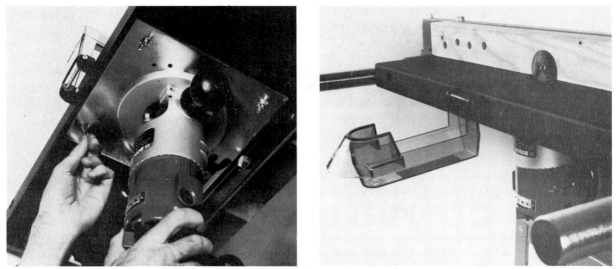

Illus. 406 (above left).   *First mount any router to an adapter plate, which, in turn, can be quickly attached to the leaf with four wing nuts. Illus. 407 (above right). A premachined wood fence bolts to the saw fence, and a swing away transparent guard allows a clear view of the cutting action.*

Illus. 408.   *Here the guard is shown in use for an edge-shaping operation with a pivot-guided bit.*

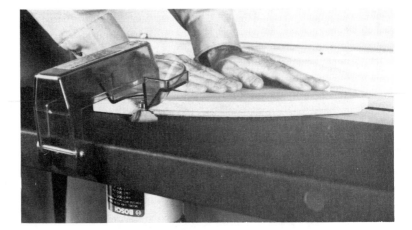

Part V
Shop-Made Jigs, Fixtures, and Useful Devices

Probably one of the most pleasant and satisfying aspects of woodworking is confronting a particular machining problem head on, knowing that there must be some way the router can be used to solve it. Sooner or later the inspiration comes, and you eventually have a jig or fixture that solves the problem. The more ideas you read about or come across, the easier it becomes to solve the problem.

Another reason for making jigs and fixtures obviously includes just seeking a better way to do the job at hand, that is, making the job safer, easier, faster, and more precise—in short, more productive and efficient—than it has been done before. Now that you've read about many commercially produced gadgets, jigs, and routing machines, the next step is to show you how to apply some of these concepts to making your own jigs or fixtures.

It's preferable to make the kind of jigs that can be used more than once or for a number of different projects. I have often come across jigs that are limited to doing only one job for just one project. Making these jigs is sometimes even more work than actually making the project itself; and, once the project is completed, the jig either remains to clutter up the shop or is eventually thrown away.

Some of the jigs presented in the following chapters might actually fall into this category. However, they are included because they are either unique, easy and inexpensive to make, or incorporate an idea or technique that can be applied to other potential problem-solving situations.

Preparing this section was a great deal of fun, but, at the same time, it was also somewhat frustrating because there are always more new ideas to think out, test and revise. Even after a jig has been remade a second or third time, it can be further improved and streamlined. Consequently, some of the ideas and plans presented in this section can, and should, be modified or improved as you see fit.

Furthermore, space limitations simply do not permit including every potential shop-made router jig or idea that exists. Some of the basic and commonly known jigs are not included to avoid needless repetition. My intentions here were essentially to present a number of new and fresh ideas. Therefore, in the following chapters you'll discover techniques and jigs to convert your plunging router into a dowel-joint boring tool, a jig that permits you to cut perfect and precise ovals in various sizes, and a presentation about the advantages and disadvantages of making vacuum chucks and templates like those used in industrial settings.

One of the most disturbing and annoying aspects of router jig and fixture work is the difficulty of fastening shop-made bases, jigs, and guides to the bottoms of the routers on the market today. The worst offenders in the industry are the manufacturers of plunge-type routers. On one hand, they provide us with routers that have the capabilities to make fantastic controlled, perfect vertical bit entries and quick, safe bit retractions, yet the majority of plunge routers today either don't have enough threaded sockets in their bases or have sockets that are too small to permit attaching shop-made devices to. Maybe someday those who design routers will be people who actually use them on a daily basis in a variety of creative and practical ways. Until the manufacturers make the appropriate improvements (which would, in fact, be easy and inexpensive), we will have to do the best we can with what is available.

19

Making Special Router Bases

There are improvements that I'd like to see manufacturers make to router bases. First of all, subbases should be made of transparent plastic so that the work area can be seen better. Center holes in the subbases should be larger so that bits with larger cutting-edge diameters can be used; and it follows that there should be larger-diameter template guides to accommodate the larger, special bits, and subbases to accommodate these larger-size template guides.

As I've mentioned previously, there is a definite need for good threaded sockets, to make it easier to secure shop-made bases and other devices to the bottom of routers to increase router versatility. I could make many other suggestions, but since here I am concerned solely with making router bases, I will concentrate on showing you how to make them with some of the necessary conveniences.

Most of the foreign routers have metric threads in the screws that secure the plastic subbases. A good hardware dealer or industrial supply company will be able to provide longer metric screws when required. Otherwise, it might be practical to consider drilling out the existing threads, getting a tap, and rethreading the holes with larger United States pitch threads and getting larger screws. So far

I have not resorted to this tactic, but if I didn't own a variety of routers, I would do this to some of the foreign routers I do have.

Illus. 409 shows some of my growing selection of special shop-made router bases, but only those that are made from clear plastic. Clear acrylic and polycarbonate are both used for these bases (cheaper acrylics are too soft and difficult to machine), but the polycarbonate (Lexon or Tuffak brands) is greatly preferred because of its superior overall toughness. It is almost impossible to break or shatter, and it machines so much easier. Illus. 410 depicts a test that compares the two. I drilled identical holes through the corners of acrylic and polycarbonate pieces at the same locations in stock of equal thicknesses. I then attempted to crack off the corners. The acrylic corner snapped off quickly. The polycarbonate, however, would not snap or crack, not even when I placed it in a vise and hit it with a 16 ounce hammer. The worst I succeeded in doing to it was bending it.

Incidentally, most sheet plastics are available locally in almost all metropolitan areas. Check your phone directory for a good source. Grades, prices, and quality vary among manufacturers and suppliers.

Illus. 409. Some of my special subbases made of clear plastic.

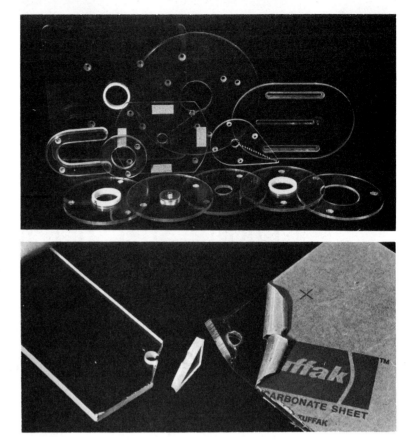

Illus. 410. A little test comparing the toughness of acrylic (at left) to polycarbonate sheet plastic. The latter will bend, but not shatter like the acrylic.

Adjustable Circle-Cutting Base The router base I recommend that you make first, before any others, is an adjustable one designed to make accurate circular cuts of fairly *small* diameters. (See Illus. 411–413.) This routing jig, with which you can make very accurate circular cuts in plastic and wood, is very useful for many router jig- and fixture-making jobs, and has many different project-making uses. (See Illus. 414 and 415.) The one shown in these illustrations was designed specifically to fit onto the Ryobi 1 horsepower plunge routers, Models R-150 and R-151. You'll have to adapt this base to fit other plunge routers, but this should not be difficult. Although my primary intent was to make a precision small-hole cutting device, this base also has the capability to make larger circular cuts of up to $7\frac{1}{2}$ inches in diameter very quickly. Illus. 416 gives the essential dimensions and construction details.

The adjustable circle-cutting base is designed to be used with a $\frac{1}{4}$-inch-diameter straight- or

spiral-cutting bit. Notice that in the section view of Illus. 416 $\frac{3}{8}$-inch-thick plastic (polycarbonate) is specified. This provides a sufficient thickness to anchor a pivot pin and permit roundhead screws to clear the lower surface when they are set into the $\frac{1}{4}$-inch-deep recessed slots, which are also shown in the section drawing.

Cut the slots into the plastic with the

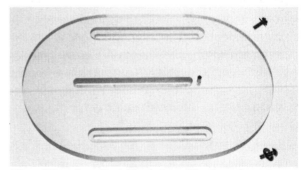

Illus. 411. An adjustable circle-cutting base for a plunge router will very accurately cut diameters as small as 1 inch.

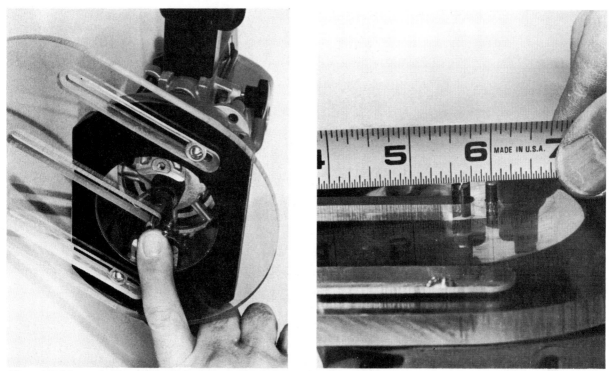

Illus. 412 (above left). View of the adjustable circle-cutting base mounted on a plunge router. Note that the pivot pin can be adjusted very close to the cutting edge of the bit. Illus. 413 (above right). Here's another view showing a setup for making a 1-inch-diameter hole.

Illus. 414 (above left). The circle-cutting jig in use. A hole for the pivot pin must be drilled into the workpiece. Illus. 415 (above right). Here is a 1-inch-diameter hole that has been cut through a board 1½ inch thick. The cut was made from both sides. The shallow cuts at left are the test holes used to check the precise diameter adjustment.

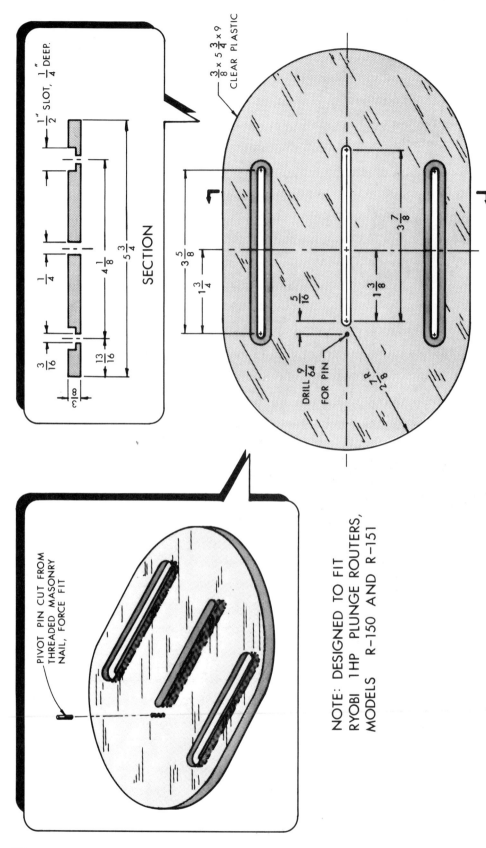

SECTION

$\frac{3}{8} \times 5\frac{3}{4} \times 9$
CLEAR PLASTIC

$\frac{1}{2}''$ SLOT, $\frac{1}{4}''$ DEEP.

$5\frac{3}{4}$

$4\frac{1}{8}$

$\frac{1}{4}$

$\frac{3}{16}$

$\frac{13}{16}$

$\frac{3}{8}$

$3\frac{5}{8}$

$1\frac{3}{4}$

$3\frac{7}{8}$

$1\frac{3}{8}$

$\frac{5}{16}$

DRILL $\frac{9}{64}$ FOR PIN

$2\frac{7}{8}$R

PIVOT PIN CUT FROM THREADED MASONRY NAIL, FORCE FIT

NOTE: DESIGNED TO FIT
RYOBI 1HP PLUNGE ROUTERS,
MODELS R–150 AND R–151

Illus. 416. Details for making an adjustable circle-cutting base for Ryobi 1 horsepower routers.

assistance of a router table. Illus. 417 shows how a fence is used to guide the work. Note the two marks drawn vertically on the fence that indicate the diameter of the bit. The exact location of these lines can be found by placing a try square against the fence and extending the cutting edges of the bit back to the fence. These vertical lines simplify the establishment of stops that can now be clamped to the fence to limit the length that the slots will be cut. Trial cuts can also be cut partway into the waste areas of the plastic so that you can be sure that the fence is located so that the resulting slots will be cut the correct distance from each other. (See Illus. 417 and 418.)

Illus. 416 specifies a ¼-inch-wide slot that runs down the middle. The slot should be slightly more than ¼ inch, which is likely to happen automatically if you run both edges of the workpiece against the fence; such a maneuver will also center the slot perfectly. (See Illus. 419 and 420.)

Illus. 417. Cutting the ³⁄₁₆-inch-wide slots on a router table. Make trial cuts partway into the waste areas, and check the measurements before cutting the actual slots (which are shown in the photo) through.

Illus. 418. After you have cut through both ³⁄₁₆-inch slots, insert a ½-inch-diameter bit. Do not move the fence or stops. Now, cut only to a ¼-inch depth using the same fence and stop settings you used for the ³⁄₁₆-inch slots.

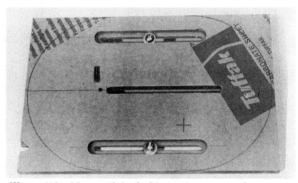

Illus. 419. Use a ¼-inch bit again to cut the center through slot, as shown. This slot can be slightly more than ¼ inch wide. Running both edges against the fence will center the slot exactly, and probably provide the slight extra width of cut needed for bit clearance.

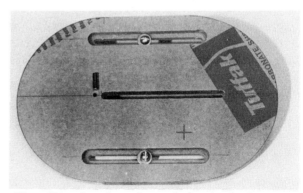

Illus. 420. Saw the ends round after the slotting operations are completed because the corners are needed to register the placement of stops on the router table fence for machining the slots. Note the pivot pin ready to be inserted.

The pivot pin used for this base was cut from a section of a 3-inch threaded masonry nail, as shown in Illus. 421. Other pins, called tension pins or split pins, will also work. They are available in $\frac{3}{16}$- and $\frac{1}{4}$-inch diameters, but must be ground to length rather than hacksawn. They are made of spring steel, which is tough on hacksaw blades.

You will find that this adjustable circle-cutting base is well worth the effort it takes to make it. This device will cut holes as accurately as a precision, and more expensive, circle-cutter. (See Illus. 422.) You can also utilize flat-cutting bits to make circular rabbet cuts of any diameter and depth around the inside of the holes cut; with this technique, you can make precise recessed rabbet cuts in shop-made, clear-plastic router bases to accept various template guides. I discuss this in greater depth on pages 199–200.

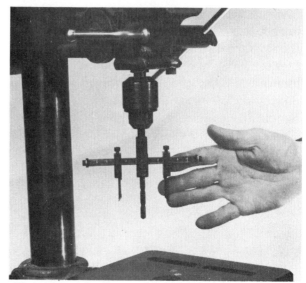

Illus. 422. *A shop-made circle-cutting jig for your plunge router is a good alternative to this circle cutter, which is more expensive, more difficult to adjust, and, obviously, much more dangerous to use.*

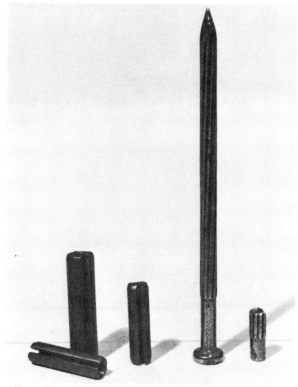

Illus. 421. *A section of a "threaded" masonry nail makes a perfect pivot pin. The serrated part is driven into a hole drilled into the plastic. Split pins (also called spring-steel tension pins) of different sizes are available for similar uses.*

Here are some tips regarding the use of your adjustable circle-cutting base: First, find a drill bit that will make exactly the same-size hole as the pivot pin. The actual diameter of the pivot pin is not as important as the relationship of the pin and the hole drilled for it. The pivot pin must fit snugly into the hole that must be drilled into the workpiece center of the circle or area that is to be cut. You may have to purchase a special-numbered bit from a hardware dealer or an industrial supply house if a "fractional" bit makes a sloppy hole.

When using the adjustable circle-cutting base for making holes completely through the thickness of the workpiece, make a trial cut in scrap stock to ensure that the adjustment is exact. (See Illus. 413 and 415.) Be sure to attach the work securely to a flat surface with double-faced tape. Apply the tape so that both the workpiece and the center do not move or float as the core is freed from the rest of the workpiece at the completion of the cut. Some practice pivoting the router quickly (to make cooler cuts) and a knowledge of the best depth of cut per pass for cutting various materials will give you the necessary confidence to tackle any job.

Clear Bases For Template Guides Your adjustable circle-cutting base will cut to the very accurate diameters required for making clear-plastic router bases to carry any commercial brand or size template guides. Some of the jigs discussed later on that require the use of template guides can be more easily used if they are mounted to subbases that are made of clear, transparent plastic. (See Illus. 423.) Illus. 566 shows a clear base with a template guide for cutting letters.

Illus. 423. Template guides would be a lot easier to use to follow templates if the router subbase were transparent rather than opaque, as this one is.

To make these clear bases correctly, make sure that the rims of the template guides are perfectly concentric to the axis of the router bit when they are installed or attached to the base. To do this, first remove the existing subbase from the router. Use it as a pattern to locate the mounting holes, as shown in Illus. 424 and 425. Carefully locate and drill the mounting holes only, as shown in the illustrations. Do not attempt to locate the center template guide hole until after you fasten the plastic blank to the router with the mounting holes just made. (See Illus. 426.) Install any point-cutting bit, such as a V-bit. With the power on, carefully plunge the bit, lowering it just to a distance at which the point of the bit makes a starting hole suitable for drilling the pivot-pin hole of the adjustable circle-cutting base. Remove the subbase blank and proceed to cut a rabbeted hole to any appropriate size for any template guide of your choice. (See Illus. 427–430.) Use the adjustable circle-cutting base, of course. Make some test cuts in scrap before going to

the workpiece, and everything will turn out fine.

Illus. 424. Existing subbases removed from the router provide the pattern. Here, only the screw-mounting holes are marked.

Illus. 425. Give the holes a starting "punch" with a sharp scratch awl.

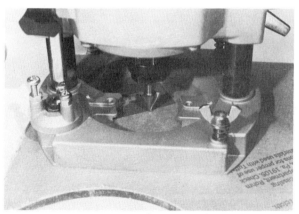

Illus. 426. Lowering this V-bit marks the center precisely and makes a starting dimple for drilling the pin hole for the pivot pin of the adjustable circle-cutting base.

Illus. 427. Some blank bases made with the adjustable circle-cutting base. Note the inside holes and rabbets cut to receive the template guides.

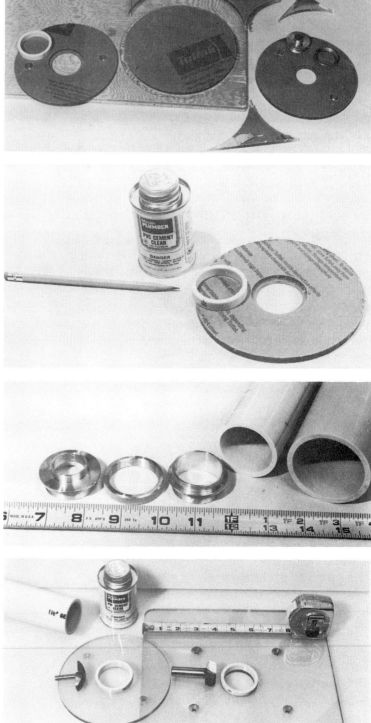

Illus. 428. Here's a closeup look at a round base rabbeted inside to receive a section of glued-in plastic pipe that will serve as a large template guide.

Illus. 429. Some of the largest inside diameter metal template guides available, at left, are not as large as that provided by the plastic pipe, at right.

Illus. 430. One-quarter-inch clear-plastic bases with template guides of 1½-inch plastic pipe that have been cemented into rabbeted holes. The base at left is 5¾ inches in diameter, and the one on the right is 10 inches square.

Plunge-Router Boring Base With this base, you can almost convert your plunge router into a portable drill press (Illus. 431); I say almost because there are some obvious and definite limitations. However, the perfect 90-degree bit-entry feature provided by the plunge-router mechanism can be sufficiently exploited to do highly accurate boring jobs.

Illus. 431. *A shop made "boring base" made of clear plastic and pads of sandpaper that have been applied with double-faced tape. The scribed lines cross at the center axis of the router bit. This allows accurate positioning of the router on the work so precisely located holes can be made with the plunging mechanism. The pads of sandpaper eliminate any slippage between the base and the work.*

Illus. 432. *When the "cross hairs" scribed in the base are aligned with similar marks drawn on the workpiece, they locate the router for the plunge-boring operation.*

To make a plunge-router boring base you need a plunge router and bits with end-entry geometry of specific sizes that satisfy your requirements. If you are considering using regular boring tools, be extremely careful, make sure that whatever bit or boring tool you use is rated for the high-speed RPM's of the router. If it is not, you must use a speed control (see pages 79 and 80) to dial-down the spindle speed of the router.

The boring base for plunging routers is fairly easy to make. It can be done accurately if you use the same steps to locate the exact center of the base as those used to make bases to receive the template guides, and which are discussed and illustrated in Illus. 424–426. Drill the router's mounting holes and countersink them. Then mount the plastic base to the router, which is carrying a pointed bit in its collet. Now, lower the bit to locate where its exact center on the plastic blank is. This is simple using the plunging mechanism of the router. Then remove the base workpiece you are working on from the router, and scratch the "cross-hair" reference lines into the bottom surface of the base with a scratch awl, as shown in Illus. 433. Drill a very small hole completely through at the center of the base. This transfers the exact center to the bottom surface of the base. Make the "hair" lines extend completely to the edge of the base. Fill the scratched-in lines with a black enamel and wipe off the excess with a dry rag. Small pads of 60-grit garnet should be applied to the base with double-faced tape. (See Illus. 434.) This will hold the router steady during the boring operation, thus preventing oval-shaped holes or holes that are not on their intended marked center.

Corner-Boring Base Illus. 435 shows a ¼-inch-thick hardboard base with two guides (stops) that position the router so that holes can be identically plunge-bored at predetermined corner distances from the edge and end of the board; with this technique, identical hole locations can be bored on a production basis

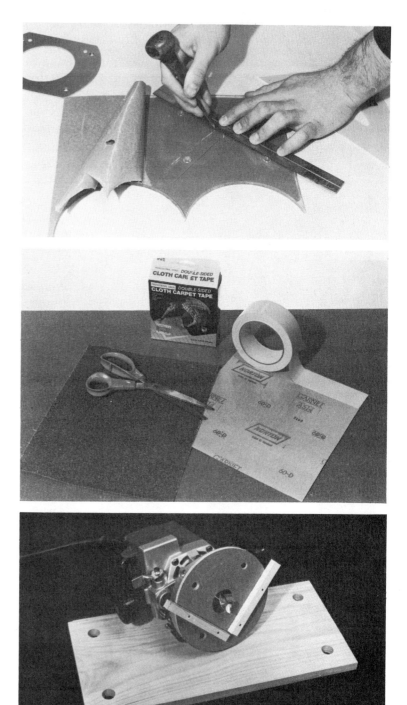

Illus. 433. Locate the precise center of the bit, as shown in Illus. 426; then remove it and drill a small hole through the center. Scribe cross lines on the bottom of the base with a scratch awl, as shown, fill them with black enamel, and wipe them clean. Note: Here it shows that the mounting holes were first drilled and countersunk.

Illus. 434. Strips of sandpaper backed with double-faced tape can be applied anywhere. In this operation, they were applied on the clear-plastic boring base shown in Illus. 431 to prevent any slippage.

Illus. 435. A plunge-boring base made specifically for boring certain identical distances from the corners of boards. The stops, glued to a hardboard base, locate holes in relation to the ends and edges of the board(s). Thus, you can plunge-bore all four holes identically without having to measure or lay out the location.

without requiring any measured layout markings. See Chapter 24 for more router-boring techniques.

Self-Centering Mortising and Slotting Base
This is another easy-to-make ¼-inch-thick sub-base for plunge-routing perfectly centered mortises and slots. (See Illus. 436 and 437.) The idea is elementary, but works very well. The illustrations show a 5¾-inch-diameter router base with two ³⁄₁₆-inch diameter × ¾-inch spring-steel tension pins located 3 inches apart,

Illus. 436. *A self-centering mortising and slotting base made of ¼-inch plastic and two spring-steel tension pins.*

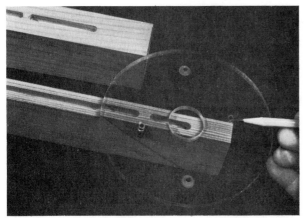

Illus. 437. *When using the router, hold it so both pins contact the surfaces of the work, as shown, which automatically centers the bit over the edge regardless of the thickness of the board.*

centered on each side of the bit on a line that extends through the center of the bit or collet. Drill ³/₁₆-inch-diameter holes in the plastic, and drive the pins in.

To use this base, simply make cross marks on the edges of the wood workpiece indicating where the slots or mortises should start and stop. Position the router on the work, holding it so that the base with both pins is against the board, as shown in Illus. 437. Plunge and cut to the desired length. The slot or mortise will be cut perfectly centered.

If this base is made to be used with stock of narrower thicknesses, position the two pins

closer together. This will permit center cuts to be made closer to the end of the board.

Plug Flush-Trimming Bases If you use wood plugs or pegs that must be trimmed flush to the surface, a router with a special base can do the job very quickly and accurately. (See Illus. 438–441.)

The idea behind trimming plugs flush is simple. Support the router on two runners approximately ³/₄ inch over the work. Drop the bit to a depth that's level with the bottom of the runners, and cut flush to the work surface. Slide the router over the work so that the bit cuts away the plug(s), making them perfectly flush. A special base can be made with the runners atached to it. (See Illus. 439.) Illus. 440 and 441 show this plug-trimming base in use.

Another version of the same idea is to simply attach two strips of wood equal in thickness to the existing subbase with double-faced tape. (See Illus. 442.) Still another type of base for the same kind of work is designed for a small trim router. (See Illus. 443–445.) It is used to trim plugs in the same way. The small size of a trim router permits a one-handed operation.

In other parts of this book you'll find more specialty bases for specific operations. Pages 215 and 216 discuss a "long-reach base" used for straight-line cutting. The "floating" base described on pages 217–219 permits variable prespaced dado and grooving operations with

Illus. 438. *One-inch-diameter plugs that have to be trimmed flush to the surface. The base with the runners above does the job.*

one straightedge setup. On pages 243–247, you will learn about another special base designed to either cut any one of four different-length tenons or make predetermined spacing cuts along a straightedge. Finally, on pages 224–227 there are ideas for refining the fairly standard shop-made, circle-cutting compass-type bases.

One fact that clearly shines through in this discussion of router bases—and in any ideas about router bases you may make on your own or read about in woodworking magazines—is that the only way to achieve complete router versatility is to have a router on which you can mount interchangeable bases.

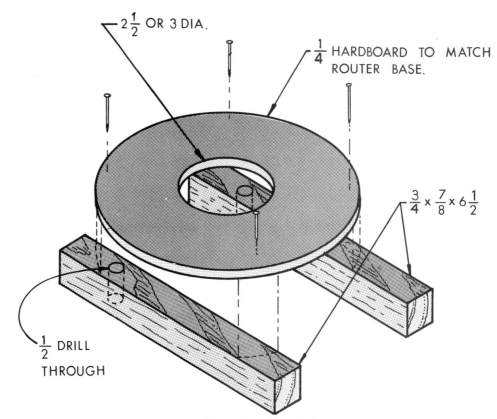

Illus. 439. Details for making a plug trimming base.

Illus. 440. Trimming plugs.

Illus. 441. A closer look at trimming plugs.

Illus. 442. Two strips of wood atttached to the router base with double-sided tape also work.

Illus. 443 (above left). Another version of a plug-trimming base. This one is made of ⅜-inch-thick polycarbonate plastic. Illus. 444 (above right). A full bottom view.

Illus. 445. A plug-trimming base designed to fit a small laminate trim router permits one-handed flush-cutting of pegs and plugs.

20
Straight-Cutting Guides

One of the most common operations performed with the portable hand-held router is the making of any one of a variety of possible cuts in a perfectly straight line. In this type of operation, you will clamp or hold the jig or guide steadily against the work surface and move the router against it over the work, as opposed to moving the work over a stationary router as is done on a router table.

Typical straight-line work includes making carcass dadoes, sliding dovetails, or grooves, and other work that might be involved in making large tenons, raised or engraved sign letters, border designs, etc. Straight-line cutting can also be applied to accurately trim and true various edges that have been sawn to a rough size and to trim the rough-cut surfaces of hand- or band-sawn mitres. Some of the jigs or straight-cutting guides presented in this chapter can also be used to do the same task a jointer does in truing an edge in glue-joint preparation. Large pieces, especially veneered plywoods or panels, can be easily and accurately machined with a portable hand-held router.

Various ideas for making straight-line guides are shown in this chapter; some of the specific sizes and dimensions are not given because router makes and requirements vary from person to person or from job to job.

Simple Straightedges These can be anything as elementary as a plywood cutoff or a strip of straight wood. The only requirement is one straight, true edge of the length needed to do the job at hand. To use the straightedge, simply clamp it to the workpiece in the appropriate location to facilitate making the cut. Sometimes it's helpful to make a few special straightedges with particular features for specific kinds of work.

Illus. 446 and 447 show two straightedges used to make quick cuts in all of the various angular directions used in sign-carving, as, for example, the vertical and slanted straight cuts used to make M's and W's. In this job, hold the edge guide steady on top of the work with one hand and move the router, which will be operated entirely with the other hand, against it. Do not use clamps because they take too much time. Instead, use either strips of sandpaper applied with double-sided tape or pointed nails that project slightly through; they will grip and hold the straightedge steady during the routing operation. Obviously, the nails grip better, but they leave their marks on the wood, which might or might not be objectionable, depending upon the particular situation. Sandpaper or protruding nail-points can also be used on other kinds of straightedges or templates.

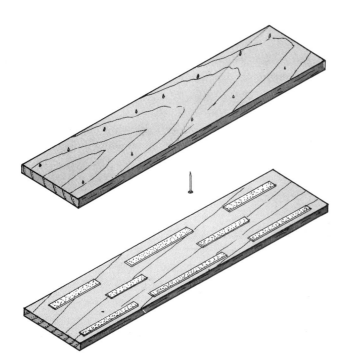

HINGED   SPACER

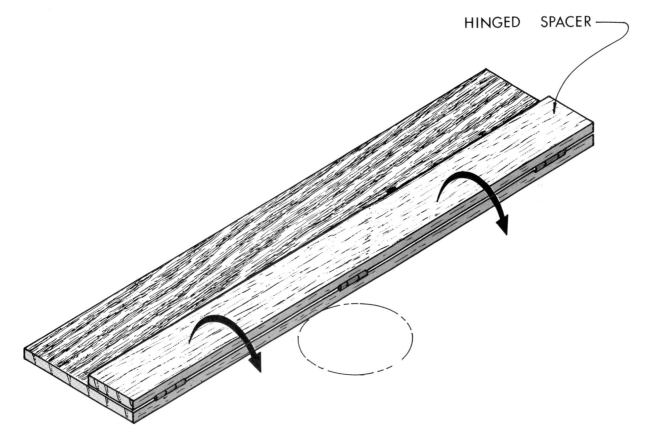

Illus. 447.   The hinged spacer is exactly the same width as the distance from the cutting edge of the bit to the outer edge of the router base.

Illus. 447 shows a straightedge with a hinged spacer. The spacer automatically locates the position where the straightedge must be held. The width of the spacer flap must be equal to the distance from the cutting edge of the bit to the outer edge of the base (where it contacts the straightedge).

Hinged spacers can also be applied to other kinds of straightedges. The commonly used T square, shown in Illus. 448, is a typical example of one that could be fitted with a hinged spacer, which will make it quicker to get accurate positioning.

Another practical idea is to use stops in conjunction with a straightedge. (See Illus. 449.) They help to make identical blind cuts such as stopped dadoes.

Dado-Spacing Straightedge This device is useful when repetitive dado spacings must be made exactly the same distance apart. (See Illus. 450.) This type of straightedge jig can be used to make dadoes for the supports of multiple-drawer banks, as well as pigeon-hole pockets and shelving, all of which must be equally spaced. If carefully made, it can be used to produce a choice of two different spacings, as indicated in Illus. 450. To use it, attach a strip the same size as the dado to the bottom of the straightedge; this strip will fit neatly into each previously cut dado. No clamping or measuring is required once the first or starting dado or groove has been cut.

Parallel Straightedges These types of straightedges are very useful and versatile because with them you can feed the router in either direction. (See Illus. 451 and 452.) They must be made carefully so that the edges are spaced from each other a distance that equals the diameter of the router base. There must be some clearance to permit free movement of the router. To avoid making the spacing too tight (which would restrict movement) or too loose (which would sacrifice accuracy), clamp and glue the assembly together against the base, with the thickness of a piece of paper in between them.

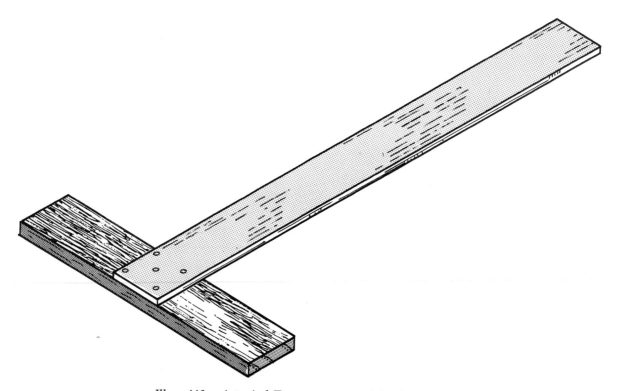

Illus. 448. A typical T square-type straightedge can be made to any convenient size.

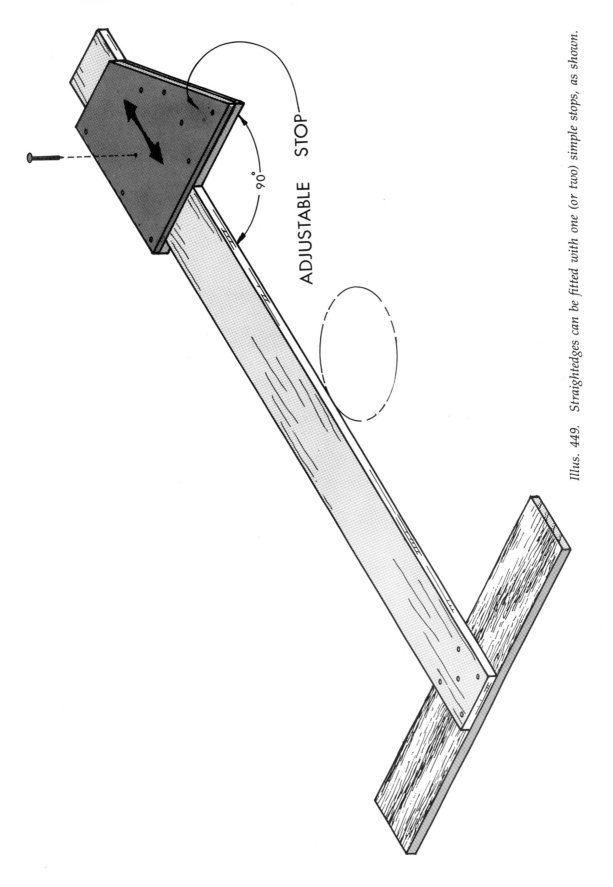

90°

ADJUSTABLE STOP

Illus. 449. Straightedges can be fitted with one (or two) simple stops, as shown.

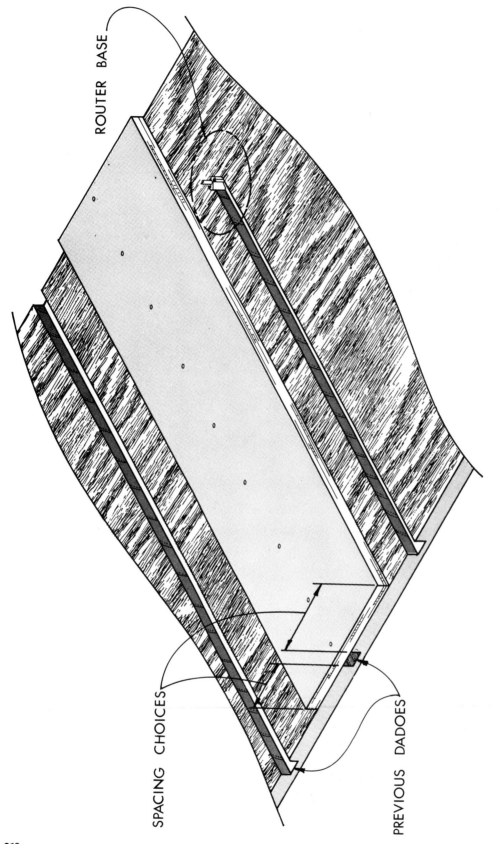

ROUTER BASE

SPACING CHOICES

PREVIOUS DADOES

Illus. 450. When you use a dado-spacing straightedge, you are ensuring identical openings for drawers, shelves, etc., without having to measure or make another layout after you have made the first or starting dado cut.

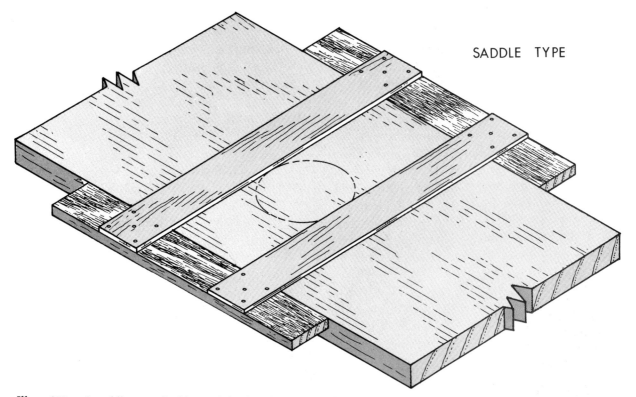

Illus. 451. A saddle-type double straightedge is made to fit a specific board or panel width, as shown here.

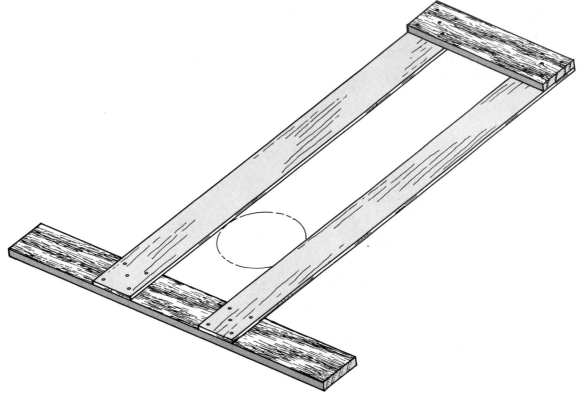

Illus. 452. Here is another double straightedge that can be used on stock of any width, narrow or wide.

Use a good grade of ¼-inch hard-wood plywood for the straightedges. The longer they are, the wider they should be to avoid any deflection during the cut. The cradle type of straightedge shown in Illus. 451 is more accurate but it can only be used on a panel or board of one maximum size. It obviously can be used with narrower panels or boards.

The double straightedge type shown in Illus. 452 is more versatile in that it can be used on narrow or wide work, as well as to make cuts that run at an angle from the edge of the work. Of course, it must be clamped to the work like all straightedges, unless other holding provisions are involved.

Straightedge and Trimming Guides These devices can be used for a variety of common and unusual routing jobs. (See Illus. 453 and 454.) Woodworkers with years of experience will note that the idea is somewhat like that of a "shooting board" for a hand plane. However, instead of clamping the work to the "board," you clamp this straightedge to the work; also, obviously, the tool you use is a router instead of a hand plane.

These straightedge and trimming jigs are actually made to be used with router bits of a specific size. The selected bit is used to make the jig's precise spacing from the line of cut to the fence or straightedge part of the jig. The straightedge jigs shown in Illus. 453 and 454 are made with ⅛-inch-thick plastic bottoms, but ⅛- or ¼-inch hardboard or plywood can also be used for the jig bottoms. The specific details for making this type of straightedge are left to the discretion of the builder. (See Illus. 454.)

With a straightedge, you can perfectly trim angle cuts, mitres, glue-joint edges, etc., by guiding the router to make a true finishing cut. Illus. 455–457 demonstrate how to trim a mitre-

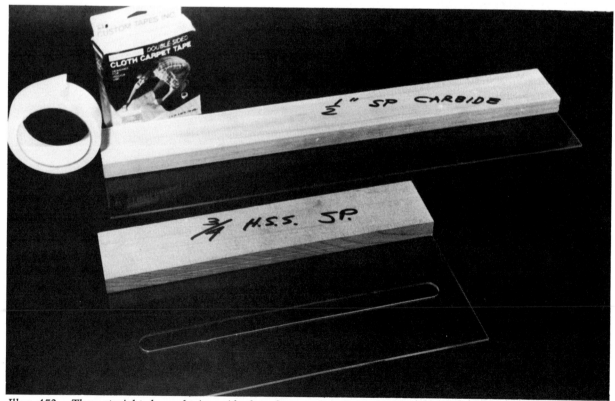

Illus. 453.   *These straightedge and trim guides have been made to be used with specific bits. The one above, as marked, is made for a ½-inch spiral carbide, and the lower one is made for a ¾-inch HSS spiral.*

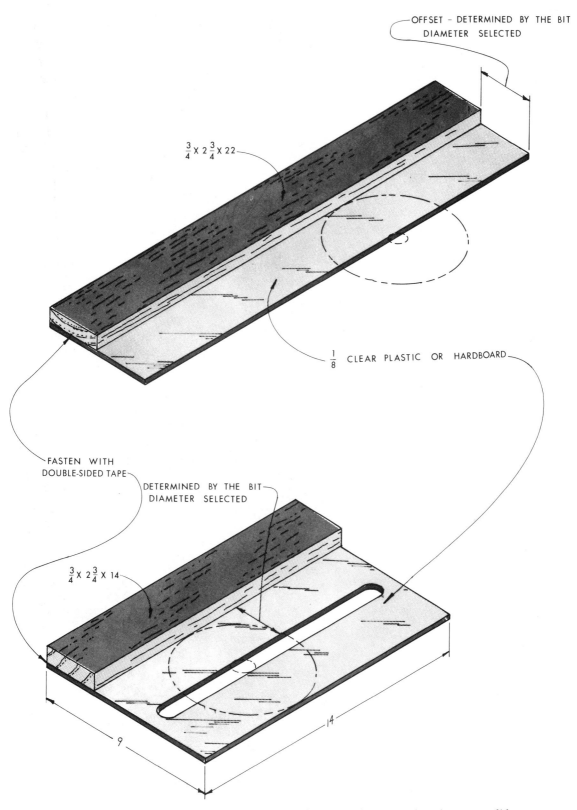

OFFSET – DETERMINED BY THE BIT
DIAMETER SELECTED

$\frac{3}{4}$ X 2 $\frac{3}{4}$ X 22

$\frac{1}{8}$ CLEAR PLASTIC OR HARDBOARD

FASTEN WITH
DOUBLE-SIDED TAPE

DETERMINED BY THE BIT
DIAMETER SELECTED

$\frac{3}{4}$ X 2 $\frac{3}{4}$ X 14

14

9

Illus. 454. General details for making straightedge and trim guides. Note that the router slides on top of the plastic spacer—the distance from the bit to the fence or straightedge.

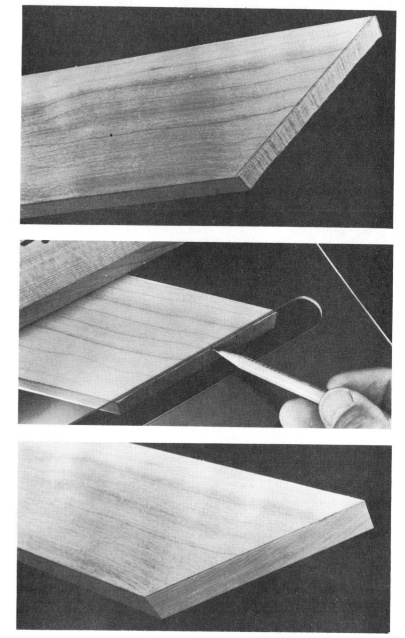

Illus. 455. You can make a rough-sawn mitre cut safely away from the layout line.

Illus. 456. Clamp the straightedge trimming jig to the work so that the line of cut (which is the edge of the slot of the jig) is directly on the layout line.

Illus. 457. The rough-sawn cut has been removed, cut clean and true with the router. The plastic base allows you a choice of saving the layout line, splitting it, or removing it entirely for the ultimate provision of accuracy.

cut with this jig. In a cut such as this, the plastic base of the jig is an advantage. You can place the straightedge so that the line of cut by the bit will either remove the layout line, split the line, or save the entire line, whichever degree of accuracy you wish. (See Illus. 456.)

Another practical use of this jig is making surface cuts at any place or angle desired. To do this, make sure that the layout on the workpiece is a single straight line, and that an

X is marked to indicate which side of the layout line the cut is to be made on. (See Illus. 458 and 459.)

Extended Base with Straightedge This device is very useful for handling those jobs that are beyond the reach of the straightedge guide that comes with many routers. (See Illus. 460.) The primary function of the edge guide is to make cuts parallel to an edge. The commercially made versions are excellent for cuts made relatively close to the working edge of the work, such as edge rabbet cuts. However, they do not have long-reach capacities, which are often necessary. With the shop-made version shown in Illus. 460 and 461, you can make dados, grooves, and similar cuts as far as 18 or more inches away, and parallel to an edge.

Illus. 458. A layout for routing an angular stopped dado with the straightedge trim guide.

Illus. 459.   The completed cut is perfect.

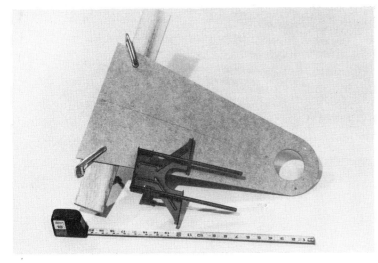

Illus. 460.   The commercial straightedge guide has limited reach, as it is shown here compared to the shop-made ¼-inch hardboard extended base that has a straightedge clamped to it.

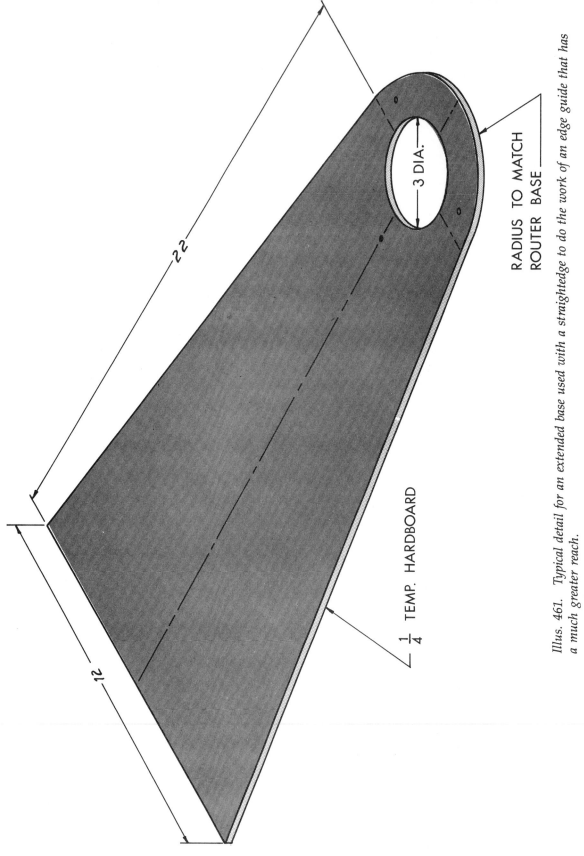

22

12

3 DIA.

RADIUS TO MATCH
ROUTER BASE

$\frac{1}{4}$ TEMP. HARDBOARD

Illus. 461. *Typical detail for an extended base used with a straightedge to do the work of an edge guide that has a much greater reach.*

Floating Router Base This base, used for multiple straight-line work, is designed to be used with your regular subbase and any template guide of appropriate size. This easy-to-make jig is used to cut a series of grooves or dadoes of predetermined spacing very quickly with only one straightedge setup, which is an ideal method for medium-run production jobs.

Illus. 462 shows a typical workpiece that contains several spaced stopped-dado cuts and the "floating" base (it is called a "floating" base because it is not attached to the router). This base is used in unison with the router during the cutting operation; it is connected to the router only by a template guide that projects into one of the holes that were prespaced in the floating base.

Incidentally, today template guides come in a wide selection of different inside and outside diameters, and lengths of projection. (See Illus. 463 and 464.) There are a number of template guides that have barrels or extensions too long to be used with normal templates ¼ inch in thickness, but they have other desirable-size dimensions. If using these guides, simply hack-saw them off to a useable length—usually a distance slightly less than ¼ inch.

Plunge routers work well with floating bases. If the manufacturer of your plunge router has a limited template-size selection, look for adapters with which you can use competitive brand name template guides. (See Illus. 464.)

Illus. 465 shows a typical layout for a floating base. The inside diameter of the template guide is not important as long as it is big enough for the bit to pass through it. However, though the holes bored in the base are obviously spaced wherever you want your cuts to be made, they must tightly fit the outside diameter of the template guide. See Illus. 466–468, which depict how stopped cuts can be made.

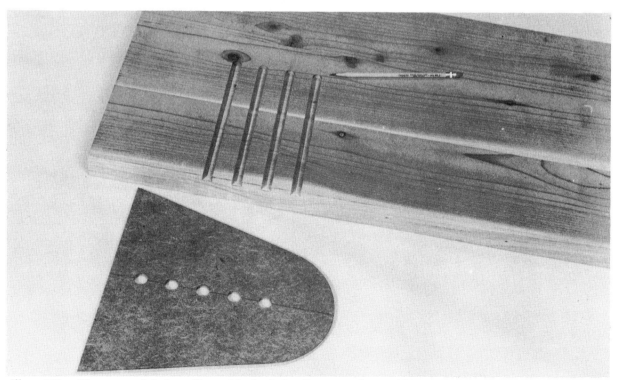

Illus. 462. These spaced dadoes align with the holes (for a template guide) in this "floating base" used to make these cuts.

Illus. 463. Template guides come in a wide selection of inside and outside diameters, and of various projections as well. If any are too long for a particular use, cut them off to a slightly less than a ¼-inch projection.

Illus. 464. Some adapters for plunge routers are available that permit the use of template guides from other manufacturers.

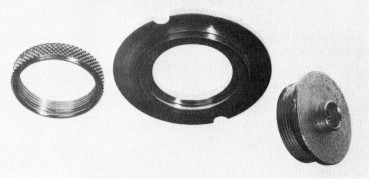

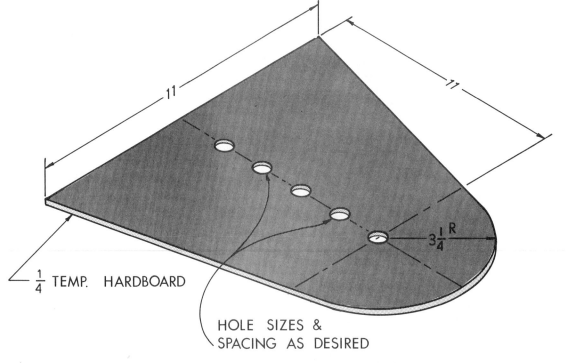

11

11

$3\frac{1}{4}$ R

$\frac{1}{4}$ TEMP. HARDBOARD

HOLE SIZES &
SPACING AS DESIRED

Illus. 465. A typical floating base. The dimensions given are only suggested for up to the 11-inch range of work shown.

Illus. 466. You can "reference" stopped cuts by marking the straightedge clamped to the work. Note the relationship of the subbase, template guide, and bit.

Illus. 467. Making the cuts. Pressure is maintained towards the straightedge throughout each cut. All cuts in this operation were made with the straightedge in the same location. A different hole in the floating base was engaged by the template guide during each pass.

Illus. 468. The cuts and components employed to make multiple dadoes quickly with a floating base.

21

Adjustable Square/Rectangle Guide

A router template guide that adjusts to a variety of rectangular and square openings (Illus. 469) offers a wide range of uses for the creative woodworker. The jig discussed in this chapter, which is constructed according to the specifications in Illus. 470, adjusts to any size from its smallest inside opening of $2\frac{1}{4} \times 3$ inches up to $17\frac{3}{4} \times 21\frac{1}{2}$ inches. It can be used for jobs like making border inlays in the smallest of box tops and for large jobs like routing decorative panel designs in cabinet door and drawer fronts, as shown in Illus. 472.

The four frame pieces should be made from good hard wood stock, such as quarter-sawn ash or oak milled to exactly $\frac{3}{4}$-inch thickness. Cut a $\frac{1}{4} \times \frac{1}{4}$-inch continuous through groove along one edge of each piece. Then cut some areas of these grooves all the way through the full $1\frac{1}{2}$-inch width of each of the four frame

pieces, thus making a series of slotted openings. These full-through slots are shown in Illus. 470. Full-through slots can be most accurately and easily made on a router table or with a pin router. You can tell from Illus. 470 that the series of full-through slot cuts are stopped, and result in separating spaces or "bridges" that can carry the weight of the router without deflection.

Machine a $\frac{1}{4} \times \frac{1}{4}$-inch tongue on the ends; a $\frac{1}{4} \times 3$-inch hanger bolt should be carefully inserted in the center of each tongue, as shown in the details in Illus. 470. Drill a $\frac{3}{16}$-inch pilot hole prior to installing the hanger bolts.

All pieces must be carefully machined with the ends and edges square in order for this jig to function effectively. The inside corners will always be square, regardless of what size-opening you adjust the frame to.

Illus. 469. The adjustable square/rectangular guide at its smallest adjustment measures inside $2\frac{1}{4} \times 3$ inches.

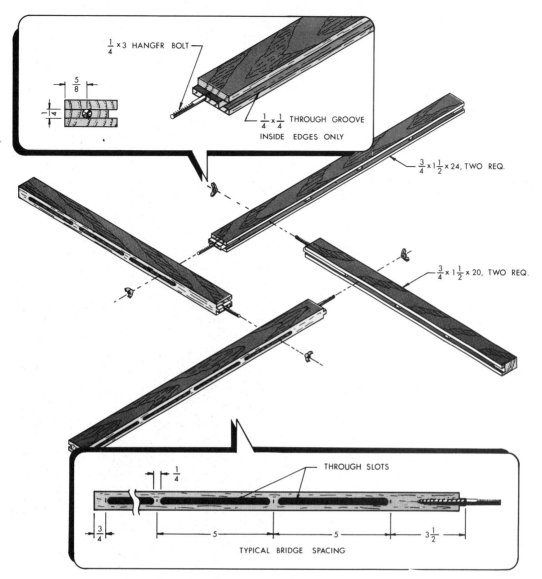

$\frac{1}{4} \times 3$ HANGER BOLT

$\frac{5}{8}$

$\frac{1}{4}$

$\frac{1}{4} \times \frac{1}{4}$ THROUGH GROOVE
INSIDE EDGES ONLY

$\frac{3}{4} \times 1\frac{1}{2} \times 24$, TWO REQ.

$\frac{3}{4} \times 1\frac{1}{2} \times 20$, TWO REQ.

THROUGH SLOTS

$\frac{1}{4}$

$\frac{3}{4}$

5

5

$3\frac{1}{2}$

TYPICAL BRIDGE SPACING

Illus. 470.   Construction details for making the adjustable square/rectangle router guide.

Illus. 471.   A closeup look at the basic tongue-and-groove construction involved in making this adjustable template.

Illus. 472. When you use the basic adjustable square and rectangle template-guide jig with inserted crown and end profiles you make these cabinet front designs. See Illus. 473–476.

There is really no top or bottom to this jig. It can be flipped over if it is more convenient to clamp it this way to the work. Remember, the inside edges of the frame pieces have the full or continuous $\frac{1}{4} \times \frac{1}{4}$-inch grooves. You can insert corner blocks or a crown-cutting template guide pieces, as shown in Illus. 473–475. Any other design shape or profile insert block will work as long as a $\frac{1}{4} \times \frac{1}{4}$-inch tongue is machined on two or three of its edges. Consequently, any number of different panel-design shapes can be made simply with shop-made interchangeable pieces of your own designs. Illus. 476 shows a variety of corner block designs cut from $\frac{3}{4}$-inch plywood. Place a piece of tape on the bottom to hold them securely in place if the tongue-and-groove fit is a little loose.

This adjustable template-frame jig is especially useful for making decorative designs and borders in all sorts of cabinetry panels, and for cutting borders on routed signs.

You can also make rectangular dishing cuts with this jig. Use a large or extended base fitted with a template guide. Suitable router bits for making rectangular- or square-recessed dishing cuts are among the bits illustrated in Chapter 4.

Because this adjustable square/rectangle guide is essentially an adjustable template, it works easiest with a plunge-type router. (See

Illus. 475.) One possible limitation worth noting is that some bits may not have the necessary "reach." Remember, the bit must reach past the full $\frac{3}{4}$-inch thickness of the jig before entering the work. There are many bits available that will work when using the jig; just make sure that you buy or select those with sufficient overall length.

Incidentally, you'll find that double-sided tape is a great help in holding this adjustable-frame template securely to the workpiece where clamps are too cumbersome.

Illus. 473. A setup for a cabinet-door design. The crown template insert has a $\frac{1}{4} \times \frac{1}{4}$-inch tongue on the three edges adjoining the frame.

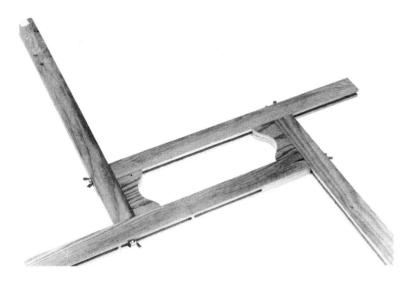

Illus. 474. Similar pieces are inserted into the adjustable frame to complete a drawer-front design template.

Illus. 475. Shown here are the template and a router with template guide and bit used to produce the decorative, incised design on the panel in the background.

Illus. 476. Some examples of various interchangeable corner templates made to fit into the grooves of the adjustable template frame.

22

Circle- and Oval-Routing Jigs

Here I present several multipurpose devices that can be used with the router to make circles, round corners, and cut ovals. Just think of the many projects that require router-cut circles, arcs, and ovals. The list is endless, I'm sure, but obvious choices include tabletops, clocks, mirrors, picture frames, sign plaques, and borders of all kinds on cabinetry panels. You can even use these jigs to make your own toy wheels in an astonishing variety of designs and sizes. All these techniques are within your

capabilities if you use the interesting, easy-to-make jigs that I'm about to describe.

Circle-Cutting Jigs   These jigs are not really a new concept. They attach to the bottom of the router; a nail provides the pivot point for a compass-like operation. (See Illus. 477.) Several companies sell commercially made plastic jigs that look similar to those shown in Illus. 477. It is very easy to make your own from $1/4$-inch sheet plastic, though $1/4$-inch hardboard or

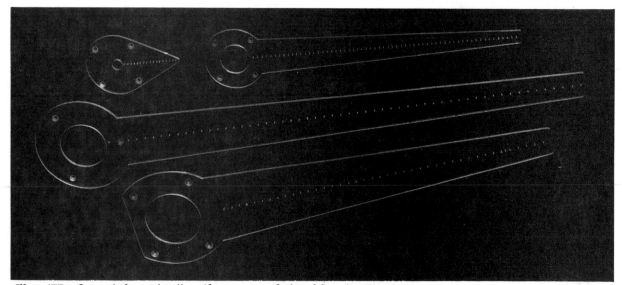

Illus. 477.   Some circle-cutting jigs. Above are two designed for trimming routers. The one on the upper left is designed for making small circles such as those used for wooden toy wheels.

plywood can also be used. The construction details for the larger circle-cutting jigs shown in Illus. 447 are given later on, along with construction details for making oval-cutting devices. These jigs are also one of the key components of the oval-cutting devices, which are discussed on pages 229–239.

Trimming Router Circle-Cutting Jig Any router can make small-radius circular cuts, such as those required for making wooden toy wheels. (See Illus. 478.) A small-sized router, such as one of the little trimming routers, is much more suited for this class of work than the full-sized routers.

Illus. 479 is a full-sized pattern of a circle-cutting base designed for a Ryobi trimming router. The design can be easily modified so that it will fit other brands of trimming routers. With the smaller trimming router, you can work in tighter-turning areas; it is also easier to perform one-handed operations when they are convenient. (See Illus. 480.)

When making any of the circle-cutting jigs presented in this chapter, you have to drive a headless nail into the center of the circular cut. For most jobs, this is not a real problem; if you have a job in which it is a problem, use a big-headed thumb tack, taped securely upside-down on the work.

To make a trimming circle jig, drill a series of $\frac{1}{16}$-inch holes, $\frac{3}{16}$ inches apart, through the $\frac{1}{4}$-inch plastic base. Use number 18 wire brad

nails for the pivots. Remove the heads with a pair of wire nippers. (See Illus. 481 and 482.)

The size of the center hole that's cut into your base for the bit is optional, though it has to be large enough to allow the largest bit you intend to use to extend through the base. However, if you make this hole too large, you will not be able to use the pivot holes for tight-radius work with other bits. (See Illus. 483.)

When you are making a number of identical cuts to predetermined depths, it would be handy to have stop features like those provided by plunge routers. These features can be improvised on most little trimming routers, as shown in Illus. 484. Simply tape a small wooden stop to the motor housing. When the motor is lowered to the point where the wooden stop strikes the base, you are precisely at your preset depth.

When making toy wheels, you can give them a realistic touch by cutting grooves around the edges to represent tire treads. The setup for this operation is very simple. Clamp the small, plastic circle-cutting base into the jaws of your bench vise, as shown in Illus. 485 and 486. You have to make a simple V-block jig to guide the circular-disc wheel as it is pivoted into the rotating bit. (See Illus. 487.)

You can establish the horizontal depth needed to make the V-shaped tread cut with the router's depth-cut mechanism. You can establish the spacing of the tread grooves by raising or lowering the router in the vise.

Illus. 478. *A variety of toy wheel designs and even wooden checkerboard pieces that were made with a small trimming router and a simple circle-cutting jig.*

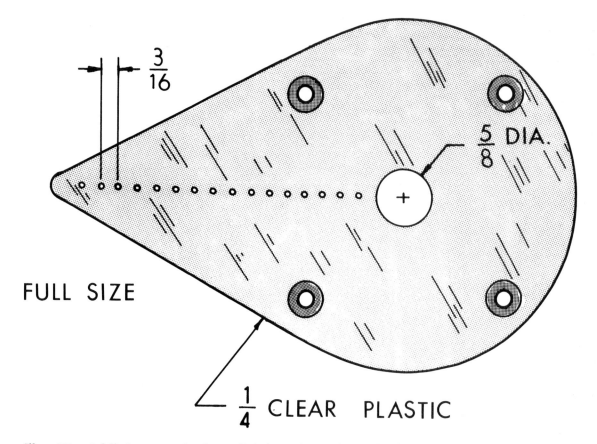

FULL SIZE

$\frac{3}{16}$

$\frac{5}{8}$ DIA.

$\frac{1}{4}$ CLEAR PLASTIC

Illus. 479. *A full-size pattern for the small circle-cutting jig designed to fit a Ryobi trimming router. Modify as required to fit other brands.*

Illus. 480. *Making toy wheels with the one-hand convenience possible with the small trimming router.*

Illus. 481 (above left). One-sixteenth-inch holes in the plastic base fit over a number 18 nail with the head cut off. Illus. 482 (above right). Toy-wheel making in progress. Note the checker pieces on the right.

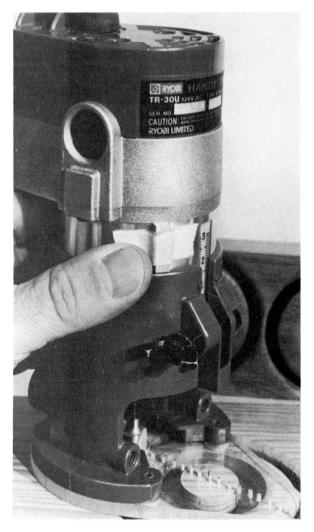

Illus. 483 (above). A closer look at circular surface cuts. Illus. 484 (right). This trimming router has been converted into a mini-plunge router. A small piece of wood taped to the motor housing acts as a stop. It hits the base to limit the depth, permitting quick, identical cuts of the same depth.

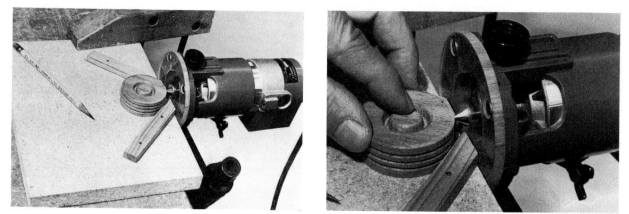

Illus. 485 (above left).   When the small circle-cutting base is clamped in the bench vise and is used with this simple jig, you can cut threads on this toy wheel. Illus. 486 (above right). Raising or lowering the position of the router in the vise spaces the tread grooves.

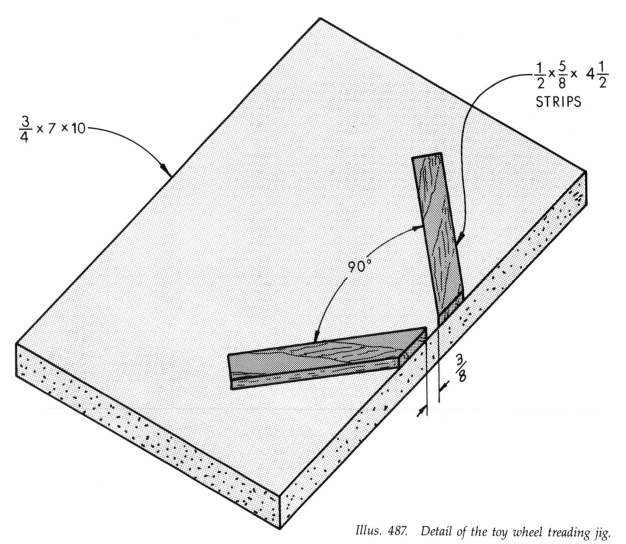

$\frac{1}{2} \times \frac{5}{8} \times 4\frac{1}{2}$ STRIPS

$\frac{3}{4} \times 7 \times 10$

90°

$\frac{3}{8}$

Illus. 487.   Detail of the toy wheel treading jig.

Oval-Cutting Jigs These are some of the most spectacular and fun-to-use jigs in this book. (See Illus. 488 and 489.) If you've ever experienced the difficulty involved in just attempting to draw a perfect oval on a piece of paper, you will indeed appreciate the performance of the two oval or ellipse jigs presented here. If you do any type of work with ovals, you'll want to make one or both of the two jigs detailed in Illus. 488 and 489. Where layout and cutting were once considered difficult, perfect results are now surprisingly easy and precise without any sort of tedious effort.

You can also use these jigs as a layout or elliptical drawing device. As you can see in photos, a regular router circle-cutting jig is used with two controlled sliding centers that move in dovetailed channels.

Here I will give plans for two different oval jigs. The smaller one is designed for use with small trim routers. Also included is a version designed for use with either the larger-sized regular routers or plunge routers. (See Illus. 490.) A plunging router is easier to use for both shallow decorative-type cuts and especially when making deeper cuts. However, standard-type routers will also work. By making successive passes at shallower depths, you can cut out oval tabletops or make openings in mirrors, picture frames, etc. Other good applications for these jobs include decorative, oval borders on architectural panels, cabinetry, and wood signs. You'll find many other uses for the jig(s), once they are made.

The structural details for both the small and larger size jigs are essentially the same; only the dimensions differ. As you can determine from the illustrations, one of the integral parts

Illus. 488. All of these oval cuts are perfect and so easy to make with this jig that employs a typical plastic circular-cutting jig as the variable-centered extension arm.

Illus. 489. The plastic arm is held on two moveable pivot points that slide in dovetail channels. Here a small trimming router allows one-hand operation. This jig will cut ovals with minor and major diameters of 10 × 20 inches up to 22 × 32 inches.

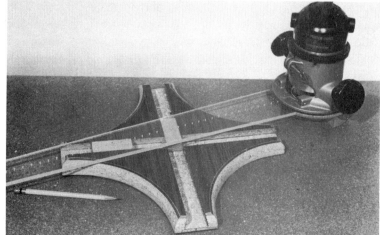

Illus. 490. Here is an oval jig designed for a regular router. With this setup you can cut perfect ovals that range from 15 × 27 inch up to 24 × 60 inches in minor and major diameters, respectively.

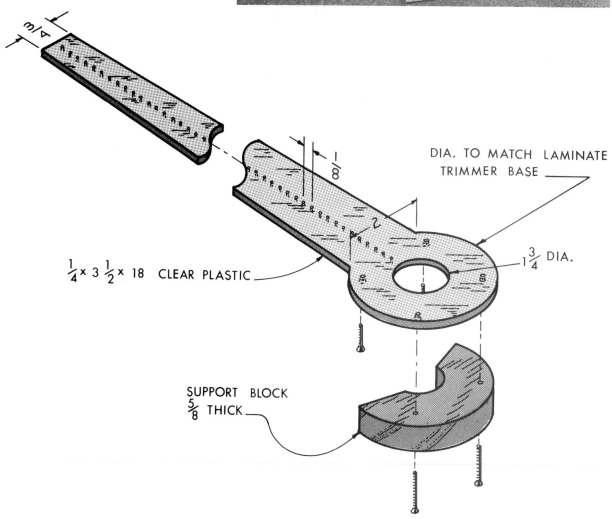

$\frac{3}{4}$

$\frac{1}{8}$

DIA. TO MATCH LAMINATE TRIMMER BASE

$\frac{1}{4} \times 3\frac{1}{2} \times 18$ CLEAR PLASTIC

$1\frac{3}{4}$ DIA.

SUPPORT BLOCK
$\frac{5}{8}$ THICK

Illus. 491. This circle-cutting guide designed for a small trimming router doubles as an arm for the small oval-cutting jig. (When used strictly for circle-cutting, it will make circles ranging from 2¼ inches to nearly 32 inches in diameter.)

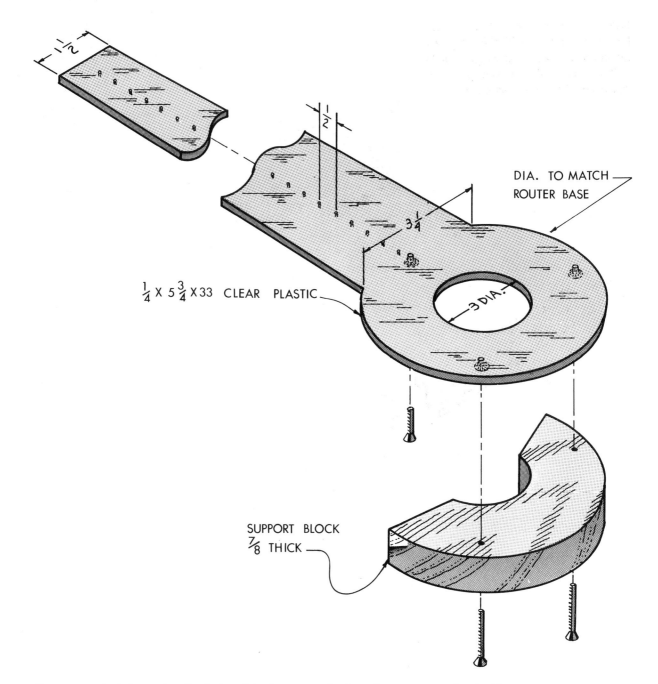

$\frac{1}{2}$

$\frac{1}{2}$

DIA. TO MATCH
ROUTER BASE

$3\frac{1}{4}$

3 DIA.

$\frac{1}{4}$ X 5$\frac{3}{4}$ X 33 CLEAR PLASTIC

SUPPORT BLOCK
$\frac{7}{8}$ THICK

Illus. 492. A circle-cutting jig designed for larger standard or plunge routers also doubles as an arm component of the large oval-routing jig. (When used strictly for cutting circles, it will make circles from 3½ to almost 60 inches in diameter.)

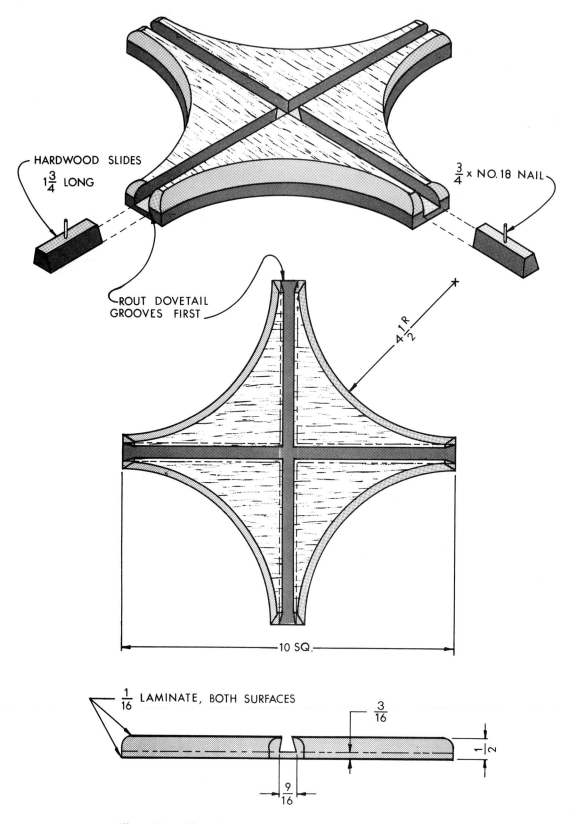

HARDWOOD SLIDES
$1\frac{3}{4}$ LONG

$\frac{3}{4}$ × NO. 18 NAIL

ROUT DOVETAIL
GROOVES FIRST

$4\frac{1}{2}$ R

10 SQ.

$\frac{1}{16}$ LAMINATE, BOTH SURFACES

$\frac{3}{16}$

$\frac{1}{2}$

$\frac{9}{16}$

Illus. 493. Plans for the dovetail base and slides for the smaller oval-cutting jig.

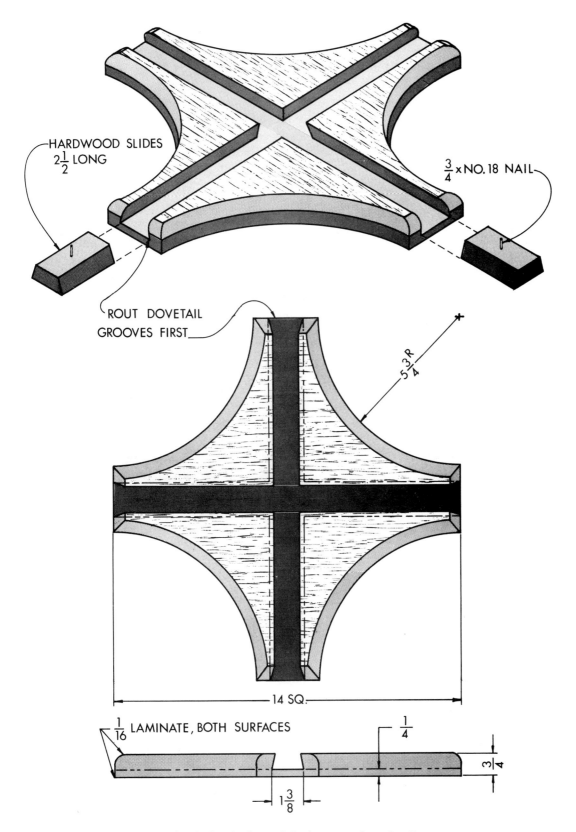

HARDWOOD SLIDES
2½ LONG

$\frac{3}{4}$ x NO. 18 NAIL

ROUT DOVETAIL
GROOVES FIRST

5 $\frac{3}{4}$ R

14 SQ.

$\frac{1}{16}$ LAMINATE, BOTH SURFACES

$\frac{1}{4}$

$\frac{3}{4}$

1 $\frac{3}{8}$

Illus. 494.   Construction details for the base of the larger oval-cutting jig.

on each jig is a typical, plastic circle-cutting jig. The dimensions for these jigs are suggested in Illus. 491 and 492. Some modification may be necessary where the holes are made, so that you can mount the jig to your own router. The details for making the dovetail-channeled bases are given in Illus. 493 and 494.

The smaller jig base is made of sheet material $\frac{1}{2}$ inch thick. MDF (medium-density fibreboard) was used in the example shown in Illus. 491. Particle board $\frac{3}{4}$ inch thick was used to make the base of the larger oval jig. Note that both surfaces (top and bottom) of both bases are covered with standard decorative laminate, $\frac{1}{16}$ inch thick. This laminate is there to stabilize the material and keep it flat and free from warping; however, sometimes it does not work so well because of the dovetail cuts made into the top surfaces. Otherwise, the laminate surfaces, because of their hardness and smoothness, improve the jig bases.

Once you've applied and trimmed laminate to the square base material, make preliminary, grooved relief cuts in the areas that will be cut away with the dovetail bit (Illus. 495); the reason is that the dovetail cuts, which have to be made in one pass at full depth, are too heavy unless part of the cut has been previously roughed out. You can do the dovetailing on the router table, but other, hand-held, methods should work well if you don't have one.

Make the dovetail-shaped slides out of hard wood to fit into the dovetail channels. They should fit fairly tight, but make sure that they still slide easily. Keep all surfaces in the dovetail channel and the slides covered with a generous application of paste wax to ensure free movement. If the hard wood slides fit too tightly, cut a thin shaving off of the bottoms. Use $\frac{3}{4}$ inch by No. 18 wire nails, with their heads cut off, for the pivot-point pins. (See Illus. 496 and 497.)

Put support blocks under part of the router base to ensure a level, smooth operation. Either attach these supports with screws that extend into the base of the router, as shown in Illus. 491, 492, and 498, or simply attach

them directly to the plastic arm with double-sided tape. Illus. 499 and 500 show support blocks attached on a large 1½ horsepower router and a small trimming router, respectively. Note that the support blocks are only semi-circular in shape; this permits cuts to be made closer to the jig's base than would otherwise be possible with full circular-shaped support blocks. (See Illus. 501.)

One of the problems associated with using support blocks, as just discussed, is that some router bits are not long enough to provide the reach necessary for some jobs. One alternative to this situation is to put an offset bend in the plastic arm (Illus. 502) so that the router rests

Illus. 495. Cutting the dovetail slide channels into the base on a router table. Note the grooves previously cut on the table saw to permit the dovetail cut to be made in one pass.

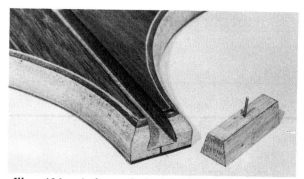

Illus. 496. A closeup look at the dovetail groove of the base and one of the hardwood slides. Note the mark indicating the centers of the dovetail slots. Note, also, how the edges of the base were rounded over.

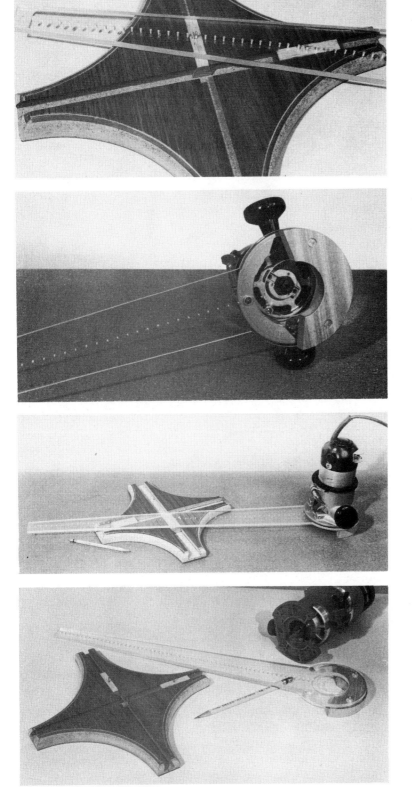

Illus. 497.   The holes in the plastic arm engage the nails in the hardwood slides.

Illus. 498.   A support block equal to the thickness of the dovetailed base is required. This one is fastened with two screws.

Illus. 499.   Here you see how a 1½ horsepower router is levelled with a support block under the base of the router.

Illus. 500.   The components for the small oval-guide jig designed for a trimming router.

Illus. 501. Support blocks are designed to permit cuts to be made close to the dovetailed jig base, as shown.

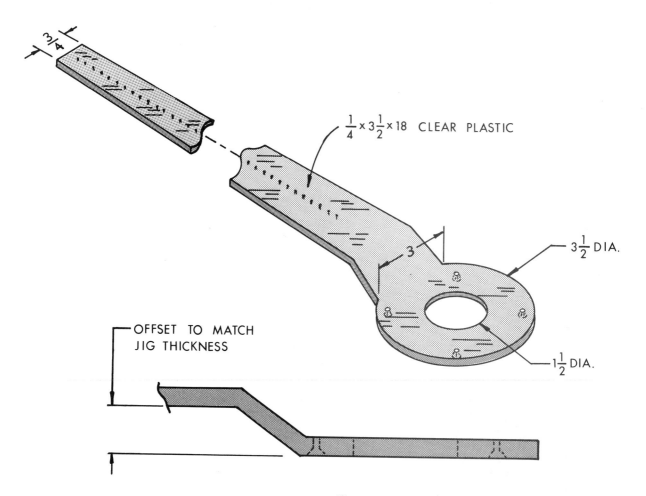

$\frac{1}{4} \times 3\frac{1}{2} \times 18$ CLEAR PLASTIC

$3\frac{1}{2}$ DIA.

3

$1\frac{1}{2}$ DIA.

$\frac{3}{4}$

OFFSET TO MATCH JIG THICKNESS

Illus. 502. The optional jig arm with a bent offset.

lower and directly on top of the workpiece. Illus. 503–507 show how this was done to make the plastic arm of the smaller-sized jig. Remember, this procedure is only optional, and if you are using it your router will not cut ovals as small as otherwise possible using the support blocks. The router bit will not be able to cut in the small paths, close to the dovetailed jig base, the way it did with the arm style with the support block. (See Illus. 503 and 504.)

It is easy to make an optional plastic offset bend. If you don't have access to a strip heater designed especially for bending plastic, simply heat it on an electric stove burner or, as I did, in the workshop wood stove. (See Illus. 505.) Clamp it to the work bench over a block of the appropriate thickness, as shown in Illus. 506. Allow it to cool for a few minutes and then you're ready to proceed.

Setting up and using the oval-cutting jigs is easy. First, locate the center of the ellipse or oval; this is where the center of the major and minor axis cross at right angles. Then make two perpendicular layout lines. Apply double-sided tape (Illus. 507) and place the base of the jig over the center point of the oval. Use the perpendicular layout line to assist in lining up the centers of the two dovetail slots on the base of the jig. (See Illus. 496 and 508.)

Once the base is set down in position on the workpiece, select the two pin holes that will produce the desired-size ellipse cut. Set one with the arm horizontal to a compass-like arrangement of a radius that equals one-half of the length of the major axis. With this one engaged, set the other radius-like point so that it equals one-half of the minor axis with the plastic arm in its vertical position. Now, keep both pins engaged during the cutting operation. One-handed operation of the router is desirable because this permits the second hand to maintain some downward pressure so that the pins do not disengage during the cut. (See Illus. 509.)

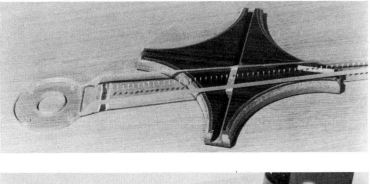

Illus. 503. The optional bend in the plastic arm lowers the router directly onto the top of the work.

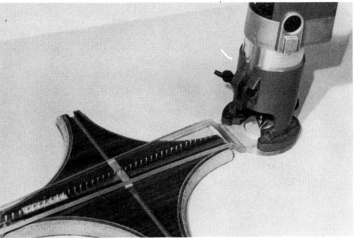

Illus. 504. With the offset arm, you cannot make cuts as close to the jig's base as when you are using a straight arm with a support block under it.

Illus. 505. To bend the offset, you have to soften the plastic for bending. Here it is held over hot coals in the workshop wood stove.

Illus. 506. Here the heated plastic is clamped with the offset bent until it cools. Note the straight plastic arm and the router above.

Illus. 507. Double-faced tape holds the jig base securely to the workpiece.

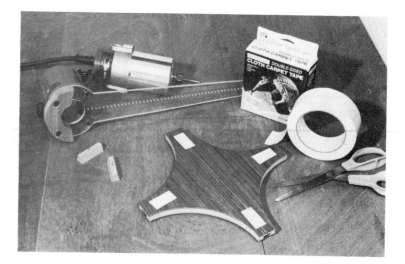

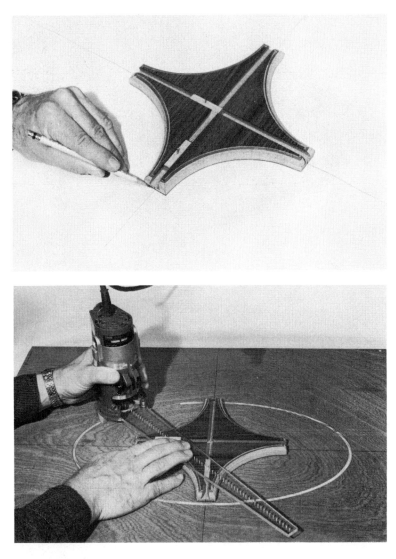

Illus. 508. Align the base to the center of the intended oval using the extended lines that represent the major and minor axis of the oval.

Illus. 509. Make relatively shallow cuts per pass and use the one-hand technique, as shown, when using both the smaller- and larger-size jigs.

Corner-Rounding Jigs These specialty devices are made to simplify the production of panels with identically rounded corners. Counter tops, tabletops, cutting boards, or any other similar type of job requiring this work can be done considerably faster if you use either of the two types of jigs discussed here. Illus. 510 and 512 give basic details for making the jigs, which are essentially templates that are clamped to the corner of the workpiece that has to be cut to a specific radius.

The jig shown in Illus. 510 and 511 is designed for use with a ball-bearing flush-trimming bit. It is referred to as a "corner-rounding trimming jig." To use this jig, first roughly cut the corners to shape with a band saw or a hand-held sabre saw. Then clamp the template under the panel, and make one trimming pass with the router to clean and true the surface of the rounded corner.

The jig shown and detailed in Illus. 512–514 is designed for use with a template guide and a straight-cutting bit. This jig is more complicated to make than the previous one, but it offers the builder at least one good advantage. The stock does not require a preliminary rough cut. Depending upon the thickness of the workpiece and the size of the router being used, the cut can usually be completed in just one pass. Two or three passes may be required for very thick stock. The resulting cut surface(s) is true and clean.

239

Illus. 510. This corner-rounding trimming jig is simply a template with stops that is clamped under the workpiece. A previously rough-cut bandsawn edge is then trimmed clean with a ball-bearing flush-trimming bit.

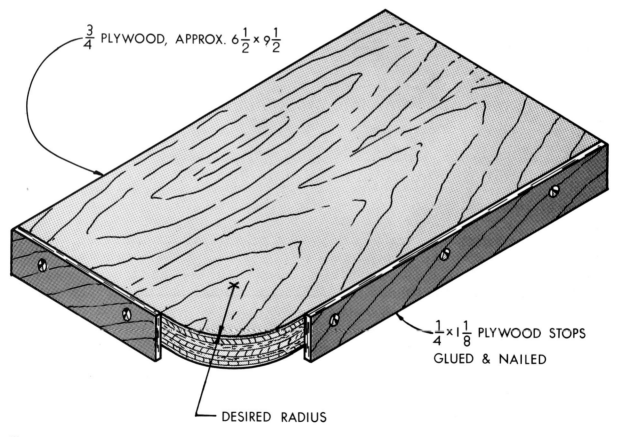

$\frac{3}{4}$ PLYWOOD, APPROX. $6\frac{1}{2} \times 9\frac{1}{2}$

$\frac{1}{4} \times 1\frac{1}{8}$ PLYWOOD STOPS GLUED & NAILED

DESIRED RADIUS

Illus. 511. A bottom view of the corner-rounding trimming jig designed for use with a ball-bearing flush-trimming bit.

240

Illus. 512.   This corner-rounding jig is also designed to be a template. It is made for and used with a template guide attached to the router base. One-eighth or one-quarter-inch hardboard, plywood, or plastic can be used for this project.

Illus. 513.   The corner-rounding jig shown here can be used to cut a true, rounded corner in one operation.

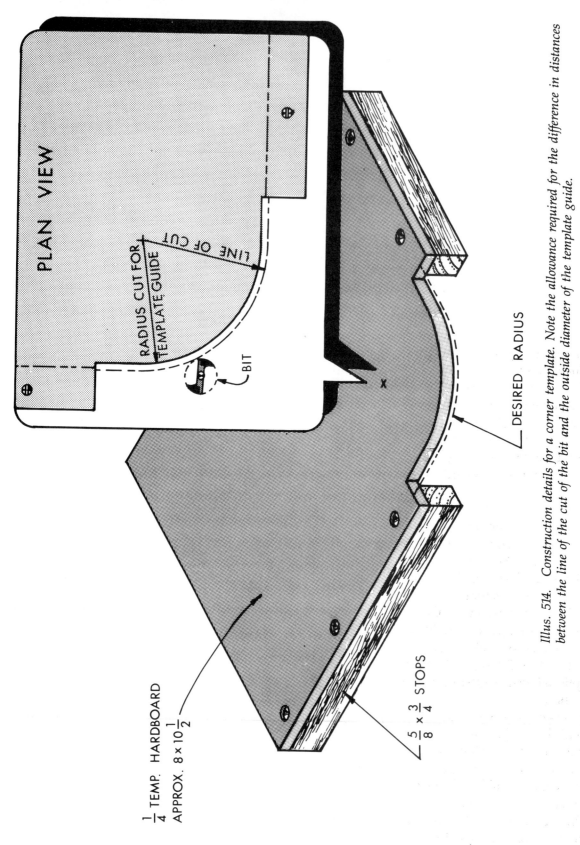

PLAN VIEW

RADIUS CUT FOR
TEMPLATE GUIDE

LINE OF CUT

BIT

x

DESIRED RADIUS

$\frac{1}{4}$ TEMP. HARDBOARD
APPROX. 8 × 10$\frac{1}{2}$

$\frac{5}{8} × \frac{3}{4}$ STOPS

Illus. 514. Construction details for a corner template. Note the allowance required for the difference in distances between the line of the cut of the bit and the outside diameter of the template guide.

242

23

Joint-Making Jigs

This book contains a number of commercially produced and shop-made devices that are used to make a variety of common and specialized joints. Here I discuss and illustrate four jigs designed to do specific joint-work jobs. They are: (1) a tenoning jig, (2) a dowel-tenoning jig, (3) a scarfing jig, and (4) a flush-trimming jig used when edge-banding panels.

Tenoning Jig The jig shown in Illus. 515 is designed to cut tenons of various lengths on stock of any thickness, length, and width up to 5½ inches. (See Illus. 516.) An optional, special router base that has four different off-set edges (four different distances from the bit) provides a quick way to make any of four different tenon lengths. (See Illus. 517.)

The details for making the jig are given in Illus. 518. Illus. 519 suggests details for making an optional offset router base that can be used with the jig.

An offset router base has other applications beyond that of just tenoning. You may want to make a special offset base for production-spacing of dadoes and grooves or for similar jobs where it would be advantageous to eliminate layout and reduce the number of setups.

When used to make tenons, the tenoning jig locates the workpiece (against some stops) and provides a straightedge guide so that one half or one side of the tenon can be cut at one time. Once this cut has been completed, flip the workpiece over and complete the tenon on the second side. When doing this, make sure that all the stock has been cut to parallel thickness and, when making identical pieces, that they have all first been prepared to the same thickness.

To use the tenoning jig, insert the workpiece under the jig and against the near guide strip. A viewing hole is provided to ensure that the edge of the workpiece is tight against the guide of the jig. Grip the end of the workpiece with pointed nails that protrude through the end stop to ensure that the part of the jig that supports the router is not deflected. (See Illus. 520 and 521.) Clamp the workpiece and the jig together against the surface of the workbench. (See Illus. 522.)

The jig-and-offset-router-base combination is designed to cut tenon lengths of ½, ¾, 1, and 1¼ inches. To do this, you have to use a straight bit with a ½-inch-cutting-edge diameter. Changing the diameter of the bit will change the tenon lengths.

To cut a 1¼-inch tenon, use the edge of the base that positions the bit the farthest from the end stop and the closest to the cross guide of the jig. Do the reverse when making the shorter ½-inch-long tenons. Illus. 523 shows the pointed nail markings that result on the end of tenons. These markings should not pose any problem for most mortise-and-tenoning assemblies.

Illus. 515. This tenoning jig will make tenons of various lengths and thicknesses on stock of any overall thickness, any length, and up to a 5½-inch-width capacity.

Illus. 516. Examples of various size tenons cut on boards of various sizes.

Illus. 517. This offset base used with the tenoning jig provides a choice of four different tenon lengths without a need for special layout measurements or a setup.

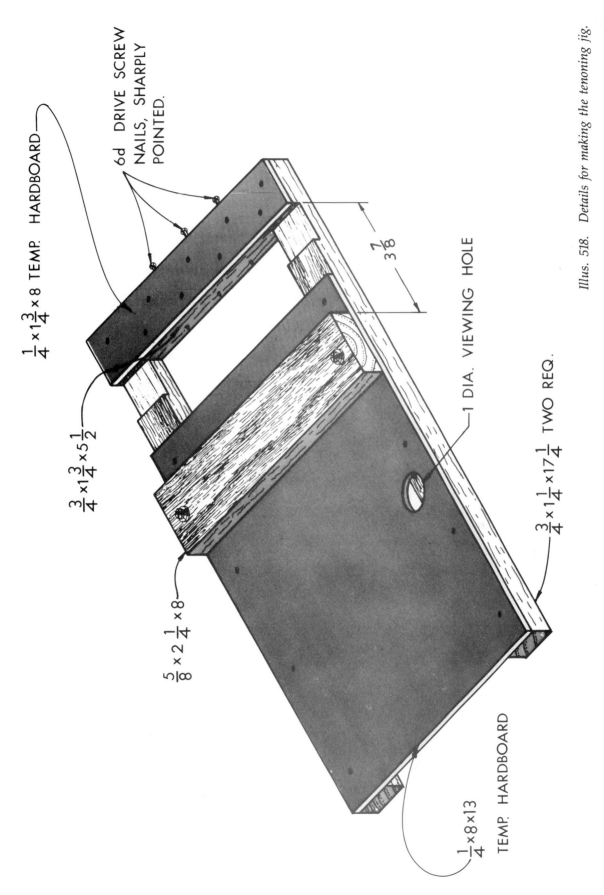

6d DRIVE SCREW NAILS, SHARPLY POINTED.

$\frac{1}{4} \times 1\frac{3}{4} \times 8$ TEMP. HARDBOARD

$\frac{3}{4} \times 1\frac{3}{4} \times 5\frac{1}{2}$

$\frac{7}{3\frac{7}{8}}$

1 DIA. VIEWING HOLE

$\frac{3}{4} \times 1\frac{1}{4} \times 17\frac{1}{4}$ TWO REQ.

$\frac{5}{8} \times 2\frac{1}{4} \times 8$

$\frac{1}{4} \times 8 \times 13$

TEMP. HARDBOARD

Illus. 518. *Details for making the tenoning jig.*

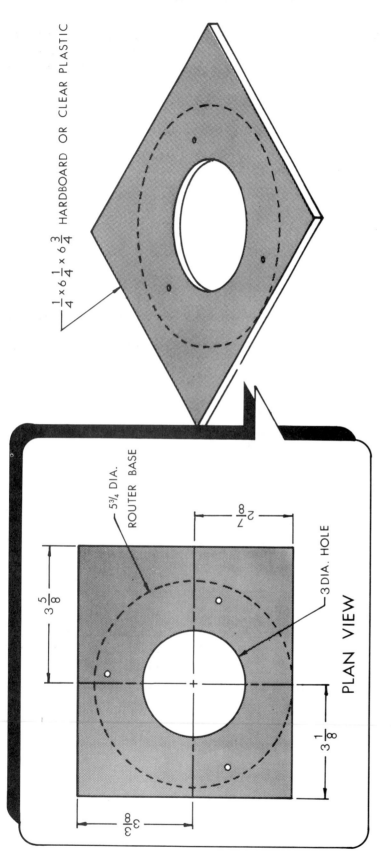

$\frac{1}{4} \times 6\frac{1}{4} \times 6\frac{3}{4}$ HARDBOARD OR CLEAR PLASTIC

5¾ DIA.
ROUTER BASE

3 DIA. HOLE

$3\frac{5}{8}$

$2\frac{7}{8}$

$3\frac{1}{8}$

$3\frac{3}{8}$

PLAN VIEW

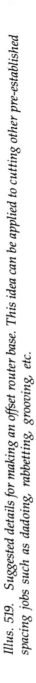

Illus. 519. *Suggested details for making an offset router base. This idea can be applied to cutting other pre-established spacing jobs such as dadoing, rabbetting, grooving, etc.*

Illus. 520.   A little tap on the end of the jig will seat the end of the workpiece on the nail points protruding through the end stop.

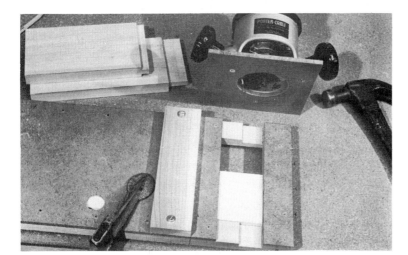

Illus. 521.   The workpiece ready to be tenoned. Note that it is tight against the near guide (checked through the viewing hole), and is also tight against the end stop.

Illus. 522.   The tenoning operation in progress. The length of the tenon depends upon the size of the router bit used and which of the four edges of the base rides against the guide (at the left).

Illus. 523. These resulting indentations from the pointed nails of the jig should not be of major significance.

Dowel Tenoning Jig This jig is designed for use with a router table or an overarm/pin router. (See Illus. 524.) The concept is straightforward. The dowel is supported steadily on a V-block, with its end against an end stop (fence). It is rotated into a stationary rotating bit. (See Illus. 525.) Illus. 526 provides the essential construction details.

The jig has an adjustable pressure bar that keeps the dowel firmly seated on the V-block as it is being rotated. A wing-nut adjustment sets the pressure bar to a suitable height that corresponds to the size of the dowel. Pressure or tension is provided by a couple of heavy rubber bands stretched over the pressure bar; this technique works very well. (See Illus. 527.)

Scarfing Jig Scarfing cuts are acute tapered bevels made on the end or edge of a member. They are used primarily to join pieces end to end to increase the length of a board. (See Illus. 529–530.) For more information concerning how to make and use scarf joints, refer to my book, *Gluing and Clamping* (Sterling Publishing Co., Two Park Avenue, New York, New York 10016.)

The construction of the jig is easy. The details are specified in Illus. 531. The two inclined side pieces have a slope ratio of 1 to 8 (thickness to length) which is the angle recommended for basic scarf joints. The workpiece is clamped with a dowel-and-wedge system that accommodates stock of various thicknesses. (See Illus. 532, which depicts a typical setup.) Because the two inclined surfaces are fairly far apart, a larger sized or extended router base is required to provide router support over the entire working area. (See Illus. 533.) Use a fairly large-diameter flat-cutting bit to speed the job and to make a smoother-cut surface.

Flush-Trimming Jig Veneered panels, hardwood sheet materials, and surfaces overlaid with decorative laminates often have solid wood edgings glued on that must be cut down precisely to the level of the abutting surfaces. The flush-trimming jig shown in Illus. 534 and 535 trims these edgings. Illus. 536 provides construction details. It is important that you attach the 1/4-inch tempered hardboard base to the bottom of the jig carefully so that no fasteners or other protrusions stem from the surface.

The jig is designed to be used with a bit that has at least a 3/4-inch-cutting-edge diameter. If necessary the jig can be modified to be used with smaller or larger bits, as dictated by personal needs or preferences. The dowel guide pin inserted into the bottom is optional. (See Illus. 536 and 537.) It gives the operator an idea of where the bit is and where the cutting is taking place when the jig is moved inward to a position where the dowel pin strikes the edging. At times, the guide pin may have to be removed, such as when working on projects where the edge-banding turns or follows around outside or inside corners.

Illus. 540 shows how the jig is held during use. A downward pressure on the jig must be constantly maintained over the inside area of panel to counteract a natural tipping action due to the weight of the router.

Incidentally, a commercially manufactured "flush trimmer," Model 180 or 185, is available complete with a Bosch or Porter-Cable-mounted router and a 1½-inch-diameter bit from Bet- terely Enterprises, 11160 Central Avenue, N.E., Blaine, Minnesota 55434. It costs $550.

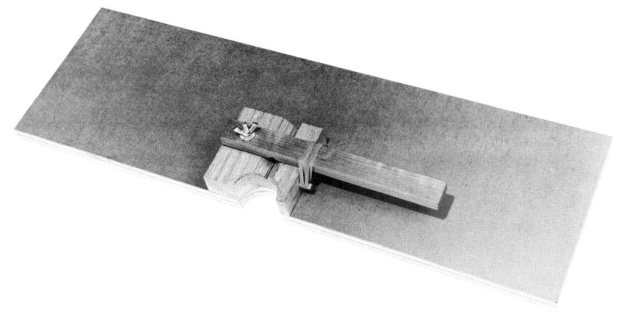

Illus. 524. Dowels of any diameter can be tenoned to any lesser diameter with this simple jig.

Illus. 525. The dowel tenoning jig in use clamped onto the router table. Note that the fence determines the length of the tenon.

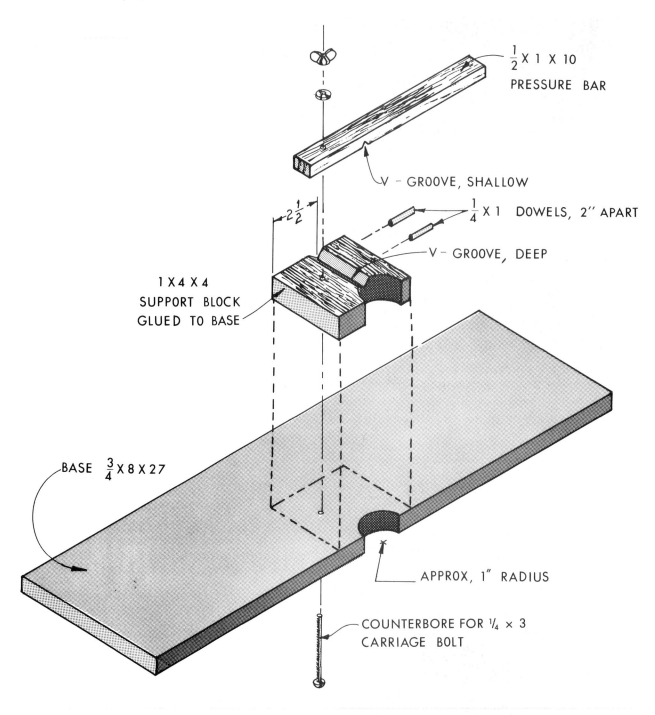

$\frac{1}{2}$ X 1 X 10
PRESSURE BAR

V - GROOVE, SHALLOW

$2\frac{1}{2}$

$\frac{1}{4}$ X 1 DOWELS, 2" APART

V - GROOVE, DEEP

1 X 4 X 4
SUPPORT BLOCK
GLUED TO BASE

BASE $\frac{3}{4}$ X 8 X 27

APPROX, 1" RADIUS

COUNTERBORE FOR $\frac{1}{4}$ × 3
CARRIAGE BOLT

Illus. 526.   Details for making the dowel tenoning jig.

Illus. 527. A close look at the essential parts. Note how the rubber bands provide pressure.

Illus. 528. A scarfing jig designed to handle stock from ½ to 1½ inch thick and up to 4½ inches wide.

Illus. 529. A scarf joint increases the length of the stock.

Illus. 530. The scarfing jig can be used to machine acute angles.

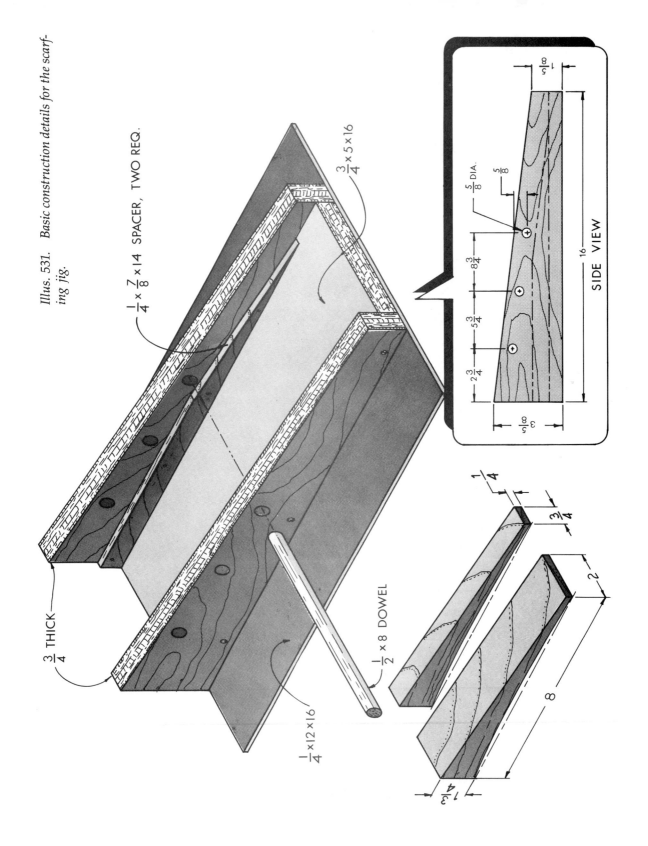

Illus. 531. Basic construction details for the scarfing jig.

$\frac{3}{4} \times 5 \times 16$

$\frac{1}{4} \times \frac{7}{8} \times 14$ SPACER, TWO REQ.

$\frac{3}{4}$ THICK

$\frac{1}{4} \times 12 \times 16$

$\frac{1}{2} \times 8$ DOWEL

$\frac{1}{4}$

$\frac{3}{4}$

2

8

$1\frac{3}{4}$

SIDE VIEW

$\frac{1}{8}$

$\frac{5}{8}$ DIA.

$\frac{5}{8}$

$2\frac{3}{4}$

$5\frac{3}{4}$

$8\frac{3}{4}$

16

$3\frac{5}{8}$

Illus. 532. *A wedge holds the workpiece steady.*

Illus. 533. *An extended or larger router base is needed to support the router.*

Illus. 534. *A flush-trimming jig cuts solid-wood edge banding precisely to the level of the adjoining surface of the panel.*

Illus. 535. *A bottom view of the jig prior to mounting the router.*

253

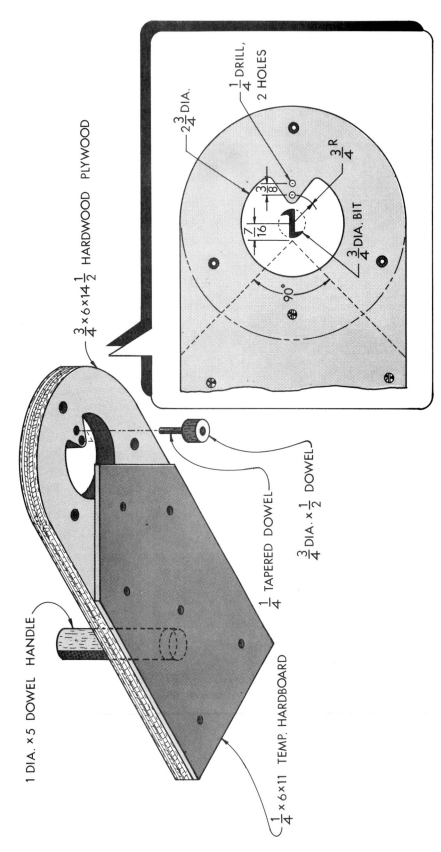

Illus. 536. A drawing that shows the bottom view details of the flush-trimming guide.

Illus. 537. The flush-trimming jig guides the cutting of the solid-wood edge band down to exactly the same level as the panel surface, as shown in progress here.

Illus. 538 (above left). *The optional guide pin is removeable, and can be inserted in a choice of two holes, as shown.*
Illus. 539 (above right). *A bottom view. Lower the bit exactly to the level of the bottom surface of the tempered hardboard. Note that all screws are countersunk well below the surface.*

Illus. 540. The flush-trimming jig in use. Maintain consistent pressure over the panel during cutting so that the weight of the router does not tip it.

24

Plunge-Router Boring Jigs

In this chapter I describe and show several jigs designed specifically to utilize the capabilities of plunge routers for boring and drilling operations.

All of the jigs discussed here use a template guide attached to the router manufacturer's standard subbase. The template guide must be of a particular size so that it fits snugly into a hole or holes bored into the jig(s). You clamp the jig to the workpiece, and make the hole or holes in the desired location simply by plunging the router. Router bits with plunge-entry ends should be used.

If you use a speed control to reduce the RPM of your router, you can even use boring tools in your router, that is, of course, if the shanks fit the collet or collet bushings of the correct size are used. Refer to Chapter 16, pages 79 and 80, for more information on devices that can be used to reduce the spindle speeds of routers and other tools.

Caution: Do not use drills or boring bits at the normal high speeds routing bits rotate at.

The true, vertical bit-entry that can be accomplished with plunge routers, and the spring retraction of the bit from the workpiece, make jig-drilling and boring quick, safe, and certainly as accurate as any other method. The key is to make the jigs accurately so that the holes in them are not only the correct diameter, but also located so that the plunge-cut hole will enter the workpiece in the desired location; one way to do this is to make the holes with a drill press.

Even though you might own a drill press and may question the concept and need for plunge-router boring techniques, I assure you that you'll be able to do some jobs faster, better, and easier with a jig and your router than with the drill press. Just consider the uses for the jigs on the following pages of this chapter, and I think you will agree. Even if you do not, you may become inspired to make a jig according to your own dimensions or design to perform a certain operation or to help make a particular project.

Four different jigs are presented in this chapter. Three of them, shown in Illus. 541, are designed for making various kinds of dowel joints, some of which include the edge-to-edge joint, butt-corner joint, face-butt joint, mitre joint, offset joint, and others. Dowelling and its boring requirements can be made so easy that you'll give renewed consideration to using dowels where they were previously considered impractical or too difficult to use efficiently.

All the holes bored in the three dowelling jigs shown in Illus. 541 are $5/8$ inch in diameter,

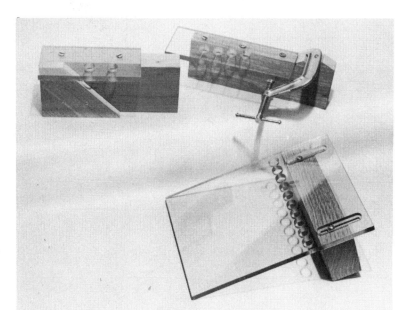

Illus. 541. Three jigs designed for making various types of dowel joints with the plunge router.

which means that you can use a template guide with a ⅝-inch outside diameter and a bit as large as ½ inch in diameter. You can also use any smaller-size bit down to the smallest size available with a large template guide. The bit will still bore in the exact center; the template guide only positions the router and its bit in relation to the center of the hole in the jig. For example, you can use ¼- or ½-inch-diameter bits interchangeably with a ⅝-inch outside-diameter template guide without having to modify the hole sizes in the jig.

In short you can also make the holes in your jig to accommodate any template-guide size; this, in turn, will permit the desired-size bit to rotate and plunge inside the template guide.

Edge-to-Edge Dowel-Boring Jig This jig is designed to be used for edge-dowelling boards from approximately ¾ up to approximately 1½ inches in thickness. (See Illus. 542.) Each of the four holes has center lines scribed on the bottom of the plastic that extend exactly through the center of the hole. (See Illus. 542 and 543.) The jig provides a choice of four different holes, each hole best for a range of different stock thicknesses. The jig requires a 2½-inch regular C-clamp; a hole drilled through it that has a screw in it keeps the clamp in position.

When using the jig, simply draw a layout line squarely across the edge of the workpiece where the dowel or hole is to be located. One of the four holes will be fairly close to the center thickness of the workpiece. Clamp the jig in position with the line of the jig immediately over the layout line drawn on the edge of the workpiece, as shown in Illus. 544. Insert the router so that the template guide is in the correct hole. Turn on the router and plunge the hole into the work to the preset depth desired.

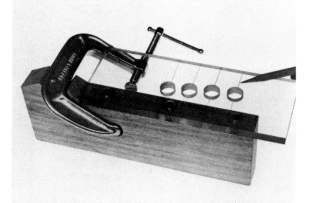

Illus. 542. A jig designed primarily for making edge-to-edge dowelled glue joints. This jig can be used with any stock between ¾ and 1½ inch in thickness. Note the scribed lines passing through the centers of each hole on the bottom of the plastic.

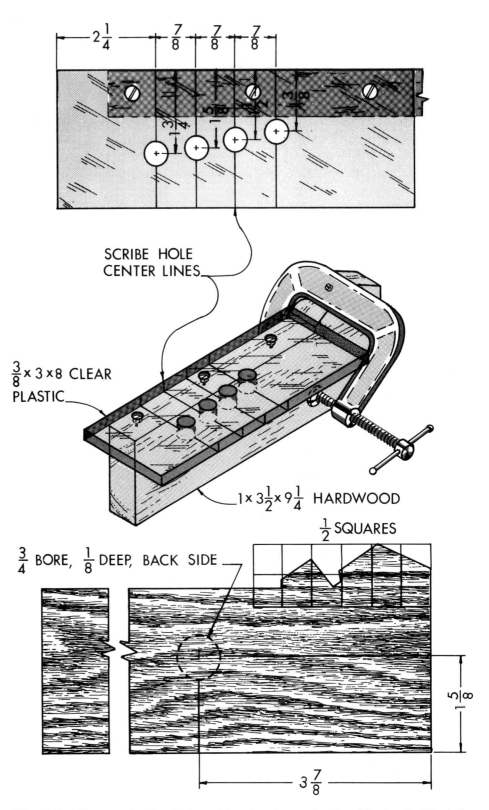

$2\frac{1}{4}$ $\frac{7}{8}$ $\frac{7}{8}$ $\frac{7}{8}$

SCRIBE HOLE
CENTER LINES

$\frac{3}{8} \times 3 \times 8$ CLEAR
PLASTIC

$1 \times 3\frac{1}{2} \times 9\frac{1}{4}$ HARDWOOD

$\frac{1}{2}$ SQUARES

$\frac{3}{4}$ BORE, $\frac{1}{8}$ DEEP, BACK SIDE

$1\frac{5}{8}$

$3\frac{7}{8}$

Illus. 543.   Construction details for making the edge-to-edge dowel-boring jig. The holes in the plastic should be sized to fit the outside diameter of the template guide of your choice.

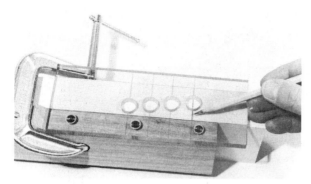

Illus. 544. Drilling a dowel hole into a piece of stock 1½ inch thick. Note that the line of jig is immediately over a line drawn on the edge to indicate where the hole is to be located. The jig is then clamped to the workpiece.

Illus. 545. This jig is designed only to produce dowel holes in mitre-cut pieces of one standard thickness.

Dowels do not have to be located in the exact-center of the board thickness when you are making dowelled-edge glue joints. However, it is important that the same faces always be clamped against the vertical part of the jig; this ensures that all of the holes will be made the exact-same distance from that face of the glued-up panel, with one perfectly flat and even face of each member of the assembly exactly flush to the next one.

Remember, this jig can also be used to make other kinds of dowel joints and for other boring jobs. If you want to make holes with offsetting locations, simply clamp a shim of the desired thickness or offset dimension between the jig and the workpiece. If the offset boring job is a production run, attach the shim to the jig with a small piece of double-sided tape.

Mitre-Joint Dowel-Boring Jig This jig is not as versatile as the others described in this chapter. As shown in Illus. 545–547, it is limited only to production-boring of mitre-joint dowel holes into pieces of a specific, consistent thickness.

The mitre dowel-boring jig shown in Illus. 545–547 was, in fact, made to drill two identically spaced holes exactly in the center of mitred pieces of stock, all exactly one inch thick. I am including it to enrich your repertoire of jigs. The concept may be of value someday when you are working on a particular job. Construction details are given in Illus. 548.

Illus. 546. Clamp the mitre dowel-boring jig to a workpiece.

Illus. 547. The dowelled mitred joint ready for assembly. Note the plunge router with the template guide mounted to the base.

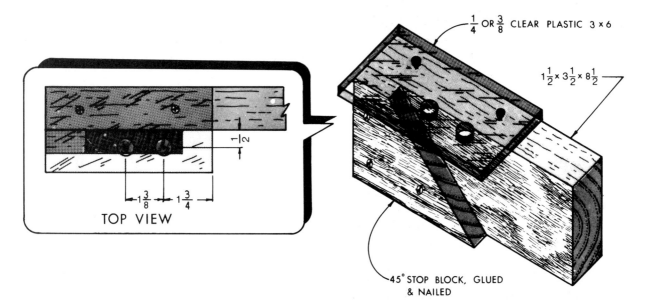

Illus. 548.   Drawing of the mitre-joint dowel-boring jig.

Multiple-Hole Dowel-Boring Jig   This is a very intriguing device for the creative router craftsman. (See Illus. 549 and 550.) You are certain to find many different and unusual dowel-joint applications for this jig. It is very easy to make, and consists of only a few parts.

Since making and using this jig, I have learned several ways it could be improved to make it even more versatile. I will point out these refinements as I discuss the jig. If you take a look at the dowel joint in Illus. 552–553, you will note that the holes align because they are perfectly spaced in distance from each other. A slight modification in the design of this jig would make the fit of the joint equally good even if one or more holes is slightly off in the jig. This I discuss later on.

To make the jig as specified in Illus. 551, begin with a squared piece of polycarbonate plastic, $\frac{3}{8}$ inch thick ($\frac{1}{2}$-inch thickness would be better), 8 inches wide and 11 inches long. Carefully cut the two grooves for the adjustable guide screws as specified in the drawing. Note that according to the drawing the double slots are only cut into one side or face of the plastic. Here is where another refinement can be made. Instead, use $\frac{1}{2}$-inch-thick plastic and cut the adjustment slots into both surfaces so that

the plastic can be flipped over when desired. Cut the slots on the router table with either a pin router or a portable, hand-held plunge router with an edge guide. Refer to pages 194–197 in Chapter 19, which discuss how to cut similar slots into an adjustable circle-cutting router base.

With the adjustment slots complete, on one surface or both, carefully lay out the holes for the template guide. The diameter of the holes should be such that the outside diameter of the template guide will just slip snugly into them. Illus. 554 depicts the drill-press boring setup used. Note that a straightedge fence ensures that the holes are made in a straight line. If you want to, you can set up an indexing pin or locating stop so that each hole is spaced exactly the same. The indexing technique *is not* shown in Illus. 554.

Before removing the paper mask on the surface of the plastic, scribe a line down both edges of the plastic that extends from the center of the holes. (See Illus. 555.) Illus. 556 and 557 show the setups used to drill the holes for making the joint shown in Illus. 552 and 553. As mentioned earlier, one optional improvement to the jig would be to make the plastic component of the jig so that it can be flipped over when desired. If you do this, you would then be able to make each corresponding hole in each member of the joint using the exact-same template hole in this jig. Consequently, the series of holes in each piece of the joint will match perfectly because they were drilled with the jig in a self-matching or mirror-image setup—even if the holes in the jig are not precisely spaced.

The multiple-hole dowel-boring jig can also be clamped to any surface at any location or angle without the wooden guide. This setup is shown in Illus. 558.

Just because there are many holes in the jig doesn't mean that you have to use every one of them in every joint. You may determine that for the job at hand it is more appropriate to use every other one, every third one, etc.

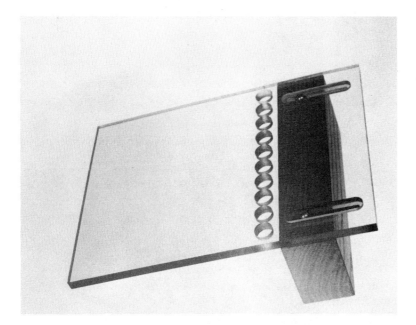

Illus. 549. The multiple-hole dowel-boring jig is easy to make and does a wide variety of dowelling jobs. Note the adjustable wood-locating block.

Illus. 550. The component parts only include one piece of plastic, a piece of wood, and two machine screws with two T nuts.

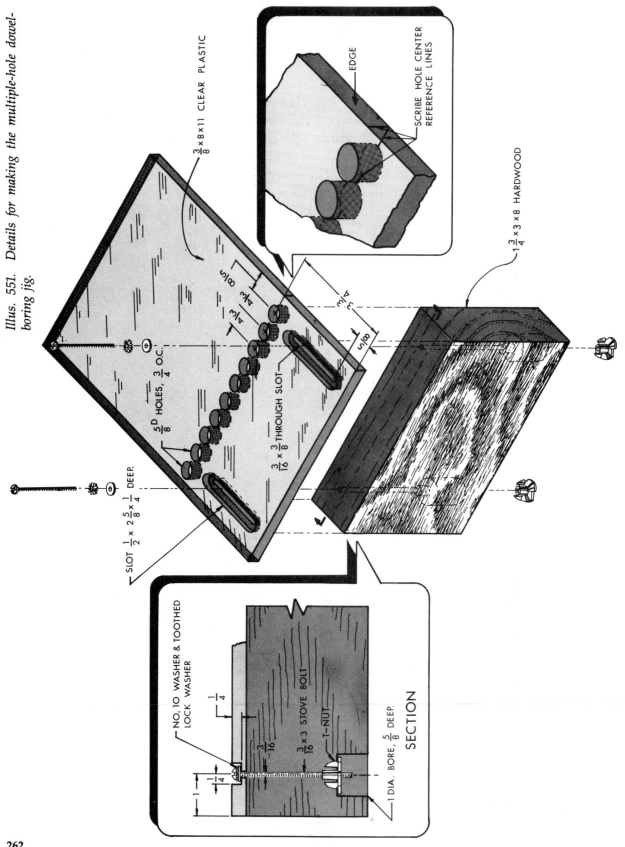

Illus. 551. Details for making the multiple-hole dowel-boring jig.

EDGE

SCRIBE HOLE CENTER REFERENCE LINES

$\frac{3}{8} \times 8 \times 11$ CLEAR PLASTIC

$1\frac{3}{4} \times 3 \times 8$ HARDWOOD

$3\frac{3}{4}$

$\frac{5}{8}$

$\frac{1}{8}$

$\frac{3}{4}$

$\frac{5}{8}$ D HOLES, $\frac{3}{4}$ O.C.

$\frac{3}{16} \times 3$ THROUGH SLOT

SLOT $\frac{1}{2} \times 2\frac{5}{8} \times \frac{1}{4}$ DEEP.

NO. 10 WASHER & TOOTHED LOCK WASHER

$\frac{1}{4}$

$\frac{1}{4}$

1

$\frac{3}{16}$

$\frac{3}{16} \times 3$ STOVE BOLT

T-NUT

1 DIA. BORE, $\frac{5}{8}$ DEEP.

SECTION

Illus. 552 (above left). Holes for this corner dowel joint were made with the multiple-hole dowel-boring jig and a plunge router. Illus. 553 (above right). The joint slides together perfectly. Doesn't it look strong?

Illus. 554. Carefully lay out and bore the template holes in the plastic so that they are all evenly spaced. Note the use of the guide fence on the drill press to ensure that all of the holes will be in a straight line.

Illus. 555. Lines scribed into the edges and faces of the plastic running through the hole centers are used to adjust and position the guide and locate where the holes will be bored into the wood workpiece. Here the guide is set ½ inch from the hole centers.

Illus. 556 (above left). Here the jig is used to bore holes into the surface of one member. Illus. 557 (above right). The setup for boring the same number of holes into the end grain.

Illus. 558. Holes can be made in a surface at any angular position. Here a single layout line on the workpiece is mated to the line scribed into the surfaces of the plastic, ensuring perfect positioning of the jig.

Special Plunge-Boring Jig This can be designed to handle a specific job: making notches in dowels used for toy-building logs. (See Illus. 559 and 560.) Once it is set up, and the template guide used to locate where the hole will be made is in relation to the workpiece, the result will be a fast, production-oriented operation. The jig shown here employs the boring features of the plunge router to cut circular notches in dowels for making toy-building logs.

The essential details for making this jig are given in Illus. 561. Use one-inch diameter dowel. A V-groove and a system of stops ensures that the plunge-router cut will be made where intended and that both cuts on the ends of each piece will be "on line" with each other.

If you take a look at Illus. 562 and 563, you will note that provisions are made in the design of the jig so that identical pieces can be made in a number of different lengths; in the particular operation the jig is being used for in Illus. 559, the result will be identical toy log parts.

The concept used in this jig design can be applied and utilized for jobs other than making notches in dowels for toy logs. Devise an elevated block to support the router, with a hole for the template guide. Use a stop (or several if required) to position and locate the workpiece(s) under the plunging bit. As Illus. 559 shows, you can use a one-handed pumping action, working the router somewhat like a punch press.

Illus. 559. This plunge-boring setup is employed to make the notches in toy building logs.

Illus. 560. The essential parts of the jig. Note the template guide on the router that matches the hole in the elevated support block of the jig.

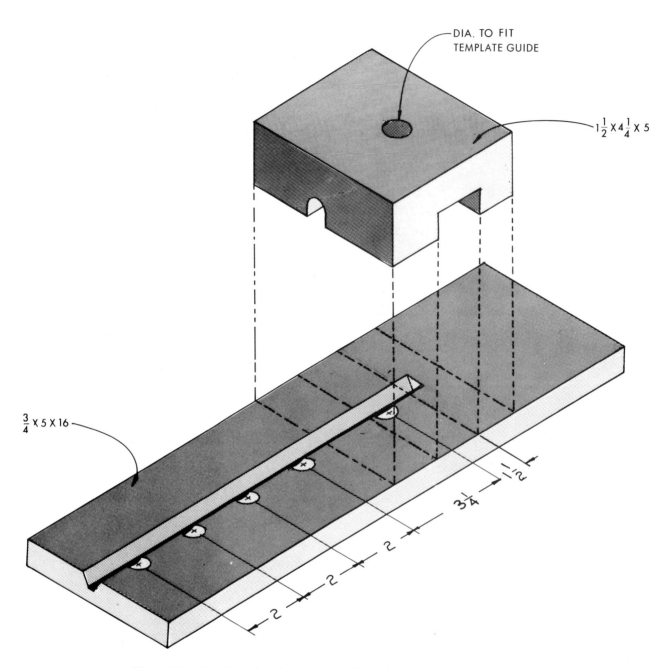

DIA. TO FIT
TEMPLATE GUIDE

$1\frac{1}{2}$ X $4\frac{1}{4}$ X 5

$\frac{3}{4}$ X 5 X 16

$1\frac{1}{2}$

$3\frac{1}{4}$

2

2

2

2

Illus. 561. Drawing of a plunge-boring jig used to cut notches on dowels for toy building logs.

Illus. 562.   A length of dowel acts as an adjustment guide to ensure that the second cut at the other end will be made "on line" with the first notch cut.

Illus. 563.   The guide peg must be used with each piece when you are making the notch on the second end.

25

Jigs for Letter-Carving and Wood Signs

In two of my previous books, *Making Wood Signs* and *Router Handbook*, considerable space was devoted to the discussion of commercial and home-made jigs for wood-sign work. Also included were tips for perfecting the techniques of freehand routing of engraved and raised letters and designs. Straightedges and similar guides are used whenever possible in these operations. Turn to Chapter 20 for a look at some jigs that help in straight-line work. If you're interested in wood-sign work, also refer to Chapters 21 and 22 for a discussion of adjustable guides that help cut various sizes of squares, rectangles, circles, and ovals.

Here I offer some ideas for making templates for sign-letter work. Included, too, is an interesting device for holding the template in place during the routing of each letter; it has a fast repositioning feature that eliminates the use of clamps to hold the template. I also include a sample set of full-sized, traceable patterns for the entire alphabet and for numbers. Simply copy them and make the set of templates shown in this book for your own use. The jigs and templates shown in this chapter can either be used as templates that assist in the actual routing or as layout tools to mark the wood for subsequent freehand routing.

Jig-and-Lettering-Template System This system produces perfect router-guided, single-stroke inclined letters. (See Illus. 564.)The templates (Illus. 565) are designed for use with any plunge router. The resulting letters are 2¼ inches high and have a ³⁄₈-inch wide stroke. Use either a ³⁄₈-inch straight roundnose bit or a special, sharply pointed V-bit, and a template guide with a ¹⁄₂-inch-outside diameter. (See Illus. 566.)

A look at the design of the templates in Illus. 565 and 566 shows that each stroke that is necessary to make the letter(s) is guided perfectly. There is virtually no chance of making a mistake. The letter A, for example, is made in two different strokes or passes. The first pass is the inverted V stroke, and the second pass makes the horizontal "slash" stroke. To make the letter A, reposition the template to the left to make the horizontal slash stroke after the inverted V has been cut. This is where the transparent-plastic template is really an advantage. With it, you can see where to accurately position the template when making those letters that requires two passes and the repositioning of the template.

Illus. 566 takes a close look at the lettering template and a special, transparent-plastic router-base made specifically to carry template guides. Turn to pages 199 and 200 for information on making this base and other specialty bases.

When making the templates, you have to use a scroll saw to cut the plastic. (See Illus. 567.) Use ¼-inch polycarbonate plastic (Lexon or Tuffak). Make a copy of the full-sized patterns (Illus. 572–575) directly from this book; use a copy machine if possible.

Glue the paper-pattern copies to the plastic with rubber cement. You can cut the plastic pieces to any length desired, but they have to be cut approximately to a 3¼-inch width with a 60-degree bevel along one edge. Use a table saw.

The key to utilizing the templates is the unique holding device that is clamped to the work surface. Illus. 568 supplies details for making it. The plastic templates are held securely in two retaining strips that are made of ¼-inch-straight-grain hard wood and epoxy-glued to the ¼-inch tempered hardboard base; they hold the templates so that they do not move vertically during routing.

The section detail in Illus. 568 shows how pointed nails are utilized to grip the plastic templates and keep them from moving laterally. Illus. 569 and 570 show how the template sits on the pointed nails that protrude through the bevelled retaining strip. The nails grip the template so that it does not move laterally; no clamps are required to attach the template to any lateral location. To reposition the template, simply raise or lift it out of the retaining chan-nels of the holder to a point where the nail points are disengaged from the plastic.

The base or holder itself must be clamped securely to the workpiece to be routed. Use any type of clamp, temporary nail or double-sided tape to secure the template holder. (See Illus. 571.)

When making the templates and holder, remember that the objective is to make the component parts so that the plastic pieces of the template snap smartly into the retaining channels of the holder. This can be accomplished by slightly narrowing the template width by running the square (upper) edges of the templates over the jointer or trimming them with very slight stock-removal cuts on the table saw. You can also control the "snap-in" tension by driving the nails in just a little further.

If using nails, grind or file them to very sharp points, and use as few as possible. Although many nails are shown in Illus. 569, only every other nail is actually being used. The unused nails are there as reserves in case the template starts to wear or slip; if this happens to you, tap another nail or two into working position. (See Illus. 571.)

Illus. 572–575 are full-size patterns for the letters. Illus. 576 and 577 are full-size matching number patterns.

This letter template-and-holder concept can be modified to satisfy your personal needs. Simply incorporate designs of other letter styles and sizes as required.

Illus. 564. *A perfect alphabet of template-guided, plunge-routed letters that are 2¼ inches high and have a ⅜-inch stroke width.*

Illus. 565. A complete set of alphabet templates designed for use with a plunge router and a ½-inch-outside diameter template guide.

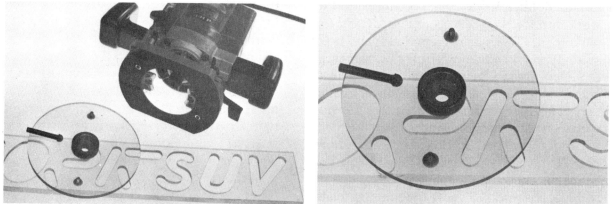

Illus. 566 A (above left). This specially made clear-plastic base that carries template guides gives you maximum visibility when you are routing. Illus. 566 B (above right). A closeup look at the clear-plastic template and router base with a ½-inch-OD template guide installed. Note the ⅜-inch core box bit that will be used.

Illus. 567. Carefully saw out the templates on the scroll saw. Drilling ½-inch holes prior to sawing makes the job a lot easier.

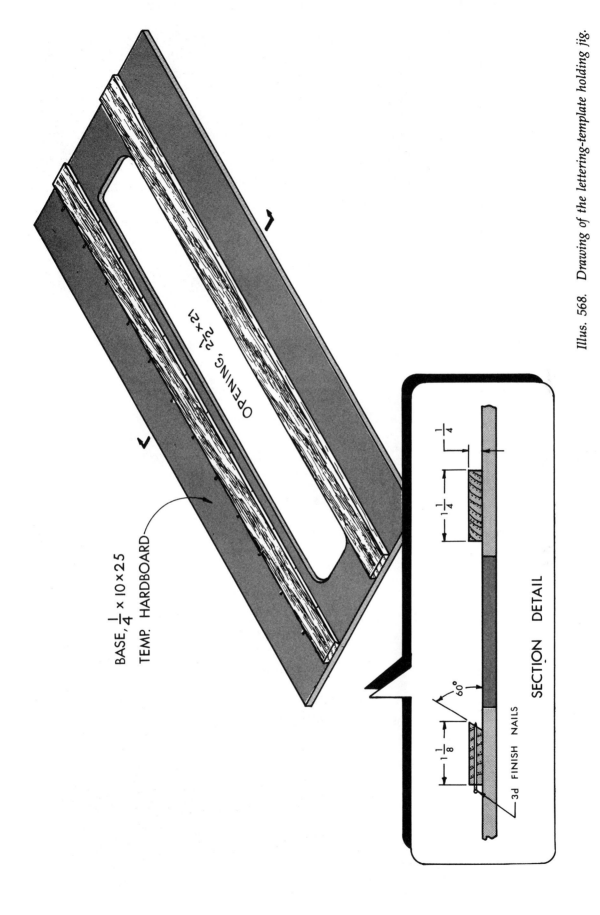

BASE, $\frac{1}{4}$ × 10 × 25
TEMP. HARDBOARD

OPENING, $2\frac{1}{2}$ × 21

$\frac{1}{4}$

$\frac{1}{4}$

$\frac{1}{8}$

60°

3d FINISH NAILS

SECTION DETAIL

Illus. 568. Drawing of the lettering-template holding jig.

Illus. 569. The template holder. Three d finishing nails extend through the lower retaining strip.

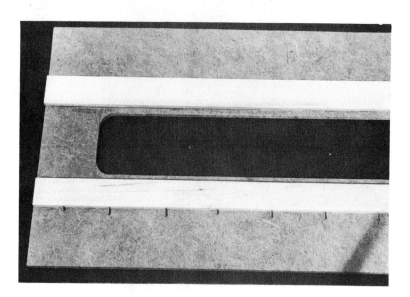

Illus. 570. A closeup look shows how the template with its bevelled edge fits into the bevelled retaining strip.

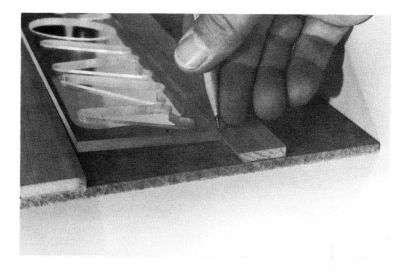

Illus. 571. The template ready for routing and quick repositioning without clamping.

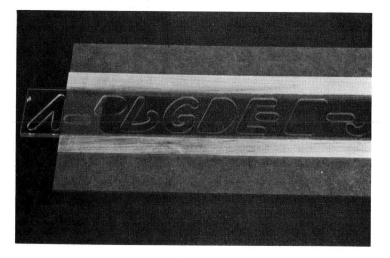

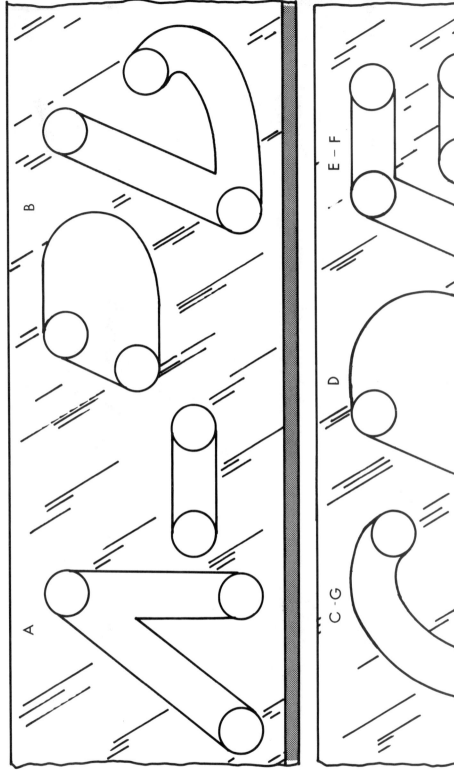
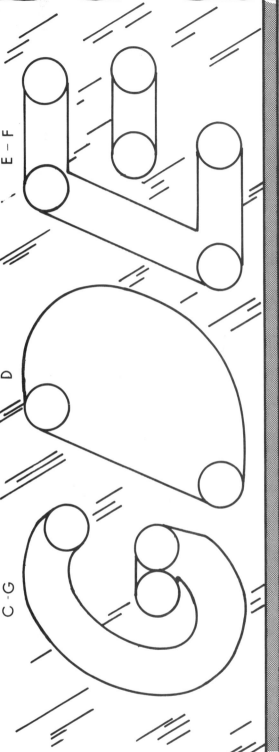

Illus. 572.

273

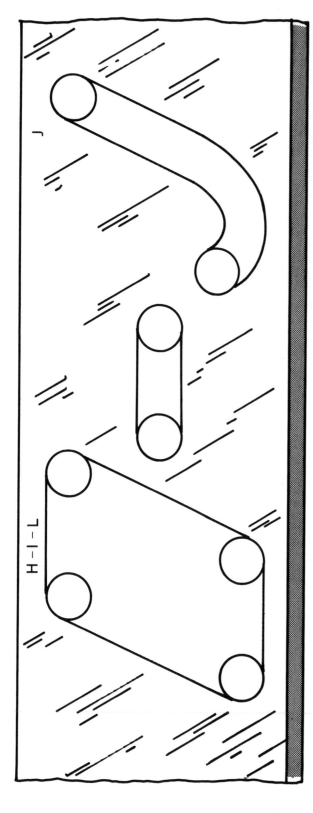

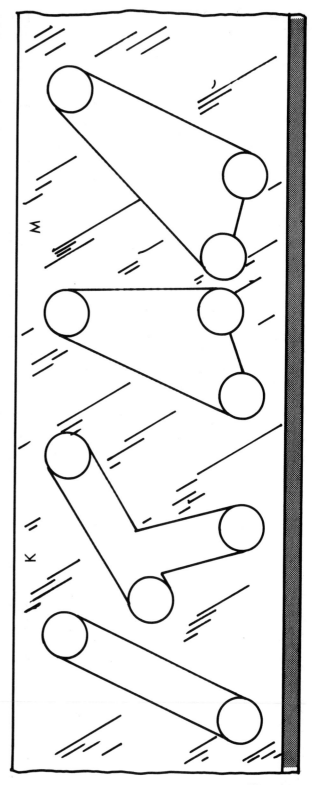

Illus. 573.

Illus. 574.

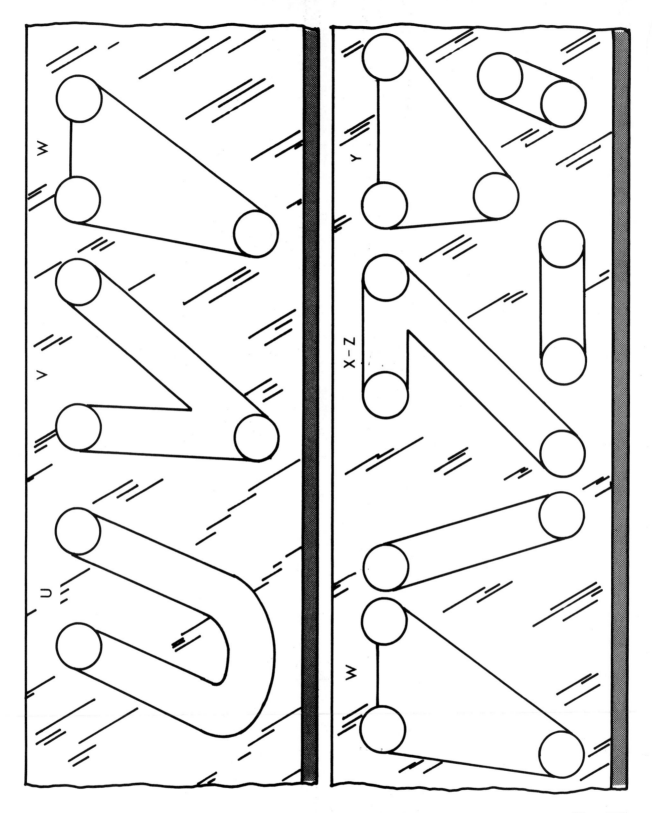

Illus. 575.

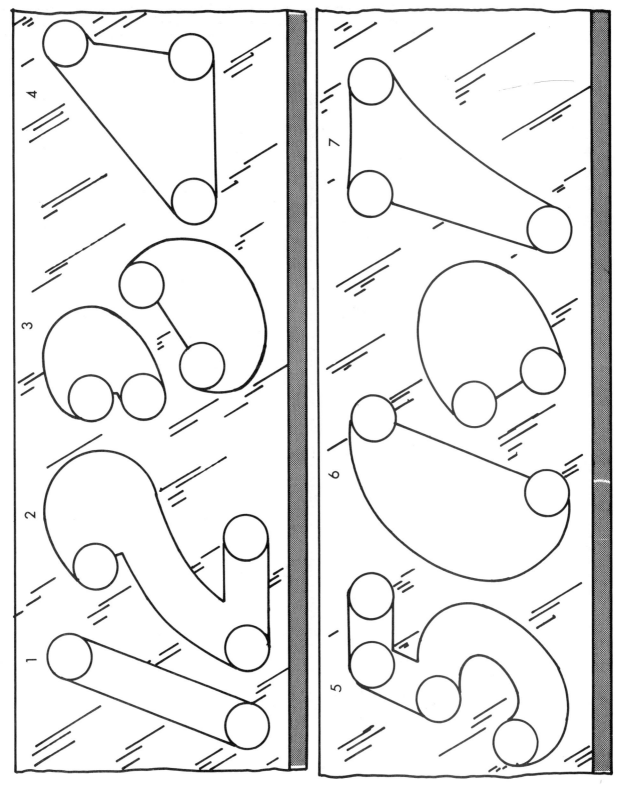

Illus. 576. Full-size number templates.

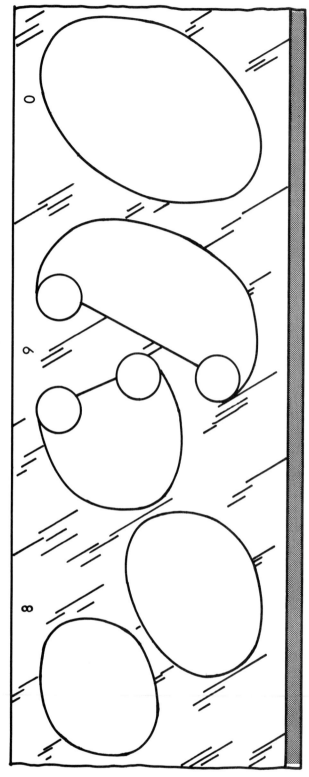

Illus. 577. Full-size number templates.

Illus. 578. Routed numbers and number templates. Full-size patterns are given in Illus. 576 and 577.

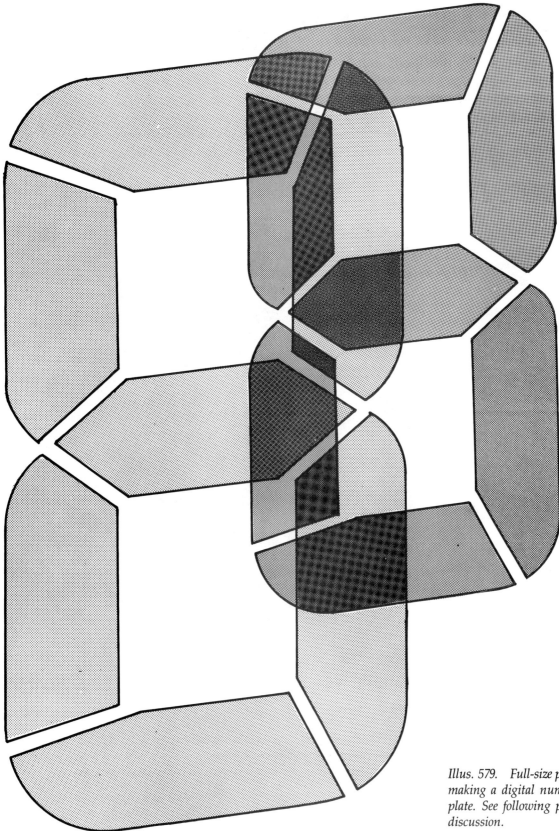

Illus. 579.   Full-size pattern for making a digital number template. See following page for a discussion.

Digital-number templates With digital-number templates, you make any digital numbers with just one template. Simply rout out the area of the template that comprises the shape of the desired number from zero to nine. The template can be made of any material, but tempered hardboard, plywood, or plastic is recommended.

Copy the full-size patterns in Illus. 579. An enlarging and reducing copy machine can be used to change either of the given sizes some-what, if necessary. Carefully cut out the template on the scroll saw (Illus. 581) and fit the router with a template guide. (See Illus. 580 and 584.) Illus. 582 and 583 depict some ideas for securing the template to the workpiece.

Illus. 585 shows lettering templates that have been scroll-sawn from clear plastic. Depending upon the number of signs involved, it is sometimes easier and faster (in production work) to make up fully worded templates.

Illus. 580. Digital number templates. Shown here are a 6-inch plastic version and an 8-inch template of ¼-inch hardboard.

Illus. 581. Cutting out the digital number template on the scroll saw.

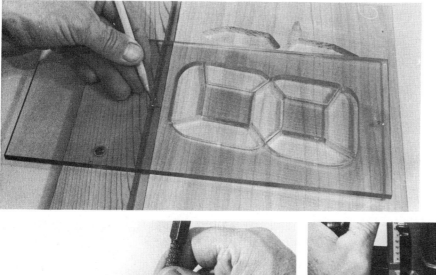

Illus. 582. An attached guide locates each letter the same distance from the edge of the board. Note the optional, pointed nail which helps prevent lateral movement of the template during routing.

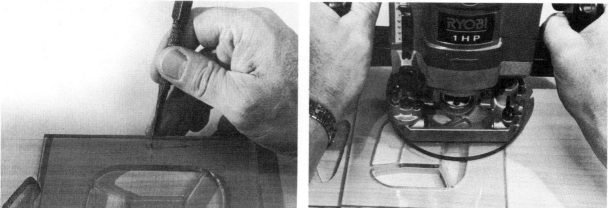

Illus. 583 (above left). *A small countersunk hole allows you to drive a small wire nail below the surface of the template to secure the template for routing.* Illus. 584 (above right). *Operator's view of routing a digital number. Note the clear-plastic base with template guide.*

Illus. 585. A couple of lettering templates. Note that the one on the left has a two-position guide for routing on boards of different widths.

26

Miscellaneous Jigs and Techniques

In this chapter I discuss and give plans for making a mini-router/shaper table that utilizes a trimming router. I include two other projects: one converts a drill press into an overarm and pin router, and another shows how to attach your router to a radial arm saw. Rounding out this chapter are ways to build and use inclined templates, a butt-hinge template, and some ideas for routing duplicate small parts.

Mini-Router/Shaper Table   A number of trimming routers on the market today have tilting bases. (See Illus. 588.) When this feature is incorporated into the design of the table shown in Illus. 586 and 587, it adds considerably to its function and value; the result is a handy little machine that can make miniatures and do model work. The high speed of the trim router and its power produces very clean cuts in many materials.

Illus. 586. The small, light-weight trimming router is perfect for this mini-router/ shaper table. Note that it is set up here in a tilt position with a simple wood guide fence.

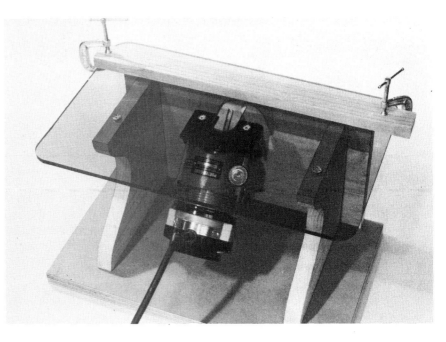

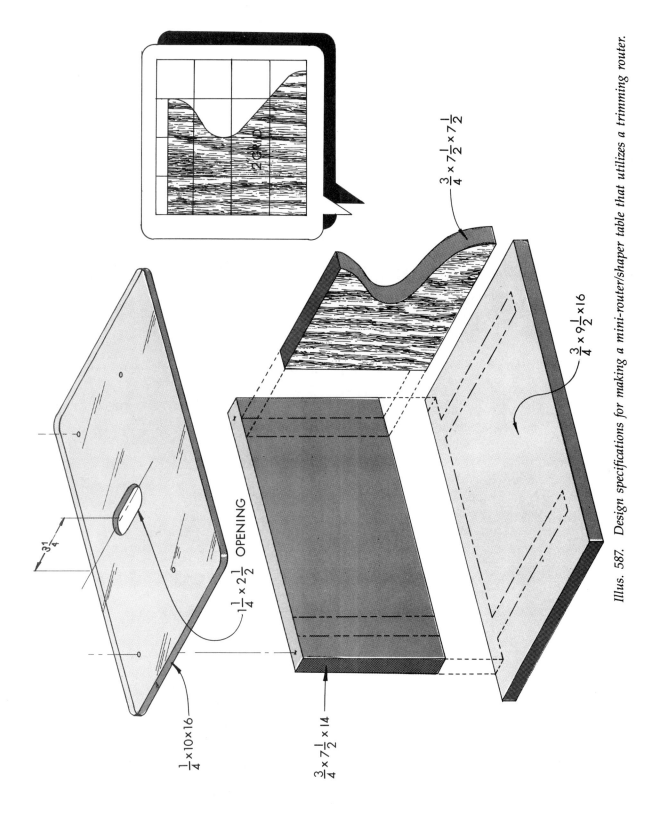

$\frac{3}{4} \times 7\frac{1}{2} \times 7\frac{1}{2}$

$\frac{3}{4} \times 9\frac{1}{2} \times 16$

$\frac{3}{4} \times 7\frac{1}{2} \times 14$

$1\frac{1}{4} \times 2\frac{1}{2}$ OPENING

$\frac{31}{4}$

$\frac{1}{4} \times 10 \times 16$

2" GRID

Illus. 587. Design specifications for making a mini-router/shaper table that utilizes a trimming router.

283

Illus. 588. Here's a look at Porter-Cable's Model 319 Tilt Base on their laminate-trimmer router.

With a bit shank-adapter, the operator can use a variety of miniature bits and other carving cutters that would otherwise require a special power-carving tool. (See Illus. 589.) When all of the possible cutting-tool shapes and profiles and the tilt capability of the router are combined, you can produce an endless variety of edge forms and cutting shapes.

In the table project shown in Illus. 586 the

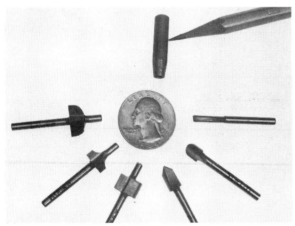

Illus. 589. A shank adapter (above) permits the use of these miniature router bits as well as a wide selection of carving tool burrs and other cutters with ⅛-inch shanks.

tabletop is made of ¼-inch transparent plastic. Tempered hardboard makes a very suitable substitute; some may even prefer it.

Drill-Press Router Overarm This device can be used with or without a simple straightedge fence. (See Illus. 590 and 591.) It can also be used to do some pin-routing and many special routing jobs that are otherwise difficult to perform. The one limitation is that it does not have a plunge-entry capability.

Part of the jig is actually clamped in the drill chuck; when this device is used, securely lock

Illus. 590. A shop-made drill-press-router overarm attachment. Here an auxiliary table is attached and a straightedge serves as a guide fence.

Illus. 591. The device is clamped to the column at the rear and into the drill chuck at the front. The quill is locked to prevent any vertical movement; this makes for a very rigid setup.

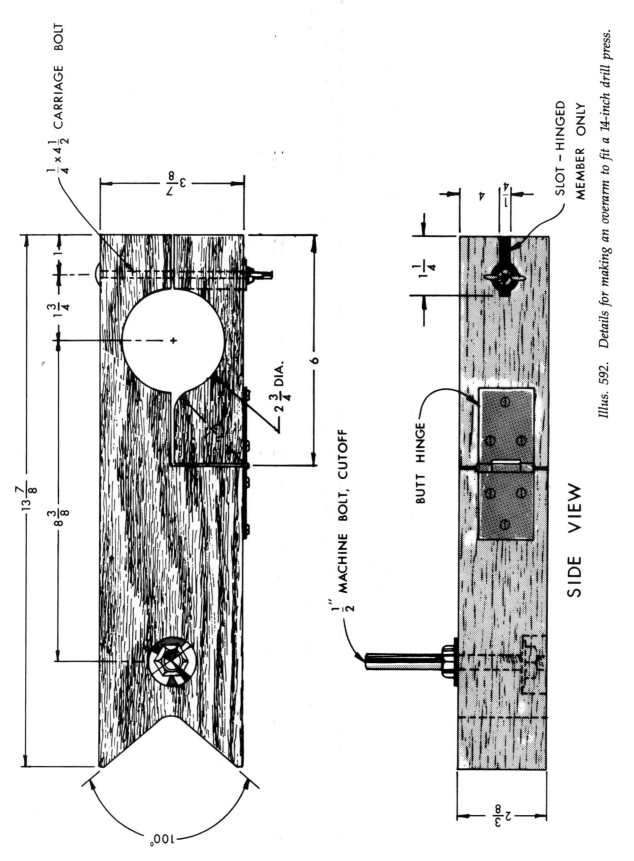

$\frac{1}{4} \times 4\frac{1}{2}$ CARRIAGE BOLT

$3\frac{7}{8}$

1

$1\frac{3}{4}$

$2\frac{3}{4}$ DIA.

6

$13\frac{7}{8}$

$8\frac{3}{8}$

100°

$\frac{1}{2}$" MACHINE BOLT, CUTOFF

SLOT – HINGED MEMBER ONLY

$\frac{1}{4}$

$1\frac{1}{4}$

BUTT HINGE

$2\frac{3}{8}$

SIDE VIEW

Illus. 592.   Details for making an overarm to fit a 14-inch drill press.

285

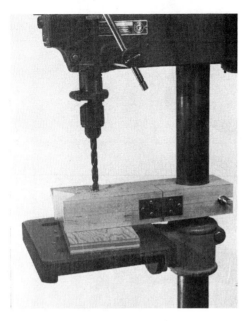

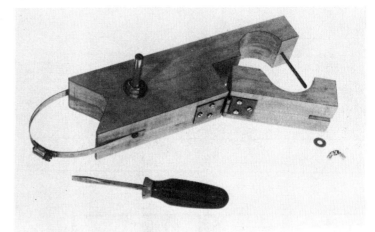

Illus. 593 (left). The best way to locate and drill the hole for the machine bolt is as shown, by making the column clamp first and securing it for this operation. Illus. 594 (above). A good look at the finished project.

the quill of the drill to eliminate any vertical movement.

Illus. 592 shows the essential details for making a router overarm that fits a 14-inch drill press. Note that the plan specifies the use of stock $2\frac{3}{8}$ inches thick; if stock this thick is not available, simply laminate three layers of $\frac{3}{4}$-inch-thick hard wood, which equals a thickness of $2\frac{1}{4}$ inches.

Make the column-clamp part of this device before drilling the hole for the machine bolt that fits into the drill chuck. Clamp the unit to the column, and then drill the hole as shown in Illus. 593. To complete the project, secure the pieces of hose clamp with two pan-head sheet-metal screws. (See Illus. 594.) Obviously, the design can be modified for a different-size drill press and to satisfy other personal needs.

When using this device, always unplug the power to the drill press. Being a creature of habit, you'll find yourself switching the drill press itself rather than the router motor unit.

Refer to my previous book, *Router Handbook*, for some other design ideas for similar jigs.

Radial-Arm-Saw Routing Attachment The attachment shown in Illus. 595–599 is also illustrated in the *Router Handbook*. In Illus. 597, however, I include suggested specifications for

this device that I did not include in the *Router Handbook*.

The bracket is made from welded strap iron. If you do not have the skills or access to metal-fabricating tooling, have the bracket made up for you at a welding shop.

Check the saw design and the hole specifications to ensure that the jig will, in fact, fit your saw. The jig shown in Illus. 596 fits some of the older model DeWalt, Delta, and Sears saws. You may have to modify the design or scrap this idea altogether if it is not compatible with the design mechanics of your radial saw.

Illus. 595. With a metal, welded bracket you can mount your router to the arbor of your radial arm saw.

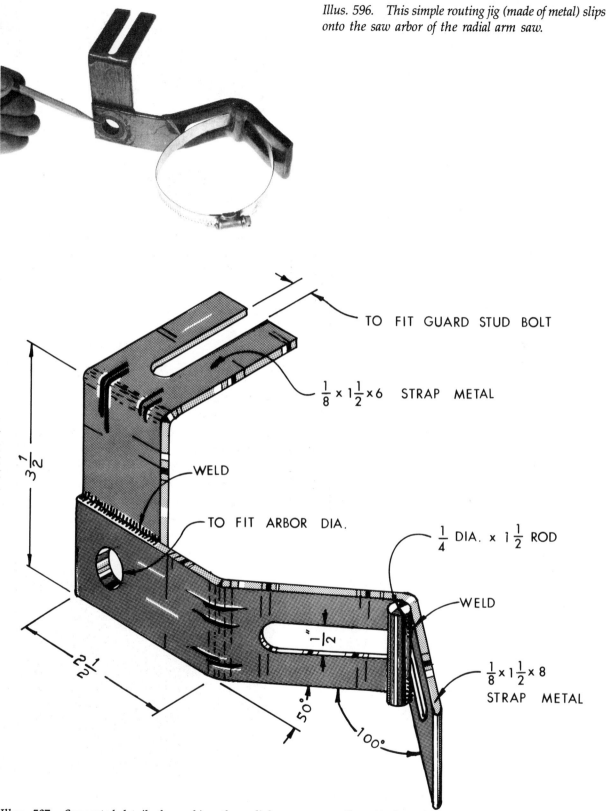

Illus. 596.   This simple routing jig (made of metal) slips onto the saw arbor of the radial arm saw.

TO FIT GUARD STUD BOLT

$\frac{1}{8} \times 1\frac{1}{2} \times 6$ STRAP METAL

WELD

TO FIT ARBOR DIA.

$\frac{1}{4}$ DIA. x $1\frac{1}{2}$ ROD

WELD

$3\frac{1}{2}$

$2\frac{1}{2}$

$\frac{1}{2}''$

50°

100°

$\frac{1}{8} \times 1\frac{1}{2} \times 8$ STRAP METAL

Illus. 597.   Suggested details for making the radial-arm-saw routing attachment.

Illus. 598.　*The bracket mounts onto the saw arbor like a saw blade, and the guard stud on the motor housing keeps it rigid.*

Illus. 599.　*The radial-arm-saw routing atachment in use. Be sure to disconnect the power to the saw when installing and using this device.*

With this device, you can use your router in all of the positions and guided-cutting directions that are possible with the design of the radial arm saw. (See Illus. 599.) It can also be set up as an overarm pin router with vertical-entry capability.

There are literally hundreds of different kinds of cuts and uses possible with this marriage of the radial arm saw and router motor. Refer to chapters 14 and 17 and to the *Router Handbook* for techniques that can be performed with this tooling arrangement.

Inclined Templates　Most surface-routing jobs performed with templates are cuts that must be a uniform depth, such as those required for a recess for a hinge or an inlay. Here I discuss two specialty templates that make cuts which are inclined or slanted.

The gun-stock butt template (Illus. 600–602) is propped up along one edge. Thus, a slanted cradle or pocket will be carved-out to receive the butt ends of guns in a gun cabinet project. If you use the same template to cut each of the side-by-side slanted recesses, they will all turn out identically. Illus. 603 shows the $\frac{3}{8}$-inch bit and standard $\frac{1}{2}$-inch-outside-diameter guide used with the template. The finished cuts are shown in Illus. 604 and 605.

A "sunburst" jig (Illus. 606) is another inclined routing guide. Though it is not strictly a template, a template guide is used on the router. (See Illus. 609.) The outside diameter of the template guide matches the width of the slot cut into the wedge; this controls the length of the inclined cut. The wedge pivots on one dowel pin as a center point, and is engaged by a second pin that holds it steady for each successive cut. (See Illus. 607 and 608.)

Illus. 600.　*The gun-stock butt template is shimmed up along one edge.*

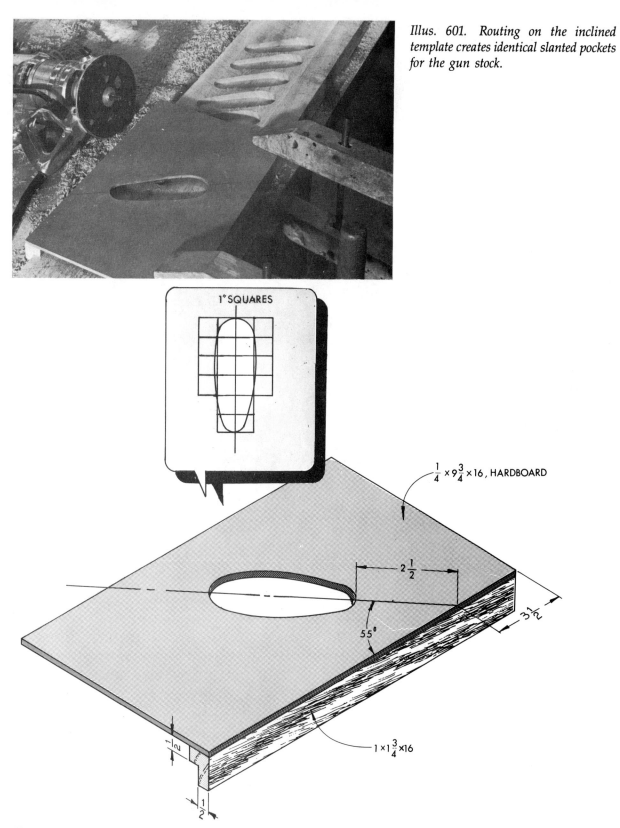

Illus. 601. Routing on the inclined template creates identical slanted pockets for the gun stock.

1" SQUARES

$\frac{1}{4} \times 9\frac{3}{4} \times 16$, HARDBOARD

$2\frac{1}{2}$

$3\frac{1}{2}$

55°

$\frac{1}{2}$

$\frac{1}{2}$

$1 \times 1\frac{3}{4} \times 16$

Illus. 602.   Details for making a gun-stock butt template.

Illus. 604. The base for a gun cabinet has slanted butt pockets so the guns will tip towards the rear of the cabinet.

Illus. 605. A close look at the routed slanted pockets.

Illus. 606. These different sunburst corner designs were all cut with the same jig.

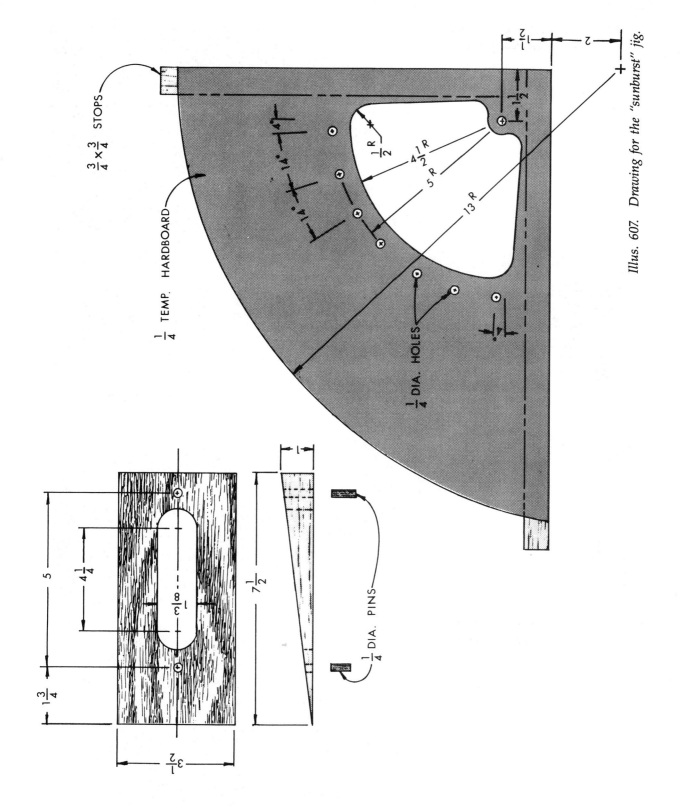

Illus. 607. Drawing for the "sunburst" jig.

291

Illus. 608.   Parts of the "sun-burst" jig.

Illus. 609.   The router rides on this slotted wedge, and the cut is controlled by the template guide in the base of the router. Note how the wedge can be pivoted for each successive cut.

This jig was made to make corner sunburst designs on wood signs and furniture panels. It can be enlarged or reduced, or expanded to make a half or full sunburst design as you may wish.

Most of the design samples shown in Illus. 606 were cut with a corebox or roundnose bit. By using other bit-cutting configurations, changing the bit sizes or diameters and using different depths, you can create an array of other interesting designs.

Door Butt-Hinge Template This device will prove to be a timesaving and useful jig when you use it to hang a number of doors. (See Illus. 611.) The one specified in Illus. 610 is de-signed for three 3½-inch butt hinges, with the top hinge spaced closer to the top of the door than the bottom one is to the bottom of the door. Simply stack three pieces of ¼ × 3¼ × 8-inch tempered hardboard together and band-saw them very carefully, saving the layout lines. File the finished opening size while they are still together.

The template is designed to be used with a ⅜-inch router bit and a ½-inch-outside-diameter template guide or a ½-inch router bit and a ⅝-inch-outside-diameter template guide. Illus. 612 shows the basic components.

Pattern-Routing Small Parts This is some-times a problem, and might be resolved by

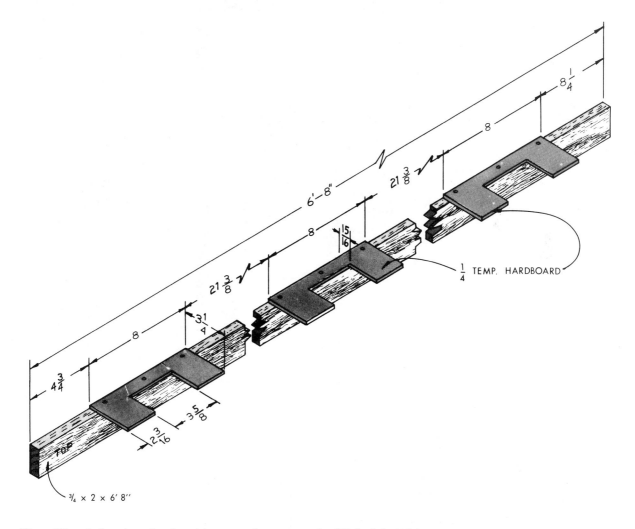

Illus. 610.   A drawing of a door hinge template system for 3½-inch butt hinges.

Illus. 611. This door butt-hinge template clamps to the door. Note the finished cut and the template guide and bit projecting from the base of the router.

Illus. 612. The basic components of a door butt-hinge template system.

either of two techniques shown in Illus. 615–617. A hard wood, such as northern maple, makes a good pattern. (See Illus. 613.) Fasten the workpiece (or thin pieces stacked) to the pattern/template with double-faced tape. (See Illus. 614.) If convenient, hold the pattern/template with the workpiece(s) in the vise for routing, as shown in Illus. 615. The type and style of bit will vary according to the shape, size, and kind of material that has to

be cut. A single-edge, carbide-tipped panel pilot-bit was used in this demonstration (shown in Illus. 616). The solid pilot tends to burn wherever feeding is slowed or interrupted, such as at the inside corners; this, however, isn't a serious problem for these pieces.

You can also hold the pattern/template to the work with double-sided tape, and cut it on the router table. (See Illus. 617 and 618.)

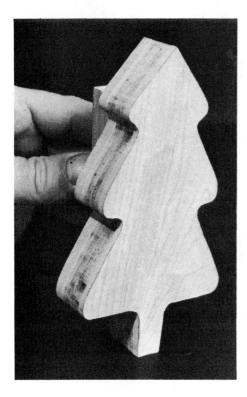

Illus. 613 (left). A hardwood pattern/template has a small block on the back. Illus. 614 (above). Secure the workpiece to the template with double-sided tape.

Illus. 615 (right). Hold the pattern/ template under the workpiece in a vise. This permits cutting the laminate with a trim router.

Illus. 616 (right). A panel pilot-bit installed in the trim router.

Illus. 617. Here the pattern/template, on top of the work, is being cut on a router table. Note how the pilot burns the pattern when it is not fed fast enough.

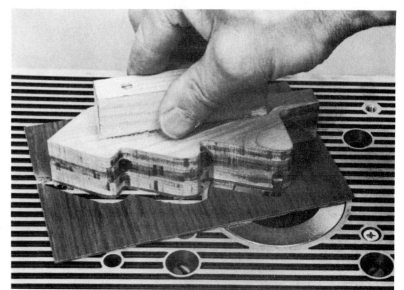

Illus. 618. Any number of identical small parts can be made.

27

Vacuum Pumps, Clamps, and Templates

An air-vacuum system that holds work and secures templates to workpieces without clamps can be used in industrial settings, small-production woodworking shops and by woodworking professionals. (See Illus. 619 and 620.) In Chapter 17, I discussed how air cylinders can be used on pin routers, with a foot-pedal control, to plunge and retract the routing head. Woodworkers who use compressed air systems can utilize them in other ways. For, example, by connecting an inexpensive accessory into the line, you can create a vacuum system with any small-shop compressor. Special vacuum pumps and related supplies are also becoming more accessible. Therefore, it's time for the serious woodworker to look at the potential uses of an air-vacuum system.

One of the major advantages of using an air-vacuum system is that you can hold workpieces securely to a worktable or hold a template tightly to the workpiece without using any conventional clamps or similar mechanical devices. This frees both hands and ensures a maximum work advantage.

Another advantage is the holding power of the vacuum clamp and chuck, which is astonishing. (See Illus. 621.)

A foot control is usually employed as the "on and off" switch for the more-elaborate vacuum systems. However, valves and other devices

Illus. 619. An air-vacuum clamp table manufactured by Safranek Enterprises, Inc. To use it, simply lay the work on it and touch the foot control; the work will be held secure for any kind of job.

Illus. 620 (above left).   Her-Saf Air-Vac is a vacuum-clamp table that permits a full 360-degree work area without interference from conventional clamps. Some models have a revolving holding plate that holds material for sanding, trimming, gluing, assembling, and routing, as shown. Illus. 621 (above right). This demonstration illustrates the great holding power of the Her-Saf Air-Vac-Clamp, which is self-contained and requires no vacuum pump. The holding plate is 36 inches from the floor and measures approximately 12 × 16 inches. This device has to be connected to a compressed-air supply of at least 85 PSI.

can sometimes be used so that every setup does not require foot controls or expensive vacuum pumps.

Illus. 619–621 show products manufactured by Safranek Enterprises, Inc., 4005 El Camino Real, Atascadero, California 93422. This company offers other air clamps, hoses, adapters, gasket material, pumps, and other components for the serious router craftsman.

Vacuum Pumps   Vacuum pumps, and related equipment, suitable for vacuum clamping systems come in two general types: very simple and fairly inexpensive systems or quite complicated and expensive systems. Air compressors and vacuum pumps employ essentially the same basic mechanisms; thus, the

equipment is very similar. The primary difference is that the air inlets and outlets are reversed. Because vacuum pressure is lower than atmospheric pressure, a vacuum pump requires much-less driving power (smaller motor) than an air compresser of comparable capacity.

The capacities of vacuum pumps are basically specified as CFM (cubic feet per minute) of free air pumped, more so than they are by horsepower. The sizing of a vacuum pump for a specific job depends upon the volume of air that must be removed. A small pump and a big pump may have the same maximum vacuum capabilities for closed systems such as clamping chucks and templates; the small pump will just take longer to reach the maximum vacuum.

298

A system with a reserve tank, which stores vacuum air just as a tank stores compressed air, will suck down the air very quickly.

There are a number of different kinds or types of vacuum pumps; some major ones are piston, diaphragm, rotary vane, and screw pumps. Each has certain advantages and limitations, which should be analyzed before buying. Consult directly with a tooling supplier or pump manufacturer. Some companies are:

C. R. Onsrud, Inc.
P.O. Box 416, Highway 21 So.
Troutman, North Carolina 28166

Gast Manufacturing Corp.
P.O. Box 97
Benton Harbor, Michigan 49022

Pneumatic Air Power Products
4601 Central Avenue
Monroe, Louisiana 71203

Safranek Enterprises, Inc.
4055 El Camino Real
Atascadero, California 93422

Magna-Lock, USA
545 Blackhawk Park Avenue
Rockford, Illinois 61125

Dayton Electric Mfg. Co.
Chicago, Illinois 60648
(Locally—Yellow Pages)

The rotary-vane vacuum pumps are basically half the cost, have somewhat lower vacuum ratings, are quieter, and provide continuous air evacuation without a storage (receiver) tank.

The chuck or template area calculated in square inches provides a basis for sizing the vacuum system. A four-CFM unit (Illus. 622) will handle chucks and templates with up to 288 square inches, or 12 × 24 inches, of non-porous material. Most home-shop needs, however, can usually be fulfilled with a much smaller total chucking- or template-clamping area. A small, rotary vacuum pump-and-chuck kit is available from Ring Master, Inc., P.O. Box 8527-A, Orlando, Florida 32856. (See Illus. 623.)

Vacuum pumps can be found in many different areas of commercial enterprise, such as in the refrigeration, packaging and wrapping, material lifting, agriculture, automotive, and medical industries. Sometimes the basic pump can either be found used or can be salvaged. An acquaintance told me how he made his vacuum system using the parts from a discarded refrigerator. My vacuum pump is a very old (and bulky) twin-piston type that was once a milking machine on a nearby Wisconsin farm. (See Illus. 624.)

If you have compressed air, an inexpensive transducing pump (Illus. 625 and 626) will con-

Illus. 622. This industrial-quality vacuum pump unit from C.R. Onsrud, Inc. features a ¼ horsepower motor, 4 CFM unit pump, reserve tank, foot-control valve, and other features.

Illus. 623. This vacuum pump and vacuum-chuck kit is available from Ring Master, Inc. It has a ⅛ horsepower air-pump motor (14 PSI/20-inch HG), two aluminum plates (chucks) measuring 4 × 4 inches and 8 × 8 inches, plus gasket material and an air hose.

Illus. 624. My big, old, clumsy, but functional, vacuum pump was salvaged from an old milk machine used on a Wisconsin farm. Note the casters which were added for portability.

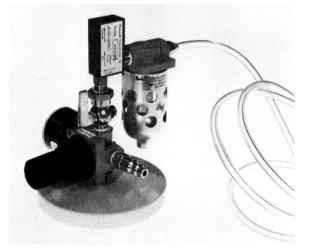

Illus. 625. This small accessory from the Allen Company essentially converts compressed air to vacuum air. The air line connects to the coupler shown at the bottom. The entire unit measures only about 6 inches high and 6 inches across.

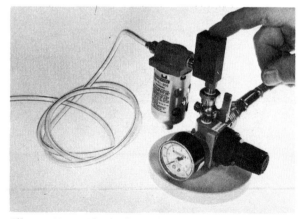

Illus. 626. The Allen Company's Li'l Octopus transducer pump provides a vacuum pull of about 6 to 8 pounds per square inch, or 600 to 800 pounds of clamping force on a 10 × 10-inch template or clamp. Placing a finger on the exhaust, as shown, shuts off the vacuum, as does the valve directly below.

vert it to vacuum air. One such item, called the Li'l Octopus, is manufactured by the Allen Company, 7505 Washington Avenue South, Edina, Minnesota 55435. This accessory is only 6 inches high and about 6 inches wide, and operates on only one CFM of free air. It has to be connected to a compressed air supply that has between 40–85 PSI. This small unit generates a pull of 6 to 8 pounds per square inch. When used with a 10 × 10-inch template, it provides between 600–800 pounds of clamping force. Do not exceed more than 120 total square inches of encircled template or chucking area. Operate the vacuum shutoff with an air valve or simply by placing your finger over the exhaust flow of the unit, as shown in Illus. 626.

Vacuum Chucks Vacuum chucks, as you already know, can be built into a table. (See Illus. 619–621.) Turn to Chapter 30, which shows a vacuum chuck inserted into a shop-made router table and how to make your own swivel or rotating vacuum clamp (or chuck).

Portable vacuum chucks are used with templates for pin- and table-routing. Illus. 627 shows a small chuck made of aluminum, which was designed to be used between the workpiece and a template. It can also be used on top of a bench and also as a work-holding plate for hand-held routing jobs, sanding surfaces, etc.

Illus. 629 shows how the horizontal hole that extends into the center vertical hole of the aluminum chuck provides the air-escape route for the vacuum that leads to both surfaces of the chuck.

The gasket material must be nonporous to make a good seal. Your local hardware dealer probably has this inexpensive material readily on hand. (See Illus. 628.) The easiest gasket material to use is pressure-sensitive closed-cell foam, which comes in rolls of various lengths, and is available in various thicknesses and widths. Try to use the thinnest available, but not so thin that a slight deflection in the workpiece (or template material) would allow it to touch down on the chuck covering the vacuum hole, thus breaking the vacuum. Depending upon the size and flatness of the workpiece, $3/16$–$3/8$-inch-thick-closed-cell foam with a pressure-sensitive backing will handle most chucking and template-making jobs. You can also string out a small bead of silicone sealer if nothing else is available.

Illus. 630–634 show how to use a vacuum chuck with a template to cut out identical shapes on a pin router. This method can be applied to other projects and with other types of vacuum chucks, so the ideas and techniques illustrated should not be considered the "final word" on this subject. I know individuals who use vacuum chucks on lathes to turn various projects on the face plate; I do not recommend this technique because there are a number of hazards and limitations involved which you may violate unknowingly.

Vacuum Templates These templates are used to make the same kinds of cuts or projects that other conventional-type templates are used for. You can use vacuum templates for reproducing decorative cuts in a surface, outlining inlays, sizing and trimming full-thickness cuts made with the band saw or scroll saw, and for actually cutting out parts, as shown in Illus. 634 and 635.

Vacuum templates (Illus. 636–649) are made of any suitable material, such as plywood, hardboard, plastic, or aluminum plate. Particle board and medium-density fibreboard that is covered with decorative plastic laminates make good, durable templates.

Lay out and cut the template material to the exact profile shape that is to be reproduced. Bore a hole through the template in a convenient area, which is usually near the center; turn into the hole a threaded plug from a push-type air-line coupler. (See Illus. 645.) If the threads in the wood hole strip or loosen, reset the plug with epoxy glue. Couplers are easy to obtain from any industrial tool supplier or anyone selling air compressors. Check the Yellow Pages.

Apply the gasket or sealing material around the perimeter on the underside of the template with closed-cell adhesive-backed foam. (See Illus. 644.) After you have connected the vacuum unit to the coupler, the template is ready to use. (See Illus. 637.)

The templates shown in Illus. 639–649 are all essentially designed to be mounted on top of the work; they work well with inverted routers, where the pin is above the work and the bit projects up from under the work-supporting table. The grooved templates shown in Illus.

639–641 can be used with inverted pin routers—such as those manufactured by C. R. Onsrud, Inc. of Troutman, North Carolina—for production-routing jobs. See *Router Handbook* for further discussion and illustration of the company's machines. Top-mounted templates can, however, also be used for router-table-routing work, where ball-bearing piloted bits can follow the template. Turn to pages 371–374 for more illustrations of vacuum templates in use and some inverted pin-routing techniques.

One advantage of the inverted router is the retracting guide-pin, which allows you to utilize the grooved templates to their greatest potential. The operator simply moves the template, and the pin follows in the grooved upper surface of the template. (See Illus. 637 and 639.) With this design, you can use an oversized working template and hold it well away from the cutting area. With this system, you do not need to hold difficult-to-clamp workpieces with clamps, hold-downs or other devices. The templates shown in these illustrations have through holes in the grooves that permit the passage of atmospheric air through the templates, which helps carry the chips downward through the worktable's built-in dust-collecting system.

Illus. 643 depicts another type of vacuum template that can be used with the inverted-pin-routing system. Note that this one is not a grooved type, but it is otherwise very similar to these templates.

Illus. 644–649 show how to make a very simple top-mounted vacuum template. In this particular project, plastic was used so that all of the components and techniques would be clearly visible. Plastic does make excellent templates, but, as you know, other materials can be used equally well.

See Chapters 28, 30, and 33 for more information on shop-made vacuum-routing jigs, accessories, and techniques.

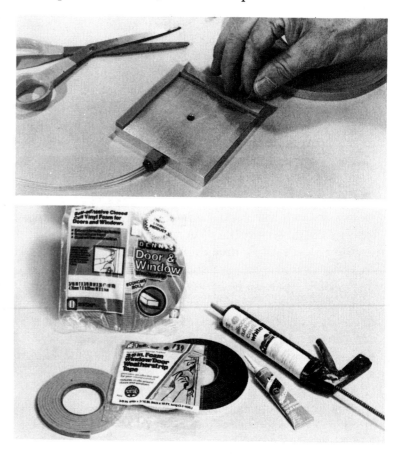

Illus. 627. This small vacuum chuck measures ½ inch thick by 4 by 4 inches. Here ³⁄₁₆-inch closed-cell adhesive-backed foam is applied as the vacuum gasket material.

Illus. 628. Gasket materials purchased at the local hardware include closed-cell foam in ³⁄₁₆ and ³⁄₈ inch thicknesses and silicone.

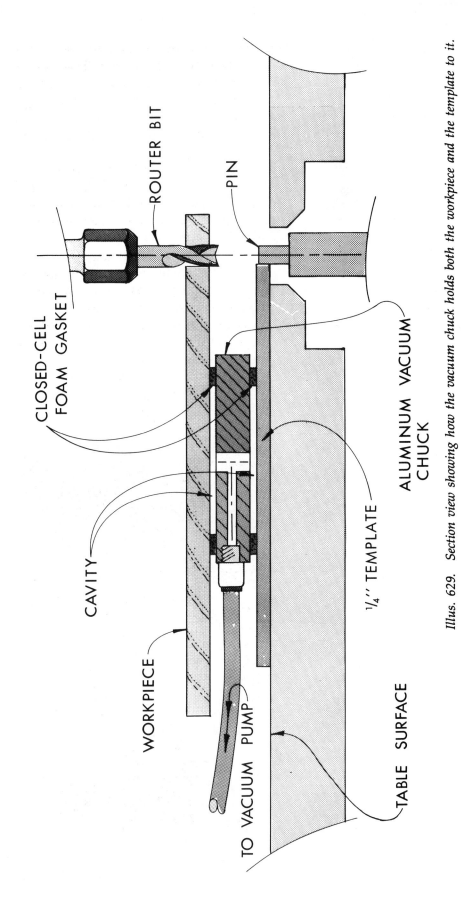

ROUTER BIT

PIN

CLOSED-CELL
FOAM GASKET

ALUMINUM VACUUM
CHUCK

CAVITY

1/4″ TEMPLATE

WORKPIECE

TO VACUUM PUMP

TABLE SURFACE

Illus. 629. Section view showing how the vacuum chuck holds both the workpiece and the template to it.

Illus. 630. Use a template material (¼-material tempered hardboard) to set the height of the guide pin.

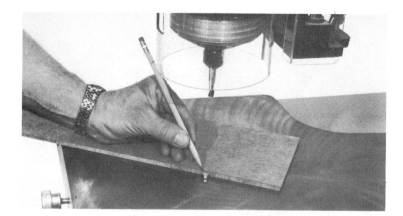

Illus. 631. The template under the vacuum chuck.

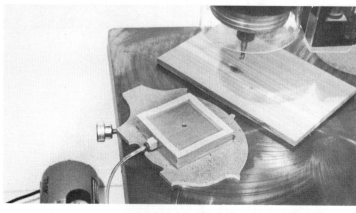

Illus. 632. The vacuum is on. Note how the pulldown force of the vacuum squashes the foam gasket material, holding the three components firmly together.

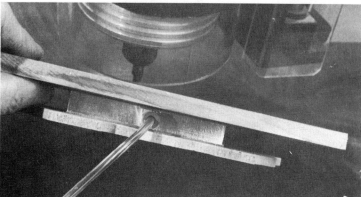

Illus. 633. A look at all of the major components involved when you pin-rout with a vacuum chuck.

Illus. 634. The operation in progress.

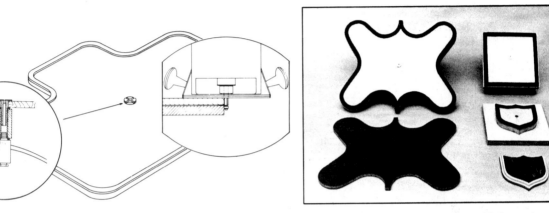

Illus. 635 (above left). A combination vacuum clamp and template. Note the gasket material around the perimeter and the adapter available from Safranek Enterprises, Inc. that connects it to the vacuum unit. Illus. 636 (above right). Some samples of vacuum templates. (Photo courtesy of Safranek Enterprises, Inc.)

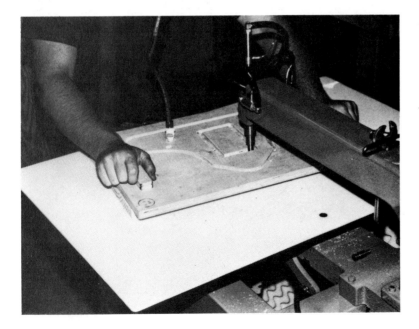

Illus. 637. Routing with a plywood vacuum template on C.R. Onsrud's inverted router. The workpiece is being cut under the template as the operator follows the groove with the pin in the top surface of the template.

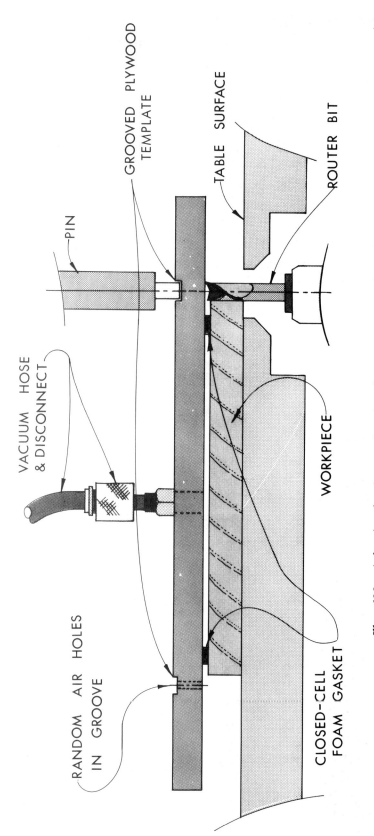

PIN

GROOVED PLYWOOD
TEMPLATE

TABLE SURFACE

ROUTER BIT

VACUUM HOSE
& DISCONNECT

WORKPIECE

RANDOM AIR HOLES
IN GROOVE

CLOSED-CELL
FOAM GASKET

Illus. 638.   A drawing showing a section view of a groove-type vacuum template routing operation on an inverted router.

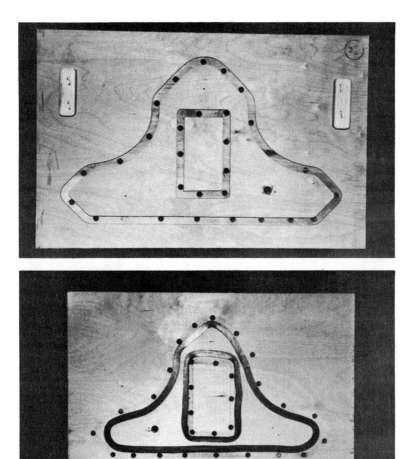

Illus. 639. The top side of a grooved vacuum template used for inverted pin-routing. Note the oversized material and two block handles well outside the peripheral of the cutting area.

Illus. 640. Bottom view of the template illustrated in Illus. 637 and 639. Note the gasket material applied. The dark dots are actually through holes along the cutting path that permit passage of air to promote chip removal with the pin router's under-the-table dust-collection system.

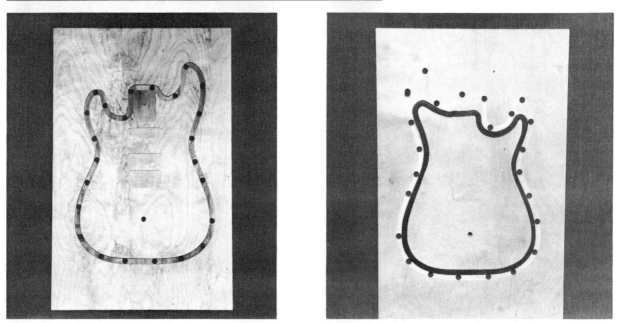

Illus. 641. Another sample of a grooved-type vacuum template designed for use on an inverted pin router.

Illus. 642.   A sample of a grooved-type vacuum template. On the left is a top view, and on the right a bottom view. Note the air nipple threaded into the wood.

Illus. 643.   Details for another typical vacuum template used with C.R. Onsrud's inverted router machines. Note the guide pin above the work, and the bit below.

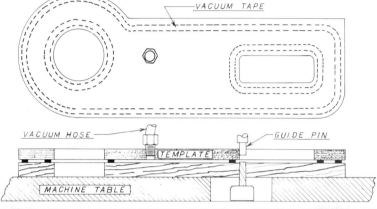

Illus. 644.   Here the closed-cell pressure-sensitive backed gasket material is being applied to a template cut out of plastic. Note the male threaded plug of a quick, push-type coupler.

Illus. 645.   Turn the male threaded plug of the coupler into the hole in the plastic or wood template, as shown.

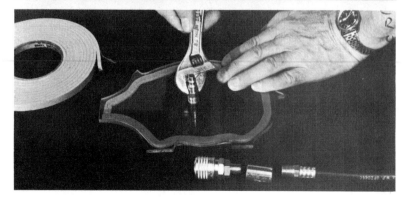

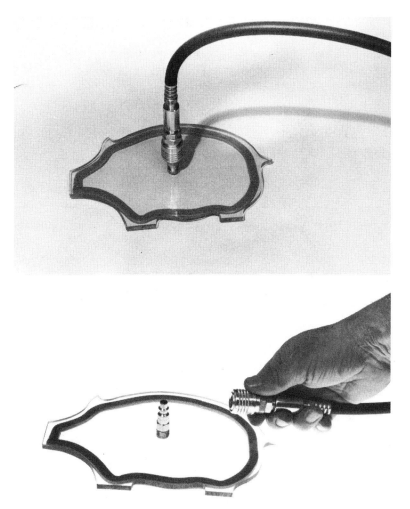

Illus. 646.   The coupler connected to the air-vacuum hose.

Illus. 647.   With the pull back on the sleeve of the coupler, you can quickly disconnect it from the vacuum.

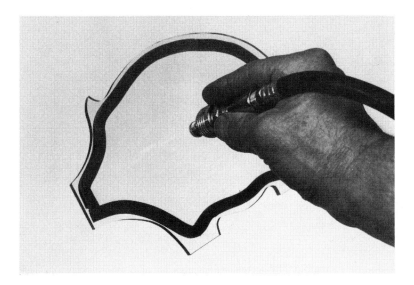

Illus. 648.   The disconnect coupler also has a built-in swivel action that prevents the hose from twisting during the router-cutting operation.

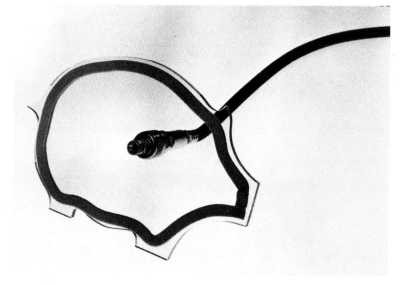

Part VI
The Ultimate Router Table

Over the years, a good number of plans and ideas for making router tables have been published in woodworking magazines and books. Most have innovative concepts; some are very unique, but others do not seem useable because the tables do not appear to be built very sturdily. I have not seen anything that is sufficiently designed and built for the new, heavy-duty routers or capitalizes on the full range of capabilities that the router seems to offer quite naturally to the creative and energetic woodworking craftsman.

The router table that I have designed especially for this book is sturdy and sufficiently heavy for safe use. It can handle the largest of the hand-held routers available today and, obviously, the smaller ones, too. You can utilize your own brand of plunge or standard routers with little modification.

In addition to being sturdy, this router table has a variety of options and features that the builder can choose to incorporate as his needs progress or his desires dictate. The basic unit is a floor-standing router/shaper table that has table-opening inserts for various-sized bits,

starting pins, a double slot for a mitre gauge, storage drawers, and other extras. Accessories include a mitre-gauge feeding guide, several different fences, and a shop vacuum hookup for dust and chip removal.

In Chapter 30, I show how to make a simple vacuum clamping plate that fits into the router/shaper table and a swivel clamping chuck that attaches to the top of the router table. Also included are plans for a joint-making attachment that holds the router horizontally at variable adjustable distances above the level of the table, as well as an accessory that works like a combination tilting-pin-and-swing-router. Finally, the last chapter includes plans and descriptions for a pin-arm attachment that make template-routing much safer and easier than any other conventional overarm pin-routing arrangement that has the router and bit above the worktable.

Many of the devices and accessories in this section of the book can be used interchangeably with each other. This further ensures that you will get the ultimate benefit and use from your router and router table.

28
The Basic Router/Shaper Table

This shop-made router table was designed to perform unlimited routing/shaping operations using any of the largest, more powerful routers available today. (See Illus. 650.) If you are going to use big, heavy routers, you need a table that provides the weight and rigidity for both safety and convenience of operation.

The choice material to use is particle board because of its normally heavy weight. (See Illus. 651–653.) Illus. 654 and 655 specify 1-inch-thick particle board for each of the two sides; this dimension can be reduced to ¾ inch if the thicker material is not available locally. Though thinner materials might be satisfactory, use ¾-inch particle board for the upper shelf, panel drawer-supports, and the back to achieve a desirable total weight.

The toe board detailed in Illus. 654 can be made from 1- or 2-inch material, as long as the outside dimensions are maintained. Glue it to the bottom of the cabinet unit and nail it from the front through the bottom drawer opening. This, along with glue blocks, makes more than an adequate assembly.

The drawers are typical flush-type construction. (See Illus. 656 for details and cutting sizes.) The tabletop, on the other hand, is something special, and considerable care and patience should go into the making of it. The

material used on the one shown in Illus. 657 is 1-inch-thick particle board, 24 × 28 inches. The top and bottom of the tabletop are covered with Formica® decorative laminate, solid color No. 961 Fog, with a matte finish. If you can't locate 1-inch particle board, either use 1-inch plywood or laminate two pieces of ½-inch-quality sheet stock together. After the final assembly, paint all exposed bare surfaces and edges with a machinery-grey enamel.

Before applying the laminates to both surfaces of the top, glue and nail two 1 × 3 × 28-inch strips along the rear, bottom edge of the top, as shown in Illus. 657. One of these pieces should be accurately predrilled (horizontally), so that you can install two ⅜ × 5-inch carriage bolts exactly 21 inches apart from center of bolt to center of bolt. Illus. 657 gives the details, and Illus. 658 and 659 show the built-up edge and the placement of the two heavy carriage bolts.

The built-up edge along the rear side provides the mounting area for three other accessory attachments that can be made later. This area should be made so that the surface of this thick edge is at a perfect 90 degrees to the top of the table; this can be accomplished by making a thin shaving cut on the table saw. Place the top upside down and shave the built-

Illus. 650 (above left).   The Ultimate Router Table was designed to carry this heavy-duty, 3 horsepower multiple-speed router, but, as you'll see, other smaller routers can also be used. Illus. 651 (above right). The base is easy to make. The basic cabinet construction consists primarily of painted ¾- and 1-inch particle board.

Illus. 652.   A view showing the underside of the top. Note that the base for the big 3 horsepower router is mounted, and that the motor is connected to a more conveniently located switch.

Illus. 653.   The left side of the base cabinet is routed particle board that's 1 inch thick.

313

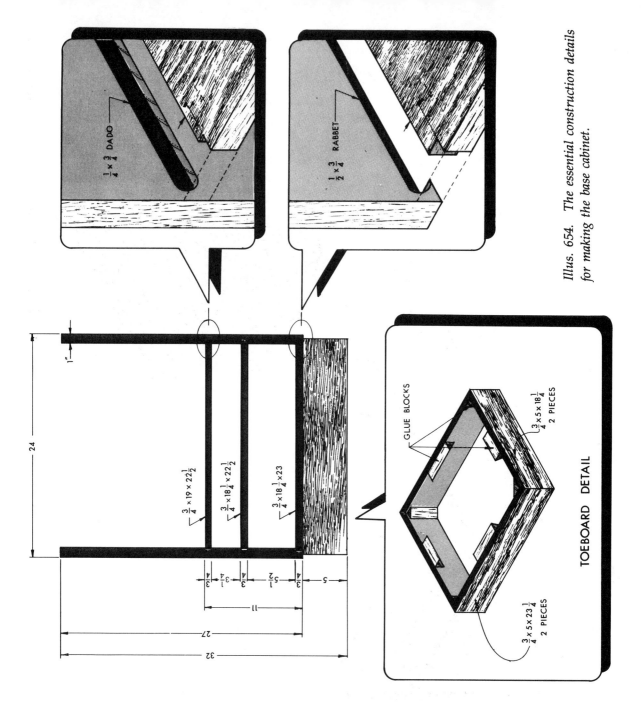

$\frac{1}{4} \times \frac{3}{4}$ DADO

$\frac{1}{2} \times \frac{3}{4}$ RABBET

1"

24

$\frac{3}{4} \times 19 \times 22\frac{1}{2}$

$\frac{3}{4} \times 18\frac{1}{4} \times 22\frac{1}{2}$

$\frac{3}{4} \times 18\frac{1}{4} \times 23$

3\frac{3}{4}

3\frac{1}{4}

3\frac{3}{4}

5\frac{1}{2}

3\frac{3}{4}

5

11

27

32

GLUE BLOCKS

$\frac{3}{4} \times 5 \times 18\frac{1}{4}$
2 PIECES

$\frac{3}{4} \times 5 \times 23\frac{1}{4}$
2 PIECES

TOEBOARD DETAIL

Illus. 654. The essential construction details for making the base cabinet.

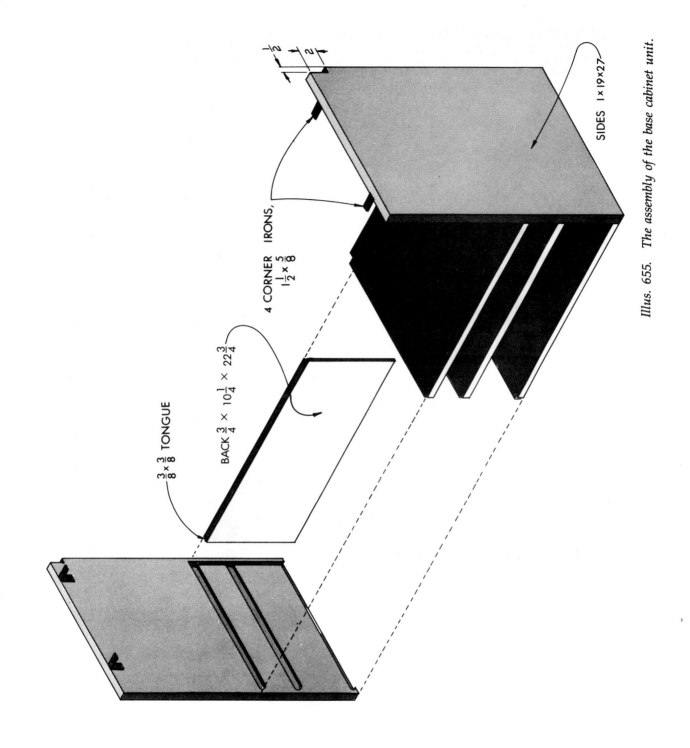

SIDES 1×19×27

4 CORNER IRONS, $1\frac{1}{2} \times \frac{5}{8}$

BACK $\frac{3}{4} \times 10\frac{1}{4} \times 22\frac{3}{4}$

$\frac{3}{8} \times \frac{3}{8}$ TONGUE

$\frac{1}{2}$

2

Illus. 655. The assembly of the base cabinet unit.

315

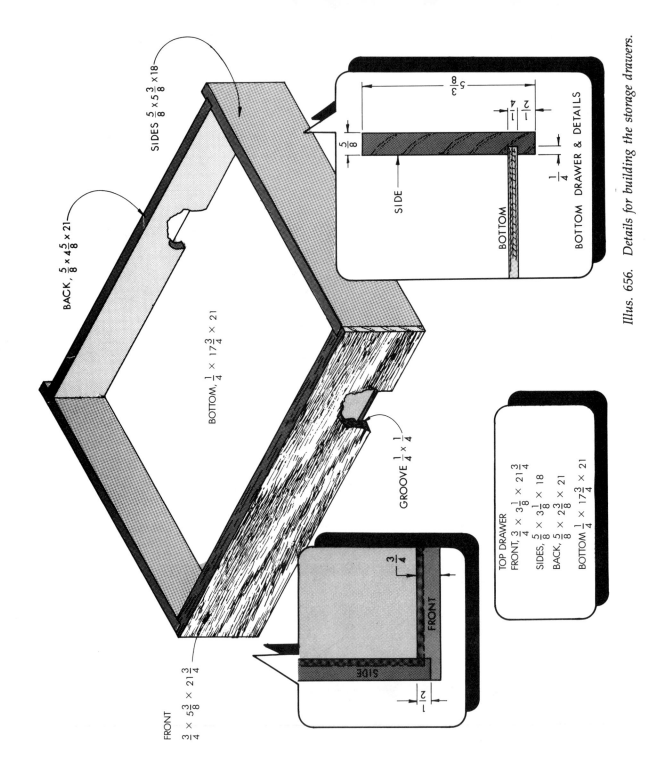

SIDES $\frac{5}{8} \times 5\frac{3}{8} \times 18$

BACK, $\frac{5}{8} \times 4\frac{5}{8} \times 21$

BOTTOM, $\frac{1}{4} \times 17\frac{3}{4} \times 21$

GROOVE $\frac{1}{4} \times \frac{1}{4}$

FRONT

$\frac{3}{4} \times 5\frac{3}{8} \times 21\frac{3}{4}$

$\frac{5}{8}$

$\frac{3}{8}$

$\frac{1}{4}$

$\frac{1}{2}$

$\frac{1}{4}$

SIDE

BOTTOM

BOTTOM DRAWER & DETAILS

$\frac{3}{4}$

FRONT

$\frac{1}{2}$

SIDE

TOP DRAWER
FRONT, $\frac{3}{4} \times 3\frac{1}{8} \times 21\frac{3}{4}$
SIDES, $\frac{5}{8} \times 3\frac{1}{8} \times 18$
BACK, $\frac{5}{8} \times 2\frac{3}{8} \times 21$
BOTTOM $\frac{1}{4} \times 17\frac{3}{4} \times 21$

Illus. 656. Details for building the storage drawers.

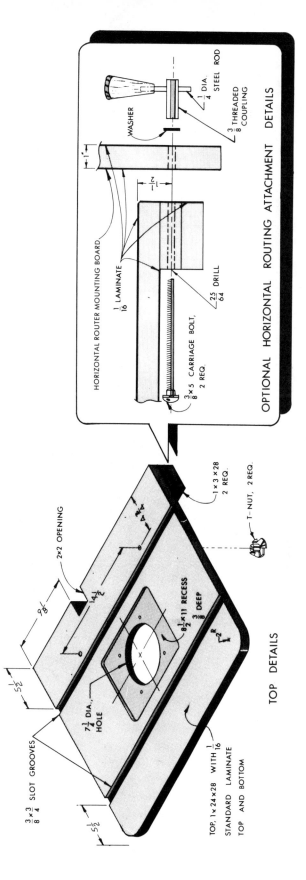

OPTIONAL HORIZONTAL ROUTING ATTACHMENT DETAILS

TOP DETAILS

Illus. 657. Details for making the router table top.

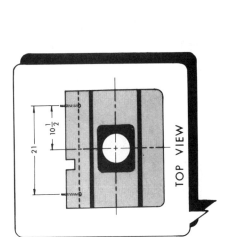

TOP VIEW

Illus. 658. Top view of the rear, built-up edge; laminate has been applied to this edge and to the top and bottom surfaces. Note the two holes for the ⅜-inch carriage bolts.

Illus. 659. The built-up bottom rear edge of the router table top with two carriage bolts about to be driven in.

up edge away from the ripping fence. When it is square and true, apply the decorative laminate to this thick edge only, and to the top and bottom table surfaces. Applying the laminate to both surfaces balances the panel and minimizes any tendency of warpage.

After the laminate has been applied, make the ⅜ × ¾-inch table slot grooves; make sure that they are perfectly parallel to each other. If you intend to share the use of a mitre gauge from your table saw, make sure that the slots are sized appropriately. Once the slots are

machined, wax them generously with hard paste wax. Do not paint inside these slots.

The table insert recess is cut a little more than a precise ⅜-inch depth to allow for painting. (See Illus. 658, which clearly shows the completed recess prior to the painting of the cut surface.) It's better to make the recess slightly too deep rather than slightly too shallow; if needed, you can always shim the insert with thin shim stock or paper placed near the screw holes.

Use a good, tough plastic such as clear polycarbonate, instead of acrylic, for the insert. Aluminum plate is a good substitute. Illus. 660 shows the specifications for making a simple table insert. The overall size is ⅜ × 8½ × 11 inches, which makes a good-size auxiliary base for other portable, hand-held routing jobs, and also works well as a "drop-in" that is seated in the recess by gravity rather than secured to it with bolts or screws. If you make a drop-in type, you may want to make the big through hole even larger than specified so that you can bring the entire router unit up through the table to quickly change a bit. However, in the interest of safety—especially when using powerful routers—fasten the table insert with four flathead machine bolts, with washers and wing nuts underneath. If you intend to do big-bit work, such as panel-raising, it's comforting to know that your unit is rigid throughout, with all the components adequately connected to each other.

The larger hole openings required in the table insert for big bits make it unsafe to use smaller-sized bits in that insert. Therefore, it is advisable to make another optional table insert. The one detailed in Illus. 661 has interchangeable hole inserts that provide hole openings for bits with 1¼-, 1¾-, and 4-inch diameters. Other sizes can be made, as desired. It is somewhat difficult to make these inserts accurately so that the rabbeted lips fit smartly together. However, if you use the adjustable circle-cutting base discussed on pages 194–195 with a plunge router, the job will be much easier than you might expect.

Illus. 662–664 show some of the key steps involved in making the optional table insert with interchangeable hole inserts. The pieces must be held to a flat supporting backup with double-faced tape. Once the holes and circles are cut with the adjustable circle-cutting base, as shown in Illus. 663, cut the rabbeted lips. Use one of the 1/8-inch rabbeting bits described on page 41 to make the circular rabbeted lips. (See Illus. 663–666.)

Two 1/4-inch-diameter holes can be drilled into either or both of the table inserts detailed in Illus. 660 and 661. These holes are for steel-rod fulcrum starting-pins, which are used when you slowly ease the stock into a revolving bit, as shown in Illus. 667 and 668. This steel rod can be purchased at most hardware dealers.

Another optional feature of the router table is actually a commercially made device, but a fairly important one: the variable-speed control that can be used with brush-type DC router motors. (Obviously, if you have one of the new multiple- or variable-speed routers, you wouldn't consider this option.) When incorporated into the ultimate router table, the variable-speed control can be a definite feature—particularly if used with medium horsepower, standard-speed routers, as shown in Illus. 669. You can easily mount the speed control to the router table by screwing a corner iron to the side of the cabinet under the switch box, as shown in Illus. 669 and 670; this arrangement permits easy removal of the variable-speed control so that you can use it with other tools or machines.

Another safety accessory that should be considered for use with the ultimate router table and any of its accessory attachments is a foot switch. Refer to page 77 of Chapter 6 for more information about the foot control, the speed control, and other safety devices that can be used with the ultimate router table.

One shop-made accessory for the ultimate

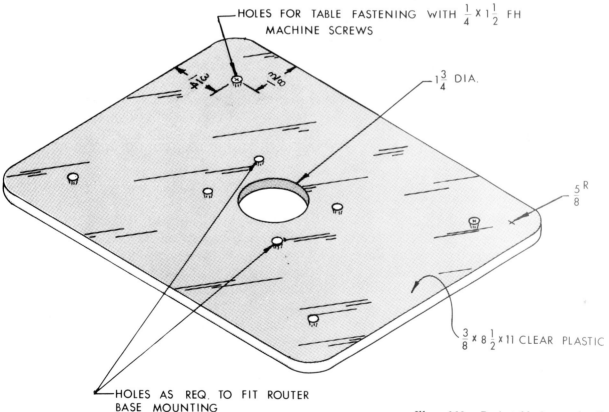

HOLES FOR TABLE FASTENING WITH $\frac{1}{4} \times 1\frac{1}{2}$ FH MACHINE SCREWS

$1\frac{3}{4}$ DIA.

$\frac{5}{8}$ R

$\frac{3}{8} \times 8\frac{1}{2} \times 11$ CLEAR PLASTIC

HOLES AS REQ. TO FIT ROUTER BASE MOUNTING

Illus. 660. Basic table insert detail.

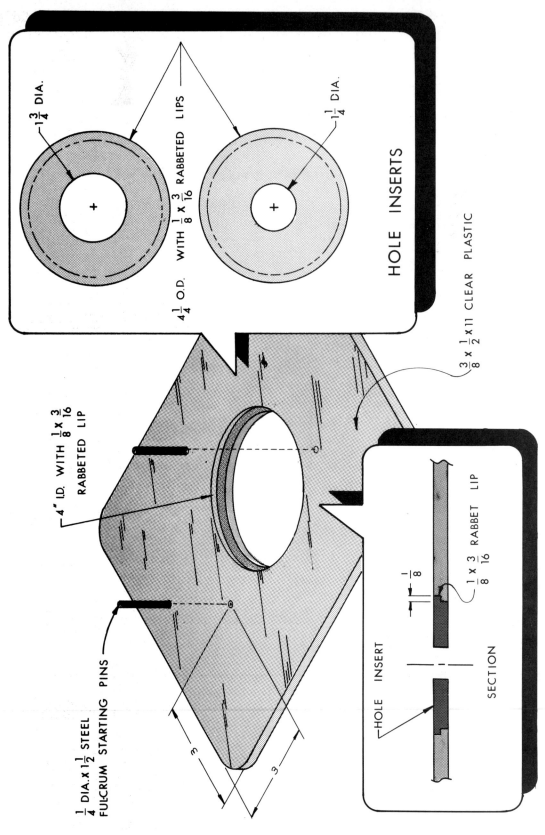

HOLE INSERTS

$1\frac{3}{4}$ DIA.

$1\frac{1}{4}$ DIA.

WITH $\frac{1}{8}$ x $\frac{3}{16}$ RABBETED LIPS

$4\frac{1}{4}$ O.D.

$\frac{3}{8}$ x $\frac{1}{2}$ x11 CLEAR PLASTIC

4" I.D. WITH $\frac{1}{8}$ x $\frac{3}{16}$ RABBETED LIP

$\frac{1}{4}$ DIA.x $1\frac{1}{2}$ STEEL FULCRUM STARTING PINS

3

3

HOLE INSERT

$\frac{1}{8}$ x $\frac{3}{16}$ RABBET LIP

$\frac{1}{8}$

HOLE INSERT

SECTION

Illus. 661. Alternate table insert detail with hole inserts.

Illus. 662. Laying out the table inserts on the masking-covered plastic.

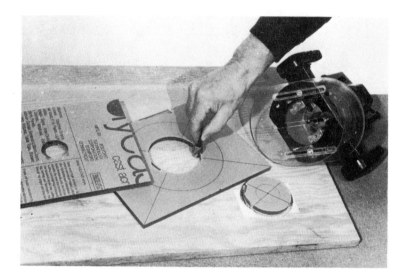

Illus. 663. The adjustable circle-cutting base discussed on pages 194–198 makes the holes. Hold the plastic to a level scrap-support panel with double-sided tape during the routing. Use the special ⅛-inch rabbeting bit (see page 41) to cut the rabbeted lips around the holes and inserts.

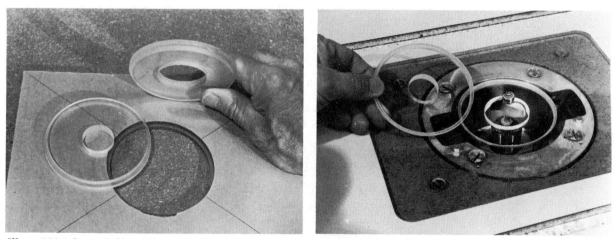

Illus. 664 (above left). Shown is the alternate table insert with ⅜-inch thick interchangeable hole inserts with rabbbeted lips and edges. Illus. 665 (above right). Here the appropriate-size insert closes the opening around the bit for safer operation.

Illus. 666. When needed, the largest opening can be used for the big panel-raising bit, as shown here.

Illus. 667. Provisions are made for two removable steel rod starting pins that are located on the operator side of the bit, as shown here.

Illus. 668. Use a starting pin to ease the work into the rotating bit with pivoting maneuver to control the feed until the stock bears against a collar or the ball-bearing guide on the bit.

Illus. 669. Smaller routers also work in the Ultimate Router table. Here an optional speed-control accessory is incorporated to make speed reductions to a standard high-speed router.

Illus. 670. *File away the back edge of the Lutron Speed Control so that its clip will catch a corner iron screwed to the side of the router table under the switch.*

router table that is a necessity for freehand shaping jobs is a guard, as shown and detailed in Illus. 671 and 672.

One distinct advantage of this table is its capability to handle the most challenging of all router operations—making raised panels. Illus. 673 and 674 show a crown-style raised panel door. Machining this particular door panel requires a total commitment to safe, prudent operational practices and an uninterrupted concentration on the task at hand. All available and reasonable safety devices and procedures should be employed, particularly the freehand shaping guard, the steel fulcrum starting-pin and, last but not least, a *reduced spindle speed* coupled with a series of multiple passes at shallow depths of cut.

Illus. 676–679 depict some of the essential techniques involved in the actual machining of the crown raised-panel. Illus. 695–698 show how to make regular straightedge raised panels using a fence on the router table.

Obviously, you can do much more with this router table than cut raised panels. You can make a multitude of straight-line routing and jointery cuts using a mitre gauge and several different choices of fences described in the next chapter. You can also use vacuum chuck-clamps and vacuum templates, as shown in Illus. 680, to rout with an inverted pin router, and much more, as illustrated in the chapters still to come.

Illus. 671. *One clamp secures a guard, allowing the operator to make freehand shaping operations. An optional spacer/ filler board is inserted when needed to raise the level of the plastic shield when shaping or routing thick stock.*

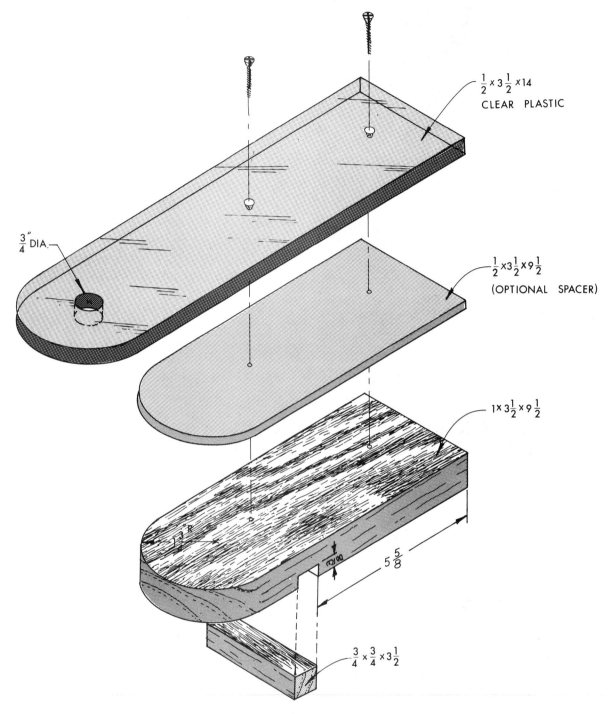

$\frac{1}{2} \times 3\frac{1}{2} \times 14$
CLEAR PLASTIC

$\frac{3}{4}''$ DIA.

$\frac{1}{2} \times 3\frac{1}{2} \times 9\frac{1}{2}$
(OPTIONAL SPACER)

$1 \times 3\frac{1}{2} \times 9\frac{1}{2}$

$5\frac{5}{8}$

$\frac{3}{4} \times \frac{3}{4} \times 3\frac{1}{2}$

Illus. 672.   Details for making the freehand shaping guard.

Illus. 673 (above left).   This typical crown-styled raised panel door, made by Mitch Olson, is very popular today.
Illus. 674 (above right). The substantial reveal on this door requires the use of a bit with a big (3½-inch) cutting-edge diameter.

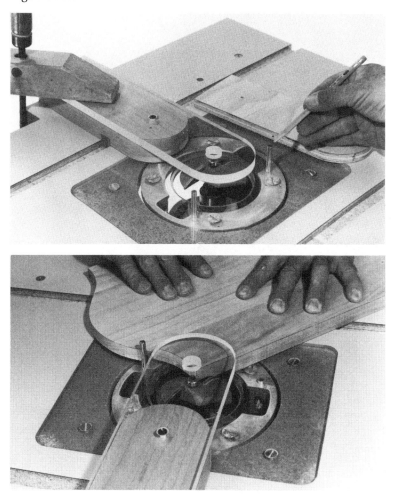

Illus. 675.   Every possible safety precaution should be employed. Safety apparatus necessary for raised-panel-shaping includes the plastic guard positioned directly over the big bit and the fulcrum starting pin.

Illus. 676.   Here the operator is starting to cut the crown raised panel. The guard is in place, the work is held tightly against the fulcrum starting pin, the bit height is set for a shallow cut, and he will machine the end grains of the panel before the other edges.

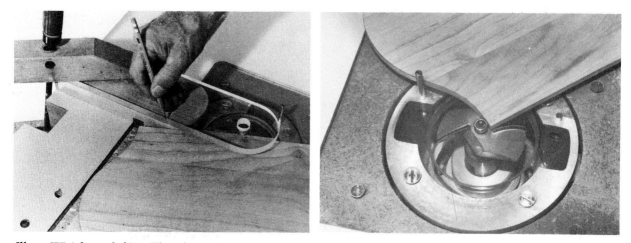

Illus. 677 (above left). *The edge grains of the panel being machined. Note how the curved block support of the guard serves as another contact point for better overall control of the operation. Illus. 678 (above right). Make successive passes at shallow depths of cut until you complete the full cut. (Guard removed for clarity.)*

Illus. 679. Raised panels and an assembled door ready for finishing. Note the big reveal on the crown panel.

Illus. 680. A typical router table operation with a ball-bearing trimming bit being used to follow a vacuum template. See pages 306–310 of Chapter 27 for more information about using vacuum templates.

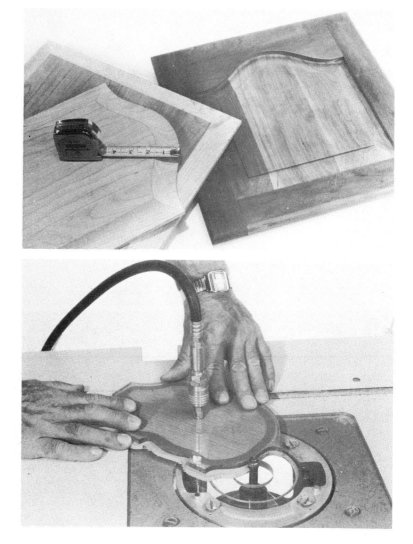

29

Special Fences and Guides

Any scrap that has one, true, straightedge makes a serviceable fence for the router table. It's easy to locate and can be easily clamped in any position with two hand screws or C-clamps. This crude arrangement works fine for a good number of short-term and limited-production jobs. One disadvantage, however, is that it sometimes does not have enough height to support some work that the operator occasionally must machine.

Straight-Line Fence Illus. 681 and 682 show a straight-line fence that's easy to make. This particular one is 3¼ inches high; it can be made higher, if necessary, to feed wide boards on edge over the router. There is an optional con-

nection for the workshop vacuum to remove dust and chips. This fence must be clamped to the table.

Adjustable Shaper Fence This is a necessity if you intend to do any jobs that involve full edge-shaping, that is, if you make any cuts that remove or reshape the entire edge of a board—unlike rabbeting, where only a part of the edge is cut away. For work of this nature, you need what is sometimes called a "split fence." (See Illus. 684.) With this type of fence, you can move out or adjust the outfeed half of the fence to support the cut edge, just like a jointer's outfeed table supports the new jointed edge.

Illus. 686 shows the component parts of the

Illus. 681.   Rear view of a basic straight-line fence.

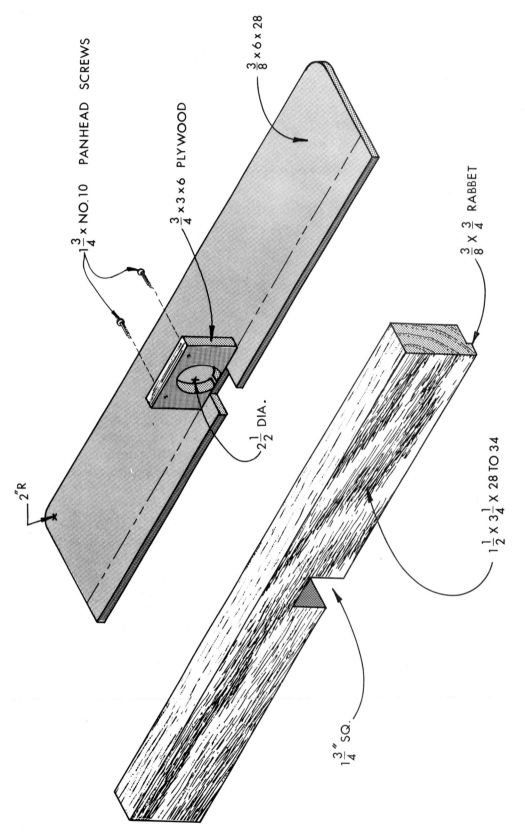

PANHEAD SCREWS

$1\frac{3}{4}$ × NO.10

$\frac{3}{4}$ × 3 × 6 PLYWOOD

$\frac{3}{8}$ × 6 × 28

2"R

$2\frac{1}{2}$ DIA.

$\frac{3}{8}$ × $\frac{3}{4}$ RABBET

$1\frac{1}{2}$ × $3\frac{1}{4}$ × 28 TO 34

$1\frac{3}{4}$" SQ.

Illus. 682.   A basic straight-line fence.

Illus. 683. The rear view of a shaper fence. The right half is adjustable from its straight-line position, as shown, outward towards the operator's side of the router table.

Illus. 684. A view from the operator's side shows the adjustable half of the fence in an out position. It is supporting the new edge that's been fully cut from surface to surface on the board.

fence and a little box for a shop vacuum connection. Use a good grade of ³⁄₄-inch hardwood plywood to make the base and two fences. Good quartersawn hard wood, such as oak, for the support blocks, and a piece of tempered hardboard are also required. Illus. 685 gives the construction details.

The adjustable clamping arrangement is provided by two shop-made hand knobs on threaded rods that go through the slots in the plywood fence base and into holes drilled into the router table; T-nuts are inserted into the holes on the underside of the table. Illus. 685 also shows the details for making the adjustment hand knobs. Make the two ³⁄₈-inch holes, with the T-nuts, in the table on 14¹⁄₂-inch centers; also machine the slots into the plywood fence base on 14¹⁄₂-inch centers.

Once the 1¹⁄₂ × 1¹⁄₂-inch hard-wood support

blocks have been glued and nailed to their respective parts, make absolutely sure that their faces will be in the same straight-line plane by clamping the adjustable half in position (with its guide strip contacting the end of the plywood base), as shown in Illus. 687. Run this assembly over the jointer; this guarantees that both working faces of the support blocks are in the same, perfectly true planes.

A working dust- and chip-removal system certainly enhances any woodworking process, and is a welcomed addition on the ultimate router table. A simple little box-like hood hooks smartly in place behind the laterally adjustable fences. (See Illus. 688 and 689.) Note that Illus. 689 specifies two different sides; the bottom "hooks" are different sizes. Illus. 690–692 show the vacuum hood and closeups of the completed fence.

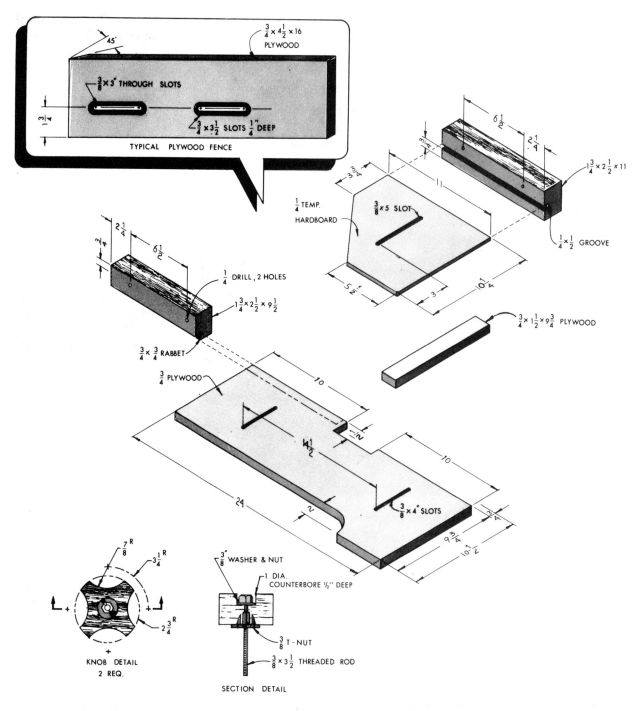

45°

$\frac{3}{4} \times 4\frac{1}{2} \times 16$
PLYWOOD

$\frac{3}{8} \times 3''$ THROUGH SLOTS

$1\frac{3}{4}$

$\frac{3}{4} \times 3\frac{1}{2}$ SLOTS $\frac{1}{4}''$ DEEP

TYPICAL PLYWOOD FENCE

$6\frac{1}{2}$

$2\frac{1}{4}$

$\frac{3}{4}$

$1\frac{3}{4} \times 2\frac{1}{2} \times 11$

$\frac{1}{4}$ TEMP.
HARDBOARD

$\frac{3}{8} \times 5$ SLOT

$3\frac{3}{4}$

11

$5\frac{1}{2}$

3

$10\frac{1}{4}$

$\frac{1}{4} \times \frac{1}{2}$ GROOVE

$2\frac{1}{4}$

$\frac{3}{4}$

$6\frac{1}{2}$

$\frac{1}{4}$ DRILL, 2 HOLES

$1\frac{3}{4} \times 2\frac{1}{2} \times 9\frac{1}{2}$

$\frac{3}{4} \times \frac{3}{4}$ RABBET

$\frac{3}{4}$ PLYWOOD

$\frac{3}{4} \times 1\frac{1}{2} \times 9\frac{3}{4}$ PLYWOOD

10

$\frac{1}{2}$

$14\frac{1}{2}$

10

24

2

$\frac{3}{8} \times 4''$ SLOTS

$\frac{3}{4}$

$9\frac{3}{4}$

$10\frac{1}{2}$

$\frac{7}{8}$ R

$3\frac{1}{4}$ R

$2\frac{3}{4}$ R

KNOB DETAIL
2 REQ.

$\frac{3}{8}''$ WASHER & NUT

1 DIA.
COUNTERBORE $\frac{1}{2}''$ DEEP

$\frac{3}{8}$ T-NUT

$\frac{3}{8} \times 3\frac{1}{2}$ THREADED ROD

SECTION DETAIL

Illus. 685. *Details for making the adjustable shaper fence.*

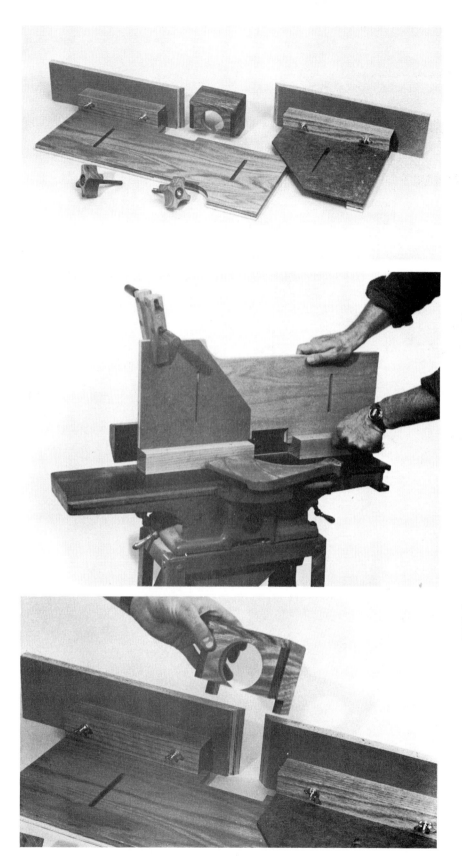

Illus. 686. The components of the adjustable shaper fence.

Illus. 687. When you run the working faces of the fence support blocks over the jointer, as shown, you are ensuring that both halves of the fence will operate in true, mating planes.

Illus. 688. The vacuum-hood connection box "hooks" in place behind the fences.

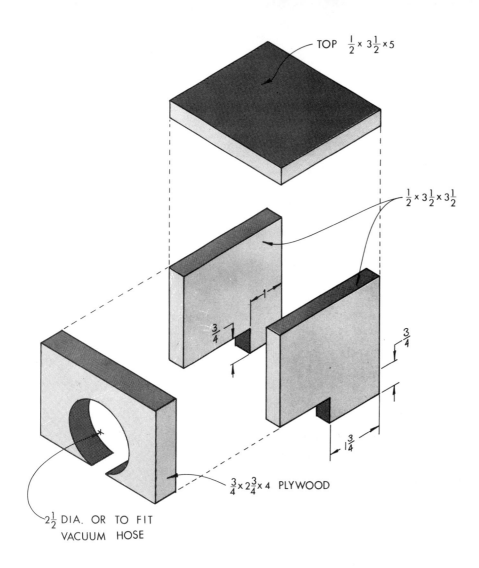

TOP $\frac{1}{2} \times 3\frac{1}{2} \times 5$

Illus. 689. Details and assembly for making the vacuum hood.

$\frac{1}{2} \times 3\frac{1}{2} \times 3\frac{1}{2}$

$\frac{3}{4} \times 2\frac{3}{4} \times 4$ PLYWOOD

$2\frac{1}{2}$ DIA. OR TO FIT VACUUM HOSE

Illus. 690. The completed vacuum hood. The opening is sawn to a friction-fit, hose connection.

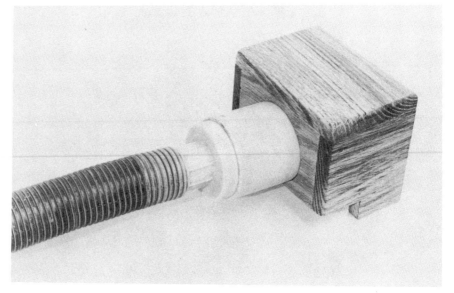

Illus. 691. The hood fits smartly behind the laterally adjustable fences.

Illus. 692. You can mount the fence quickly to the table with the two threaded adjustment knobs. The vacuum hose and box hood simply lift out when not needed.

Illus. 693. Here's a top view demonstrating the adjusting feature of this split shaping fence. Note that the vacuum hood is not affected by any of the fence adjustment possibilities.

Illus. 694. The fences each adjust laterally, here to a full 4-inch opening to accommodate this large panel-raising bit.

Illus. 695. Here the fence halves are brought into the same plane for a straight-line panel-shaping operation.

Illus. 696. Make successive passes at shallow depths when panel-raising with big bits. A slow RPM, such as 10–13,000 RPM maximum, is also essential. Here the first passes are made across the end grain.

The outfeed half of the fence is adjustable outward. Illus. 693 shows this fence and a good way to verify that the face planes of the fences are parallel to each other. The two measurements from the straightedge to the infeed fence should be equal.

The fences also adjust laterally because of their slots, carriage bolt, and wing-nut features. They will open to a full 4 inches to accommodate the big bits or close more tightly to minimize the opening around smaller-sized bits, as shown in Illus. 692.

Illus. 695–698 show the fence in a straight-line mode as it is used for panel-raising.

Hold-Ins and Hold-Downs These are important accessories, especially when you are working thin and/or narrow stock. You can make your own feather-board devices like those used with your table saw. One new device highly recommended is the feather-board and hold-down manufactured by the Universal Clamp Corporation, 15200 Stagg Street #3, Van Nuys, California 91405 (Illus. 699 and 700), which has a $3/8 \times 3/4$-inch slot aluminum bar that fits into the table groove. As the wing nut is tightened, the slotted bar expands, pressing outward against the walls of the groove until the feather-board is securely clamped in the desired position. Refer to pages 77 and 78 in Chapter 6 for a description of a similar device made of plastic.

The wheel-type device discussed on pages 77 and 79 of Chapter 6 is also very good. Illus.

701 shows it set up to rout thin and narrow edgings on the Ultimate Router Table. Illus. 702 shows the details for making a wood fence that has to be used with this particular brand of wheel-type hold-down, Shophelper, on this router table.

Illus. 699. Universal Clamp Corporation's feather board and hold-down. The slotted bar expands in the table groove, clamping the feather board firmly in the desired position.

Illus. 700. The Universal feather board in use. Note how the bar fits into the table groove. The hold-down finger is not used here.

Illus. 701. The wheel-type hold-down, hold-in anti-kickback feeds this narrow edging safely.

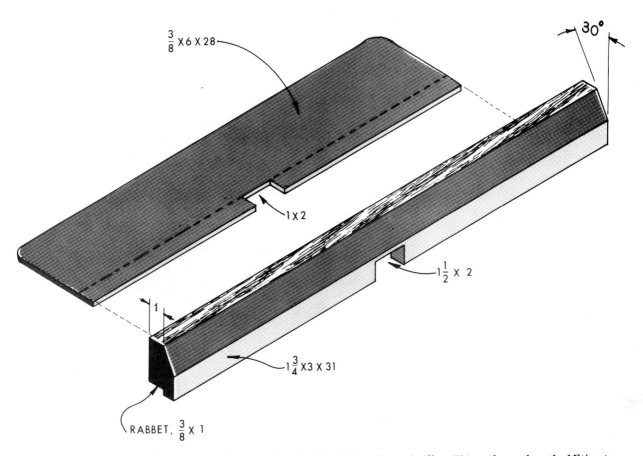

$\frac{3}{8}$ X 6 X 28

30°

1 X 2

$1\frac{1}{2}$ X 2

1

$1\frac{3}{4}$ X 3 X 31

RABBET, $\frac{3}{8}$ X 1

Illus. 702.   Details for making this wood fence so that the Shophelper shown in Illus. 701 can be used on the Ultimate Router Table.

Stock-Feeding Gauge This gauge is to the Ultimate Router Table what the mitre gauge is to the table saw, and more. This device is extremely useful and is the reason why you have two slots in the tabletop, one on each side of the bit. It should be made as precisely as possible so that you can enjoy the benefits it is intended to provide.

You'll note from looking at Illus. 704 that two hard-wood strips are needed to fit into the table grooves. Make these from quartersawn hard wood, or, better yet, use a couple of steel bars. I made mine of wood; they originally fit nicely, but later swelled during one humid day, which meant that I had to reduce them with a hand scraper.

All square joints have to be made absolute-

ly square, and the forward vertical face perfectly perpendicular to the surface of the table. To accomplish this, do the following: First, join the plywood and hard-wood facing pieces with glue and finishing nails. Countersink the heads sufficiently. Then, run this assembly over the jointer, taking a thin cut off the vertical face while holding the plywood part of the assembly against the fence of the jointer. Set the assembly in place on the router table and check the face-to-table angle with a try square.

If using the hard-wood strips, as per the plan, set them into the previously well-waxed grooves of the table. Shim them up with strips of cardboard or laminate. Run a bead of "five-minute" epoxy adhesive along the contact area.

337

Illus. 703. A stock-feeding gauge for the Ultimate Router Table works like the mitre gauge for a table saw, only with some other special features.

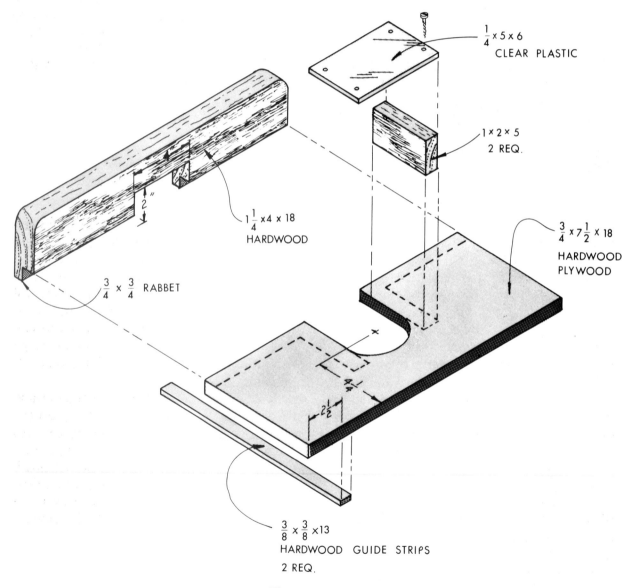

$\frac{1}{4} \times 5 \times 6$
CLEAR PLASTIC

$1 \times 2 \times 5$
2 REQ.

$1\frac{1}{4} \times 4 \times 18$
HARDWOOD

2"

$\frac{3}{4} \times 7\frac{1}{2} \times 18$
HARDWOOD
PLYWOOD

$\frac{3}{4} \times \frac{3}{4}$ RABBET

$4\frac{1}{4}$

$2\frac{1}{2}$

$\frac{3}{8} \times \frac{3}{8} \times 13$
HARDWOOD GUIDE STRIPS
2 REQ.

Illus. 704. Assembly details for making the stock-feeding gauge.

Illus. 705. *Dovetailing with the stock-feeding gauge.*

Illus. 706. *A completed dovetail. The design of the stock-feeding gauge is such that it cannot be fed entirely beyond the protruding bit. The plastic guard also serves as a window that helps you determine when to stop the forward feed.*

Carefully place the plywood and hard-wood face assembly in position on top of the glue-covered strips. Align the face of the feeding gauge to a perfect right-angle position with the table grooves. Use a big, steel framing square to check this angle. Place a weight on top and allow the epoxy to set. To complete the construction of the stock-feeding gauge, add the plastic guard and some penetrating oil sealer.

The stock-feeding gauge has many uses. You can clamp stock to the high vertical surface to do various joint-making jobs like tenoning and dovetailing, as shown in Illus. 705. Do not feed the stock-feeding gauge (in its entirety) past the protruding bit; this would cause the bit to cut into the gauge. The rear plastic guard also serves as a viewing window to indicate when the forward feed should stop. If stopping the forward feed at the appropriate place is a problem, simply clamp a stop appropriately to the table so that the stock-feeding gauge cannot be advanced farther than intended.

The stock-feeding gauge can also be used with an auxiliary board screwed to it, clamped to it, or held to it with doublefaced tape. If you feed the stock-feeding gauge so that the bit cuts into or through this auxiliary board, you will have a perfect indication of where the cut on the workpiece will be made. Then you can quickly and easily set other stops to the gauge to do operations such as indexed box-joint cutting, etc.

There are other advantages to using the auxiliary board. It minimizes splintering on the exit or trailing surface as the workpiece moves past the bit. Small pieces are better supported with the auxiliary board than without it. You'll find yourself doing more with this device than you have ever done with a table-saw mitre gauge, which, by the way, can also be used on the Ultimate Router Table.

30

Vacuum Chuck and Swivel Chuck

In Chapter 27, I explored the supply sources and equipment employed to utilize vacuum pressures to hold workpieces to tables and attach templates for routing. Here I offer two projects that utilize vacuum pressure to clamp or hold workpieces to the Ultimate Router Table for various hand-held routing jobs. The advantage of having either or both of these vacuum chuck accessories is that flat work can be held securely without clamps that might inconvenience or obstruct the routing process. The router table, in this case, becomes more of a workbench than a routing machine.

The concept and techniques associated with the design and use of these devices is not restricted to the Ultimate Router Table. The vacuum chuck projects described here can be adapted quite effectively for use with any table- or bench-like work surface. They are simply being included as accessories for the Ultimate Router Table because this is where I use them most often.

Vacuum Clamping Chuck This chuck sets flush to any worktable, but it is more specifically designed to fit into the recess of the Ultimate Router Table. (See Illus. 707.) It is extremely simple, quick and easy to make; all that's required is a piece of ³⁄₈-inch-thick plywood (plastic would be better), a plug and a quick

coupler or any connection to the air-vacuum source, and some gasket material.

Illus. 708 shows a typical section detail. When the chuck is made so that the plate sits flush with the surrounding surface, even longer or larger workpieces can be supported and clamped rigidly. (See Illus. 709.) The size of vacuum area encircled by the gasket material is optional, but remember, it's better small than too big.

If the vacuum clamping chuck is made for a workbench, it does not really have to be set flush into its surface. You could make one so

Illus. 707. *Here a vacuum clamping chuck, made of plywood, is being installed into the recess of the Ultimate Router Table.*

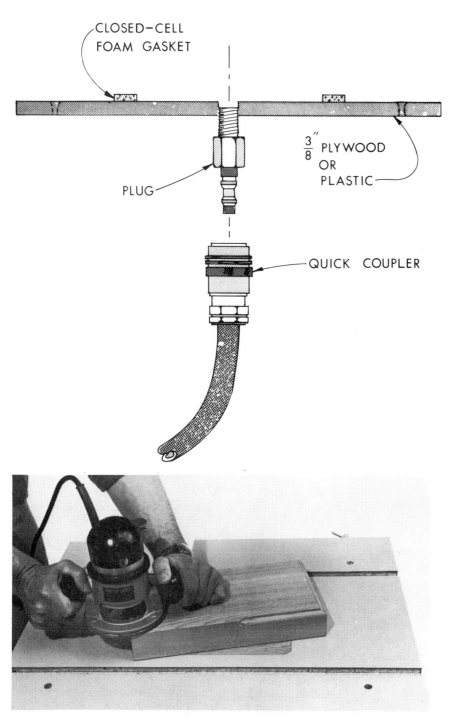

CLOSED–CELL
FOAM GASKET

Illus. 708. Typical section detail for making a vacuum-clamping chuck.

$\frac{3}{8}''$ PLYWOOD
OR
PLASTIC

PLUG

QUICK COUPLER

Illus. 709. This obstruction-free routing of a formed edge all around is easy because the work is being held in place by the vacuum-clamping chuck inset into the Ultimate Router Table.

that the plate sets on top of the workbench, over a hole for the vacuum hose. You could use scrap material that's the same thickness as the vacuum chuck plate as supporting shims, if necessary, when clamping down long or bigger workpieces.

The vacuum chuck has many uses in addition to routing. Use it to hold the work steady for sanding panels (you will be able to see the complete surface), to hold parts for boring or power- or hand-carving (such as chip-carving), in assembly work, or to hold other jigs and fixtures with flat surfaces or bases steadily to the workbench.

Rotating Vacuum Chuck With the rotating vacuum chuck not only are you able to clamp down the work, you can also rotate it 360 degrees while still maintaining the vacuum clamping action; this is often very desirable, especially when edge-forming, one-handed, all around panels or plaques, as shown in Illus. 710. The "free" hand rotates the work.

The rotating vacuum chuck is essentially self-contained in a base box; you do not have to run any hoses up through the hole in the table. (See Illus. 711.) The vacuum supply hose has a three-way ball valve mounted conveniently alongside the box base with which the vacuum can be activated or released with just a turn of the lever. (See Illus. 712.) If you do not want a swivel or rotating action, such as when doing jobs that require a two-handed operation, simply insert a stop block to stop the rotation. (See Illus. 713.)

This project is nothing more than a box with a bigger bottom and a rotating plate on its top. Illus. 714 gives the fabricating details. Illus. 715 shows that the sides of the base are four identical pieces assembled with simple butt joints to make a square box.

Depending upon the the size and type of hose going to your vacuum pump or vacuum source, you may have to buy plumbing parts such as reducers, nipples, etc. Illus. 716 shows some of these fittings, along with a three-way ball valve, a male plug, and a quick-disconnect coupler. I have used small-diameter plastic hoses that extend from the valve to the male plug screwed into the bottom of the rotating top plate. (See Illus. 717.)

Illus. 714, 717, and 718 reveal that the swivel for the top plate is simply a 6-inch Lazy Susan bearing, which is available from several mail-order woodcraft supply houses if you cannot find it at the local hardware dealer. The swivel mechanism in the air hose is in the coupler connection itself. It is a good idea to polish the end of the male plug with steel wool. Lubricate the contact areas with white lithium grease to ensure smooth operation and protection against wear or rust.

Illus. 719 shows the mounting for one type of three-way ball valve; you may have to modify this approach if you use another type of ball valve. Illus. 720, which is the bottom view of the assembled project, shows the small-diameter hose extending from the valve to the quick-connect coupler. Since this hose has to make a fairly abrupt turn, a small, flexible one works best.

The rotating vacuum chuck does not have to be used on the Ultimate Router Table. (See

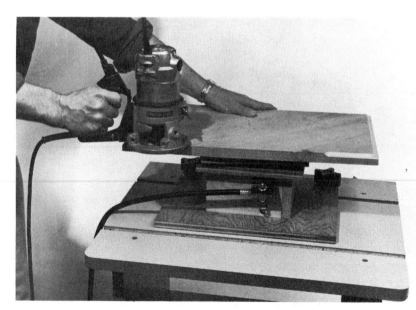

Illus. 710. A rotating vacuum chuck makes edge-forming jobs such as this even faster.

Illus. 711. The rotating vacuum chuck mounted on the Ultimate Router Table has a handy shut-off valve.

Illus. 712. A closeup look at the three-way ball valve.

Illus. 713. This stop block inserted into the matching grooves keeps the top plate from rotating.

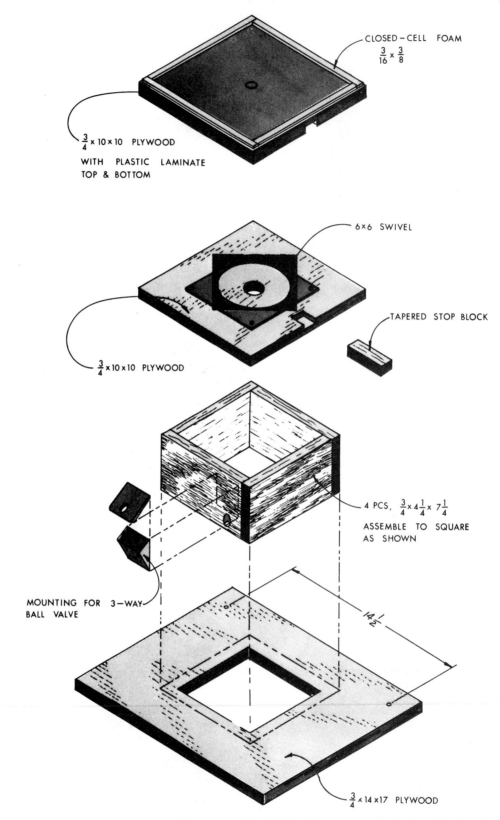

CLOSED — CELL FOAM
$\frac{3}{16} \times \frac{3}{8}$

$\frac{3}{4} \times 10 \times 10$ PLYWOOD

WITH PLASTIC LAMINATE
TOP & BOTTOM

6×6 SWIVEL

TAPERED STOP BLOCK

$\frac{3}{4} \times 10 \times 10$ PLYWOOD

4 PCS, $\frac{3}{4} \times 4\frac{1}{4} \times 7\frac{1}{4}$

ASSEMBLE TO SQUARE
AS SHOWN

MOUNTING FOR 3—WAY
BALL VALVE

$14\frac{1}{2}$

$\frac{3}{4} \times 14 \times 17$ PLYWOOD

Illus. 714. Construction and assembly details.

Illus. 715. The base is made of simple wood-box construction.

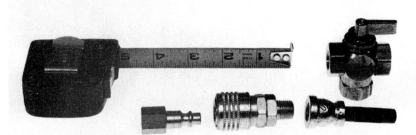

Illus. 716. Some of the "plumbing" required includes a three-way ball valve, a male plug with a disconnect coupler, and, depending upon the air line, maybe a reducer and nipple.

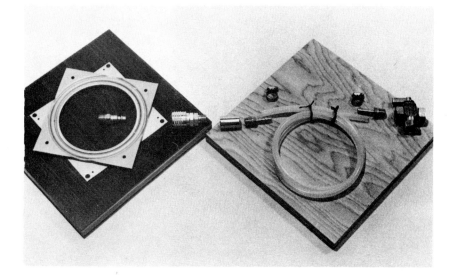

Illus. 717. Here's some of the other parts used on my model. Note the ¾-inch plywood plate on the left covered with decorative laminate.

Illus. 718. *Turning in the male plug. The swivel mechanism of the vacuum line is in the disconnect coupler itself. The male plug should be polished with fine steel wool. This and the inside of the coupler are lubricated with a white lithium grease available at most hardware dealers.*

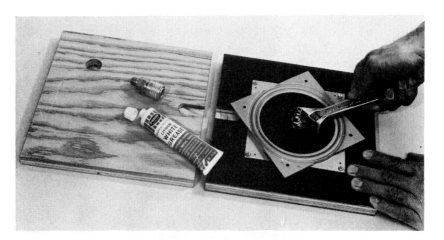

Illus. 719. *Closeup showing the mounting for a three-way ball valve.*

Illus. 720. *A bottom view of the mounting.*

Illus. 721.) The unit is portable and essentially self-contained, and can be used on tables, workbenches, sawhorses, or wherever you wish.

Incidentally, if the vacuum plate is larger than the material you have to clamp on both the vacuum clamping chuck and rotating vacuum chuck, you have two options: Either simply run another, smaller ring of foam-gasket material around the inside of the one that's there or make an auxiliary double-sided secondary plate, as shown in Illus. 722. Place this auxiliary plate on top of the standard plate, and it will be pulled down tightly to it when placing the workpiece on top and activating the vacuum.

Illus. 721. The completed rotating vacuum chuck can be clamped to any convenient table or workbench.

Illus. 722. If the vacuum plate is larger than the material you have to clamp, simply make an auxiliary double-sided plate, one with a gasket on both sides and a hole in the center, as shown, and place it on top of the standard chuck plate.

31

Horizontal Joint-Making Attachment

The router is being used more and more in a horizontal, adjustable position—especially for joint-making. This is something that I have been doing for years—even before the new machines based on this principle recently came into existence. Also refer to Chapters 11–14, which cover a multitude of related techniques with the Strong, Universal, JDS, and Ryobi radial-arm-saw machines.

The horizontal joint-making attachment (Illus. 723 and 724) is simply a router-mounting panel that attaches to the rear side of the Ultimate Router Table. It operates on a pivot to change the height of the bit protruding

horizontally over a work-supporting table. In keeping with the philosophy of heft and rigidity in design, I recommend the use of material that is a full 1 inch thick. If you are not able to get particle board or plywood this thick, one alternative is to laminate two ½-inch-thick panels.

Cut out the outside profile as specified on Illus. 725. Cover both surfaces with plastic laminate for a balanced construction that will minimize any possible warpage. The objective is to get a true, flat panel. Coat the outside edges with enamel; this seals them and gives the project a decorative touch.

Illus. 723. The horizontal joint-making attachment essentially consists only of a one-piece mounting panel that pivots to raise and lower the bit.

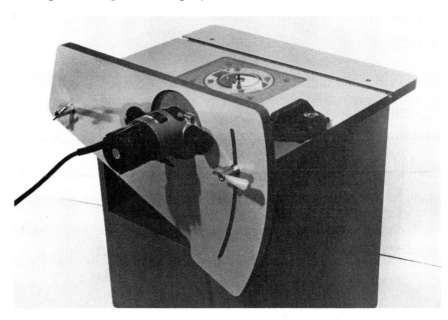

Illus. 724. The action side of the attachment. Note the use of the table saw mitre gauge and the table opening under the protruding bit.

Next, rout the ³⁄₈-inch circular slot to a 21-inch radius. This matches the two ³⁄₈-inch carriage bolt studs that protrude out of the thick, rear edge of the router table's center-to-center spacings. (See Illus. 726.) Check these spacings carefully and run a practice cut before cutting your prepared, laminated panel. Refer to Illus. 657 on page 317, which gives the appropriate specifications and details for making the router table top.

Next, cut a recess to accept the size and shape of the router base and a 2-inch hole through the mounting board. (See Illus. 727–729.) The surface of the recess can be painted the same as the edges. Simply wax the edge of the hole and edges inside the circular slot well; they could also be painted, if desired.

A good adjustment-locking knob or lever is important. One type that I have made uses a ³⁄₈-inch threaded coupling available from most hardware dealers. Drill a ¹⁄₄-inch hole near one end, as shown in Illus. 730. Slip in a length of steel rod. Then flair the steel rod on each side of the hexagon coupling so that it doesn't slip out. Using a hammer, briskly tap it once or twice with a center punch or nail set. The completed T-handled adjustment nut is shown in Illus. 731. If you like, glue on a little piece of drilled and shaped wood to make the T-handle more comfortable in your hand.

The horizontal joint-making attachment will turn out to be an unexpected pleasure to use.

There are so many different kinds of joints and creative applications on which it can be used. It is possible that you'll use your router more in this horizontal mode than the conventional vertically supported router position under the table. The popularity of the similar, commercially made machines discussed in this book is a good indication of the acceptance given to this machine by woodworkers.

Illus. 731 shows a homemade height-adjustment scale that is simply a piece of tape applied to the edge on which you can make marks that indicate certain vertical settings for special-custom jobs and cuts like tenoning and mortising cuts. The horizontal depth of cut is adjusted with the router itself. (See Illus. 732.)

Making rail-to-stile-type mortise-and-tenon joints is one of the more popular but elementary functions this device handles very effectively. Illus. 733 and 734 show some tenoning cuts. Illus. 735 shows a box joint in progress, and Illus. 736–738 show some basic steps involved in cutting slotted mortises.

The examples that I have just given you do not adequately illustrate all that is possible when using this accessory on the Ultimate Router Table. Hopefully, however, these examples and others given in this book will be a springboard from which you can launch your own ideas for utilizing this accessory with your Ultimate Router Table.

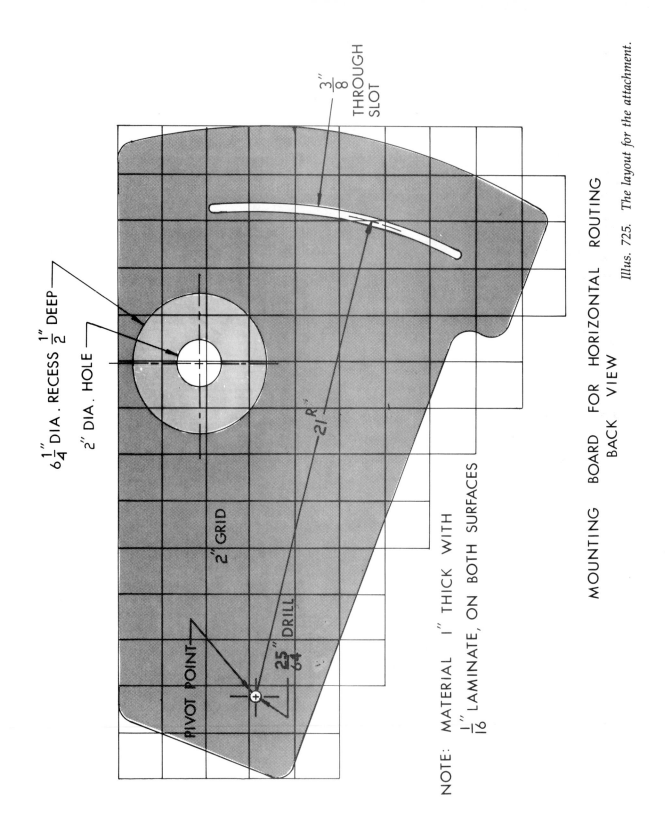

6¼" DIA. RECESS ½" DEEP

2" DIA. HOLE

3" THROUGH
8 SLOT

2" GRID

21 R

PIVOT POINT

25" DRILL
64

NOTE: MATERIAL 1" THICK WITH
1" LAMINATE, ON BOTH SURFACES
16

MOUNTING BOARD FOR HORIZONTAL ROUTING
BACK VIEW

Illus. 725.   The layout for the attachment.

Illus. 726.   A circle-cutting jig is used to cut the slot through the 1-inch-thick panel that's covered with solid-color decorative laminate on both surfaces.

Illus. 727.   Routing the recess for the router base. The method shown here, using the adjustable circle-cutting base (Chapter 19, pages 194–198), is one way of doing it.

Illus. 728.   The completed recess and cut-through bit hole.

Illus. 729 (above left). Use your base as a guide to drill the router-mounting screw holes. Illus. 730 (above right). A ⅜-inch threaded coupling makes the adjustment-and-pivot-lock screw nut. Here one is being drilled through; the result will be a ¼-inch steel rod that serves as a T handle.

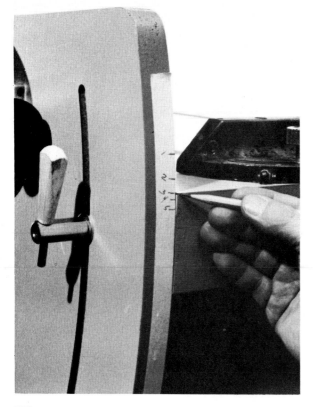

Illus. 731 (left). Note the T-handle adjustment nut on the left. The markings on the tape indicate certain special cuts referenced to the surface of the table, as shown. Illus. 732 (above). The horizontal depth of cut can be adjusted with the router itself. A system of special cutting depths can be registered with markings such as this.

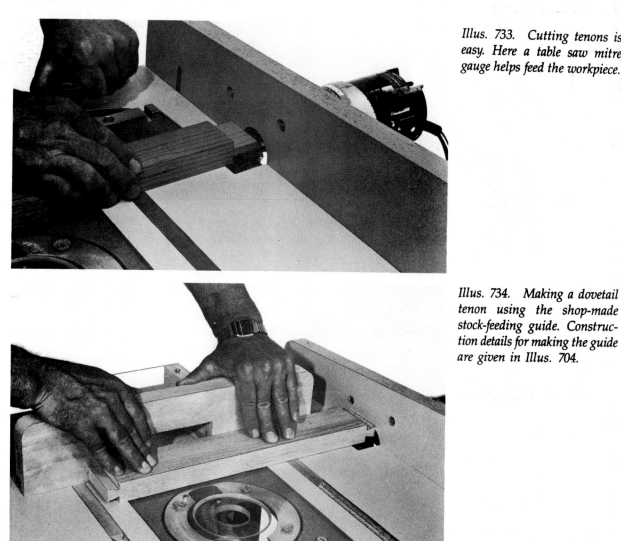

Illus. 733. Cutting tenons is easy. Here a table saw mitre gauge helps feed the workpiece.

Illus. 734. Making a dovetail tenon using the shop-made stock-feeding guide. Construction details for making the guide are given in Illus. 704.

Illus. 735. Making a box joint.

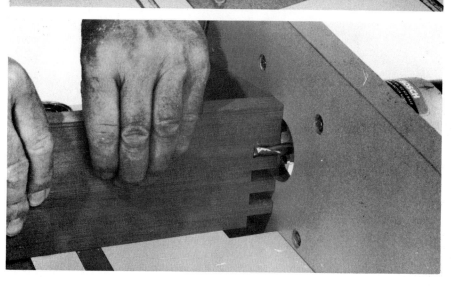

Illus. 736. Setting up to make a mortise. With the adjustment of the router height already set, this pencil mark is a reference point for ending the cut.

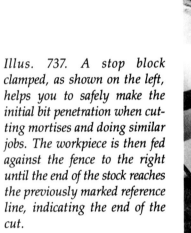

Illus. 737. A stop block clamped, as shown on the left, helps you to safely make the initial bit penetration when cutting mortises and doing similar jobs. The workpiece is then fed against the fence to the right until the end of the stock reaches the previously marked reference line, indicating the end of the cut.

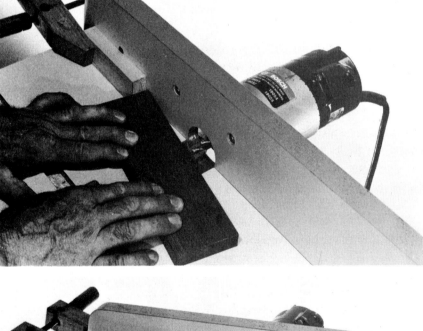

Illus. 738. The completed slot mortise and the setup used to do the job.

354

32

Swinging and Tilting Overarm Router

This accessory for the Ultimate Router Table provides several different routing modes. First, you can make the router swing smoothly through a wide range of different arc sizes that range from less than 2 inches to around a 34-inch radius. (Illus. 739–741.) Secondly, the router can be secured to a single, fixed position over the router table at one of various heights so that the bit is rotating on either a vertical axis or an angled one.

Building the swinging-and-tilting overarm router is fairly straightforward and easy. The entire vertical structure or column, as shown in Illus. 742, is a simple box construction that is nothing more than ⅜-inch-thick plywood panels glued and nailed to two 2 × 4's that are 42 inches long.

Illus. 743 shows all of the cutting and assembly details for making the column and overarms. Make the overarms from ¾-inch plywood. Cut and drill them stacked together as a pair; this ensures that all the mating holes will be located exactly the same. Use kiln-dried solid hard wood to make the lower mounting boards. The holes must be exactly 21 inches on center to fit the two ⅜-inch carriage-bolt mounting studs that project from the heavy rear edge of the router table.

Illus. 744 shows the major parts of the proj-

ect. The two long swing arms and the vertical parts of the router cradle, as shown in Illus. 745, are made of ¾-inch plywood with uniform-

Illus. 739.   *The pivot point you choose will determine the cutting arc path of the swinging router.*

Illus. 740.   Typical samples of concave surface cuts made with the swinging router.

Illus. 741.   The smallest and largest cutting arcs permitted with the swinging router are illustrated by the concave surfaces on this board. The minimum is a radius of less than 2 inches to an arc that is approximately a 34-inch radius.

Illus. 742.   The vertical column is a hollow box construction. The overarms are made from ¾-inch plywood, and the lower table-mounting boards are made of heavy hardwood.

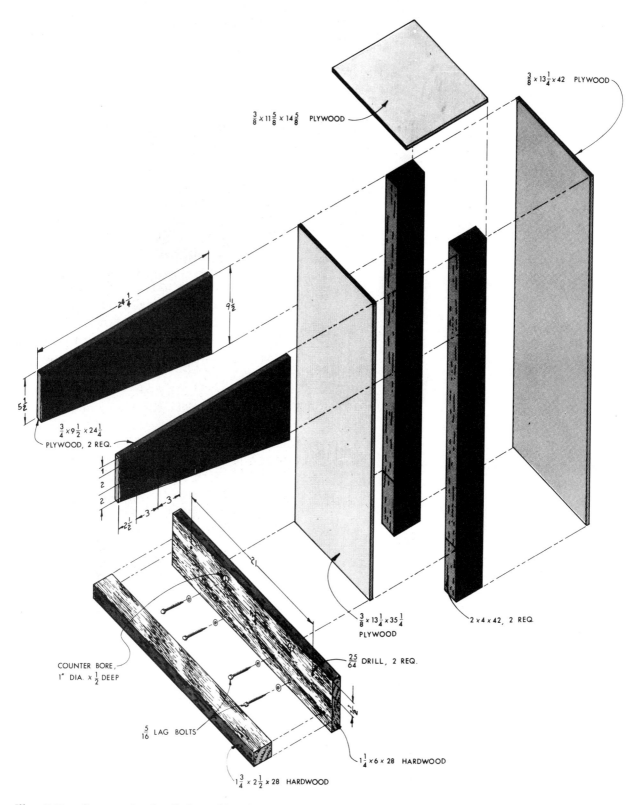

$\frac{3}{8} \times 11\frac{5}{8} \times 14\frac{5}{8}$ PLYWOOD

$\frac{3}{8} \times 13\frac{1}{4} \times 42$ PLYWOOD

$24\frac{1}{4}$

$9\frac{1}{2}$

$5\frac{1}{2}$

$\frac{3}{4} \times 9\frac{1}{2} \times 24\frac{1}{4}$
PLYWOOD, 2 REQ.

1

2

2

$2\frac{1}{2}$ 3   3

$\frac{3}{8} \times 13\frac{1}{4} \times 35\frac{1}{4}$
PLYWOOD

$2 \times 4 \times 42$, 2 REQ.

$\frac{25}{64}$ DRILL, 2 REQ.

COUNTER BORE,
1" DIA. $\times \frac{1}{2}$ DEEP

$\frac{5}{16}$ LAG BOLTS

$1\frac{1}{4} \times 6 \times 28$ HARDWOOD

$1\frac{3}{4} \times 2\frac{1}{2} \times 28$ HARDWOOD

Illus. 743.   Construction details for making the simple box column, overarms, and the mounting at the base.

357

Illus. 744.   The major parts of the swinging router.

Illus. 745.   A close look at the plywood router cradle.

ly spaced holes for height adjustments and a choice of various pivot points. Illus. 746 gives the dimensions and hole spaces.

To make the long swing arms and the vertical parts of the router cradle, stack them together and drill through both pieces at once,

thus ensuring perfectly mated holes. The base of the router cradle should be made so that you can mount your own router to it.

The long swing arms are connected to the plywood overarms with ¼-inch carriage bolts, washers, and wing nuts. Illus. 747 shows a typical setup for making small-to-medium radius arcs in the swinging-router mode. To lock the swing arm rigidly to the overarms, put two carriage bolts through the swing arms. You can also get them to pivot by using any combinations of holes in the long swing arms and holes in the verticals of the router cradle. Illus. 748 depicts the setup for routing with the smallest possible arcs, and Illus. 749 shows the setup for routing with the biggest possible arc. In the latter case, the verticals of the cradle and the long swing arms are fixed rigidly together, and the entire assembly pivots from the uppermost holes of the swing arms and the overarms.

The possibilities for making unusual and interesting surface cuts with the swinging router are expanded when you vary arc lengths, utilize bits of different shapes, or hold or support the workpiece itself in a variety of positions. Illus. 750 shows one example, in which the workpiece is simply supported on the router table by a fence that's clamped obliquely to the cutting direction of the swinging arm. Think of the cuts possible if you tilt the workpiece itself on a wedge support or if you use stopped cuts that do not swing entirely through their full arc.

Some other interesting work can be done if you make swing cuts through workpieces that will pivot on a fixed point after each successive cut. Now, visualize what cuts can be made if the workpiece can be placed on a pivot that's on a wedge support. Some interesting possibilities include making unusual surface embellishments for cabinet panels, doors and drawer fronts, etc. You are sure to invent many unique uses for the swinging router.

The tilting-overarm routing setup, frankly, is not my favorite routing mode. However, it is worthwhile to discuss some of the techniques

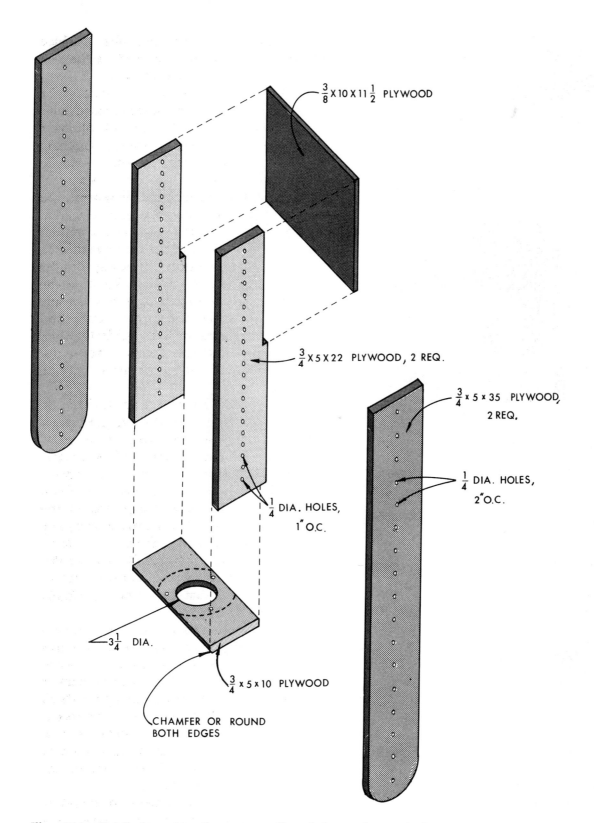

$\frac{3}{8}$ X 10 X 11$\frac{1}{2}$ PLYWOOD

$\frac{3}{4}$ X 5 X 22 PLYWOOD, 2 REQ.

$\frac{3}{4}$ x 5 x 35 PLYWOOD, 2 REQ.

$\frac{1}{4}$ DIA. HOLES, 2" O.C.

$\frac{1}{4}$ DIA. HOLES, 1" O.C.

3$\frac{1}{4}$ DIA.

$\frac{3}{4}$ x 5 x 10 PLYWOOD

CHAMFER OR ROUND BOTH EDGES

Illus. 746. Details for making the router cradle and the two long swinging arms.

Illus. 747 (above left). Small-to-intermediate-size cutting arcs are possible when the long arms are locked as desired anywhere vertically and the pivot points of choice on the router cradle are employed. Illus. 748 (above right). The setup for the smallest possible cutting arc. Note the low pivot with the long swinging arms locked above.

Illus. 749. This setup using the long swing arms makes the largest possible cutting arc.

Illus. 750. Just one example of unusual cutting produced with the swinging router. Here a roundnose bit makes identical "scooping" cuts into the surface of the work as it is supported against a fence clamped obliquely to the swing travel of the router.

possible with it. (Illus. 751.) With the addition of another easy-to-make accessory called a "stiffener" (Illus. 752 and 753), the entire setup becomes very rigid, and the vertical adjustment within the router base becomes an important feature for certain jobs. It is possible to do some overarm pin-routing jobs with the tilting router. You can make an auxiliary table from panel material like plywood or particle board. Set a dowel pin into the plywood or particle board and clamp it to the existing router table, carefully locating it in a position where the vertical center axis of the dowel pin and the router bit align perfectly. If you want to seriously explore pin-routing possibilities, you could make a special table insert of $3/_8$-inch plywood, plastic, or metal to accommodate various-sized pins that would fit neatly into the router table's recessed surface, thus eliminating the need for clamps. Once you have a suitable table pin in place, you can do typical overarm and pin-routing techniques, including template and pattern duplication work.

The fixed, tilted overarm router is also potentially useful for some particular routing jobs, like angular grooving and slotting, as shown in Illus. 755 and 756, and can make a wide variety of shaped wood mouldings. You can cut many different profiles with one bit simply by changing the tilt angle and cutting depth

Illus. 751. The swinging, tilting overarm router in a vertical fixed routing mode. Note the addition of a "stiffener" attachment that makes the overall setup very rigid.

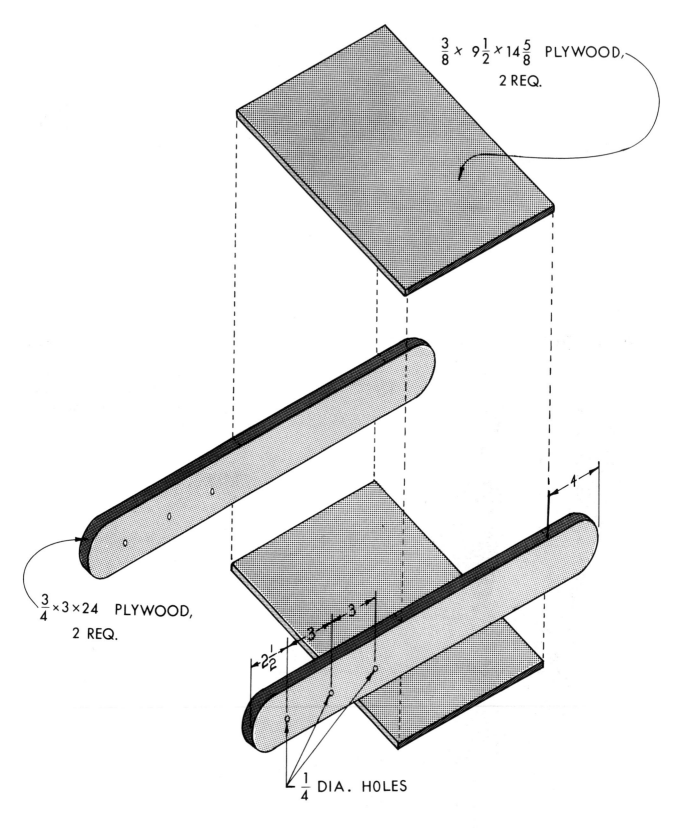

$\frac{3}{8} \times 9\frac{1}{2} \times 14\frac{5}{8}$ PLYWOOD, 2 REQ.

$\frac{3}{4} \times 3 \times 24$ PLYWOOD, 2 REQ.

4

$2\frac{1}{2}$

3

3

$\frac{1}{4}$ DIA. HOLES

Illus. 752.   Drawing of the "stiffener."

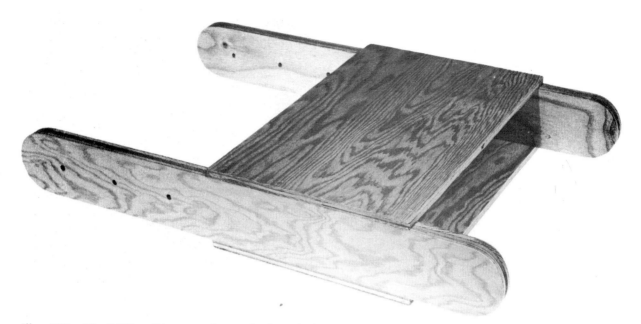

Illus. 753.   The "stiffener" is an attachment for the swinging, tilting overarm router accessory that can be quickly made.

Illus. 754.   The overarm router fixed in a tilted position. Note the use of the "stiffener" and the straightedge clamped to the table.

Illus. 755. A small sampling of angular groove or slotting cuts possible with the router in a fixed tilted position.

Illus. 756. A closeup look at angular grooving that has been made on a test piece with a spiral router bit.

of the bit. If you are machining narrow pieces, use hold-down and hold-in safety accessories. Always remember that most shop-machining accidents happen when the operator attempts to machine workpieces that are too small or too short to be handled safely.

If you follow basic safety practices and are always aware of potentially dangerous situations, you'll find that the swinging or tilting overarm router, when used with the Ultimate Router Table, will offer more viable cutting techniques and prove to be fun to experiment with.

33

Inverted Pin-Routing Attachment

It's almost impossible to restrain my enthusiasm for the concept of inverted-routing and it only follows that I am equally enthusiastic about the inverted-routing attachment for the Ultimate Router Table. (See Illus. 757 and 758.) The "inverted" process, in general, seems to embody all of the advantages of routing and eliminates or reduces the problems that are normally associated with other routing methods and techniques.

As a case in point, let's compare the overarm pin routers to inverted pin routers. As you know, in overarm pin-routing the router is always above the work; so is the entire rotating spindle collet and the fully exposed bit, with its cutting edge whirling precariously within close distance of the operator. Regardless of all efforts to effectively guard overarm pin-routers, they are just more inherently dangerous than inverted pin routers.

The inverted pin router has a nonrotating guide pin on the overarm (Illus. 758 and 759) which, obviously, is safe. The majority of the rotating bit is under the table, with only the

Illus. 757. The inverted pin routing attachment mounted to the Ultimate Router Table. This very potent combination features a 13¼-inch reach and an automatic pin engagement that improves operator safety and convenience of use.

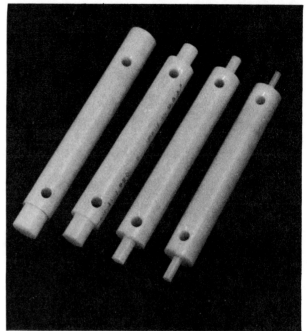

Illus. 758 (left). *The key to this effective shop-made inverted pin router is this rubber band spring-loaded guide pin, which permits a one hand clamping feature. Illus. 759* (above). *This set of shop-made, quickly interchangeable guide pins was machined from nylon rod, but birch dowels or aluminum rod will also work.*

necessary length of the cutting edge protruding above it. The stock that is being cut actually guards the bit, since the bit is engaged into the work from below, not from above.

The operator will also find inverted pin-routing much easier than overarm pin-routing when routing with a template. It is much easier to work the template (together with the workpiece) to follow along the guide pin when you can see it all from above than when the template and pin are under the workpiece.

Another distinct advantage of inverted pin-routing is the accuracy of the depth of cut. Jobs like making routing trays and cutting boards with a dishing cutter, making all kinds of flat-bottom recesses, and cutting-down sign backgrounds to raise designs and letters in relief all require uniformly accurate cutting depths. With the inverted pin router, it is impossible to cut too deeply. The worktable is the stop that prevents the work from accidentally being pushed deeper onto the bit than desired.

When overarm pin-routing, your work can "crawl" up and over shavings or chips on the table, and the bit will automatically cut deeper into the work. Often, with overarm pin-routing, I have inadvertently tipped the workpiece slightly or lifted the work, pushing it further into the rotating bit. This always seems to happen when I make the final pass.

The inverted routing accessory requires a little more effort and attention to detail to build it than the other accessories. (See Illus. 760.) However, it is worth it because it will provide many new and helpful routing techniques.

Illus. 761 provides the necessary construction details. First, make the mounting board from 1¼-inch-thick hard wood. Then drill the holes, 21 inches on center, to match the two ⅜-inch carriage-bolt studs that protrude out of the rear edge of the router table. Attach this mounting board to the router table, as shown in Illus. 762, with the T-handled lock nuts. (Refer to page 352 for information on making

T-handled lock nuts.) Then, project the center axis of the bit squarely to the top edge of the mounting board, as shown in Illus. 762. Work from the inside edges of the collet opening. Be sure to mark the space for the thickness of the arm. Also, check to be sure that the center axis of the guide-pin hole of the arm will be aligned with the collet of the router. Carefully make these necessary layout lines on the 1¼-inch-thick mounting board.

Make the arm next. Use hardwood, preferably quartersawn. When I made mine I used flatsawn stock, which could have provided some problems in stability. Fortunately (so far), I have not experienced any serious problems, even during the hot and humid summer, but I have been lucky. Square-up the arm material in thickness and width before sawing it to its profile shape. Carefully bore a ⅞-inch-diameter vertical hole for the guide pins.

Wrap some 80-grit abrasive around a big dowel and sand the hole slightly larger, making it so that a ⅞-inch dowel (plastic, aluminum, or wood) can freely drop through. Now, band-saw a kerf through the hole from the end of the arm, as shown in Illus. 759. Drill a ¼-inch hole perpendicular to the kerf in which to put a ¼-inch carriage bolt and wing nut; this makes a clamp that allows you to ad-

just and hold the guide pin at any desired height.

Make the pins as shown in Illus. 759 and as specified on Illus. 761. I have used nylon rod for them because it is strong, hard, has dimensional stability, and is easy to machine. However, birch dowelling or solid-aluminum rod should also work. Make the tenoning cuts (diameter reductions) on the ends of the guide pins with the dowel-tenoning jig described and illustrated on pages 248–251 of Chapter 23.

Make the automatic pin-plunging mechanism, as shown in Illus. 758. It employs a heavy rubber band that goes through the pin, which spring-loads it in a downward direction. Generously wax the inside walls of the guide-pin hole to make the guide-pin movement even easier. Once you have determined that the guide pin works effectively, you are ready to begin assembly.

First, lay out the two ¼ × 6-inch carriage-bolt holes on the top of one of the heavy vertical members. Clamp both vertical pieces together, and drill the ¼-inch holes through both pieces at once. After these holes are drilled, attach the vertical pieces to the mounting board with glue and lag bolts, as shown in Illus. 763.

Reattach the mounting board (now with the

Illus. 760. The inverted pin-routing attachment. Note the choice of three hole positions in the mounting board which set the arm to different height clearances when you work stock of various thicknesses.

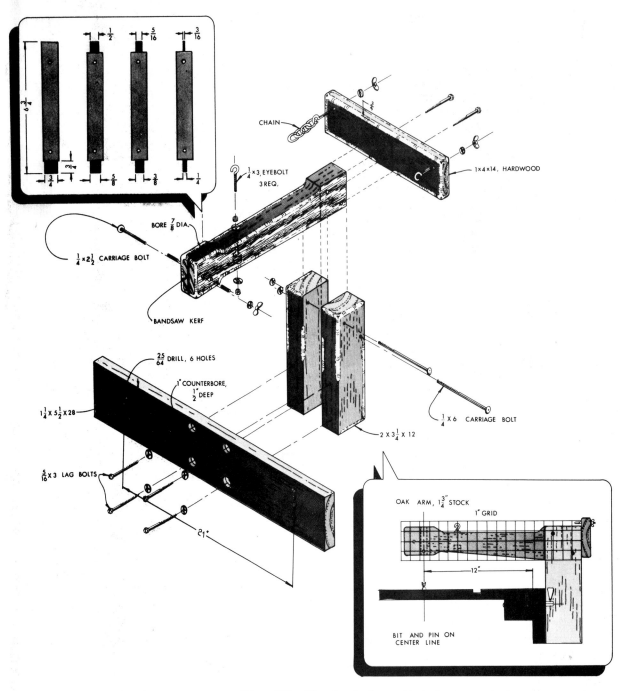

$\frac{1}{2}$ $\frac{5}{16}$ $\frac{3}{16}$

$6\frac{3}{4}$

$\frac{3}{4}$

$\frac{3}{4}$ $\frac{5}{8}$ $\frac{3}{8}$ $\frac{1}{4}$

CHAIN

$\frac{1}{4}$ x 3, EYEBOLT
3 REQ.

1 x 4 x 14, HARDWOOD

BORE $\frac{7}{8}$ DIA.

$\frac{1}{4}$ x $2\frac{1}{2}$ CARRIAGE BOLT

BANDSAW KERF

$\frac{25}{64}$ DRILL, 6 HOLES

1" COUNTERBORE,
$\frac{1}{2}$" DEEP

$1\frac{1}{4}$ X $5\frac{1}{2}$ X 28

$\frac{1}{4}$ X 6 CARRIAGE BOLT

$\frac{5}{16}$ X 3 LAG BOLTS

2 X $3\frac{1}{4}$ X 12

21"

OAK ARM, $1\frac{3}{4}$" STOCK

1" GRID

12"

BIT AND PIN ON
CENTER LINE

Illus. 761. The details for making the inverted pin-router attachment.

Illus. 762. The important first steps for making the inverted router accessory. First make the mounting board and install it to the rear edge of the router table. Make the center mark on the top edge by projecting it from the router collet, as shown.

Illus. 763. Lag and glue the two heavy, vertical members to the mounting board and space them a distance apart that equals the thickness of the pin arm.

two vertical pieces fastened to it) to the edge of the router table, as shown in Illus. 764. Using the T-handle lock nuts, make sure that it is tightly fastened to the router table.

Install the ½-inch diameter guide pin into the router collet, as shown in Illus. 765. (Use a ¼-inch diameter pin if your router only has a ¼-inch collet capacity.) Raise the router to the appropriate height. Place the arm over the guide pin, with the pin going into the hole of the arm. Clamp the guide pin into the arm with the wing nut so that the arm is at the required horizontal height above the table. (See Illus. 766.) Drill the two holes through the arm

to receive the ¼ × 6-inch carriage bolts. (See Illus. 767.)

The chain with eyebolt-and-wing-nut-tensioning system shown in Illus. 765–767 was intended to add rigidity and provide a sideways fine-adjustment feature. It does help a little, but don't count on it as a solution for careless workmanship. In fact, you may not need it at all if the bit and pin align perfectly, and the construction is stable enough to handle everything except very aggressive routing.

One of the best qualities of the inverted pin router is the way it can be used with templates. There are many different ways

Illus. 764.   Make sure that the mounting plate is tight against the edge of the table.

Illus. 765 (left).   Make sure that the rubberband spring-loaded-pin-movement-and-clamp-mechanism works faultlessly before attaching the arm to the two vertical supports. First, clamp the ½-inch-diameter guide pin snugly into the collet of the router as shown. Illus. 766 (above). Here's how to set up to drill the bolt holes through the arm. The ½ inch pin is actually engaged in the collet of the router.

Illus. 767.   After checking the working up-and-down action of the guide pin to make sure that the arm aligns it with the collet, drill two holes through the arm. Use the predrilled holes in the 2-inch-thick vertical supports to guide the hand drill straight through, as shown here.

templates can be secured to the workpiece. They can be clamped down, temporarily glued (with a spot[s] of hot melt), nailed down, either made to cradle the work or held securely with double-sided tape, and held with vacuum pressure.

Illus. 768 and 769 demonstrate one basic recess-cutting technique with an "inside" type of template, which is mounted directly to the workpiece with double-sided tape. Install a bit and a matching guide-pin of the same diameter to make a 1:1-size ratio reproduction. Set the bit-cutting depth to the appropriate height above the table. Turn on the router and carefully lower the work (with a pivoting movement) onto the rotating bit. Direct the work so that the bit enters into the central area of the design.

Once the bit is cutting at full depth, "work" with a little circular motion. Then, with one hand turn off the router, but do not move or shift the workpiece; hold it steady with the second hand. Drop the guide pin down by loosening the wing nut; retighten the wing nut when the guide pin is set before starting the router again. This is where you will appreciate the one-hand operation of the spring-loaded pin. This is also where a foot-controlled switch would be very helpful, because with it you would not have to remove your hand from the work to switch it, and you would not have to

shut off the power while dropping the guide pin into position.

Once you have set the guide-pin height, the work movement will be directed by the guide pin following the template, as the router will complete the cut. (See Illus. 760.)

To make an incised design (Illus. 770), use an "outside template" like the one shown in Illus. 771, and as explained in the caption for Illus. 772. Once you learn how to handle the rubber-band spring-loaded guide pin, the rest is easy.

A grooved template makes routing with the inverted router even easier. Once you have made it, mounted it to the work, and engaged the guide pin into the groove, it's simply a matter of feeding the work. Because the pin stays in the groove, a perfectly controlled cutting process is the only possible result.

Grooved templates are great for cutting incised-line art designs into surfaces or for making full-profile shape cutouts. Refer to pages 301–303 for more information about grooved vacuum templates. Here's how to make and use a basic grooved template:

1. Secure the pattern (or an original) onto the template material by nailing or using double-sided tape, as shown in Illus. 773.
2. Select the pin- and bit-size match and

Illus. 768. Basic template-guided cutting on the inverted router. Here, an easy-to-make inside template is mounted directly on top of the workpiece with double-sided tape.

371

Illus. 769. The completed work is a recess-cut design made from the template pattern.

Illus. 770. The inverted router can make very accurate incised designs, as on the piece of barn wood on the left, or it can be used to make entire full-profile cutouts, as shown on the right.

Illus. 771. Making an incised line design. Here the template is secured to the work—in this case by vacuum pressure. The guide pin is loose, moving freely vertically under the load of the rubber band. The work is held so that the guide pin remains against the edge of the template while the work is being lowered (with a pivoting motion shown here) onto the rotating bit. Once the cutting depth is reached, the guide pin is tightened with the wing nut.

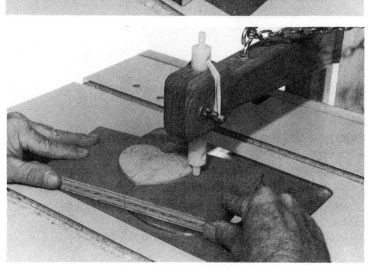

Illus. 772. Now, with the bit fully penetrated into the work's surface underneath, the guide pin is tightened. The cut is completed by feeding the template (with the work) in a clockwise direction against the guide pin.

Illus. 773. Making a grooved template. The groove is being cut into the piece of ¾-inch plywood template material below as the ¼-inch plywood pattern follows the guide pin above.

set the bit for the depth of cut. A cutting depth of ³⁄₁₆–¼ inch is sufficient.

3. Using the pivoting technique with the guide pin loose in the arm, but held against the edge of the ¼-inch-thick plywood pattern, lower the work onto the rotating bit. (Keep the guide pin against the pattern as you lower the work.)

4. Carefully feed the work, following against the guide-pin groove all around the entire outside edge of the pattern. (See Illus. 774.)

5. Shut down the router and allow the bit rotation to coast to a complete stop before removing the workpieces.

Using a grooved template is much easier than using any other kind of template. Simply secure it to the top of the workpiece with double-sided tape or by any other workable means including a vacuum. (See Illus. 775.) Loosen the guide pin, engage it into the groove of the template and slowly lower the work into the revolving bit. (Keep the pin in the groove.) Tighten the guide pin when the full-cutting depth is achieved. Proceed to complete the operation with the pin following in the groove to control the cutting path of the bit. (See Illus. 776.)

Use of this accessory is not limited to just the techniques I have described. There are many other methods and operations this accessory is capable of. In fact, once you start to use it, new different techniques will come to you simply through inspiration. This is when the effort and time involved in making the Ultimate Router Table and this accessory will really pay off and give you the ultimate in routing satisfaction.

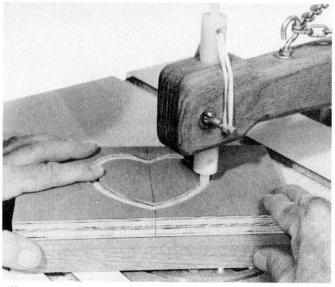

Illus. 774 (left). Another look at the pattern secured to the plywood which will become a grooved template. The ¼-inch-thick heart-shape pattern seen here will be discarded. Illus. 775 (above). Routing with the grooved template fastened to the workpiece with double-sided tape.

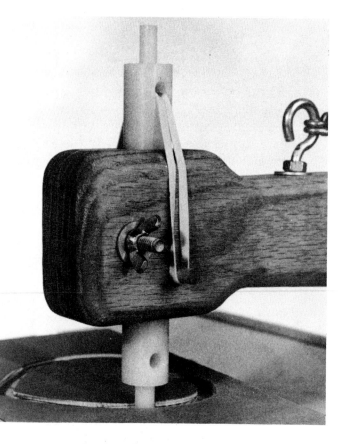

Illus. 776. The cut is completed with the pin engaged in the groove of the template during the entire operation.

Appendices

METRIC EQUIVALENCY CHART

MM—MILLIMETRES   CM—CENTIMETRES

INCHES TO MILLIMETRES AND CENTIMETRES

INCHES	MM	CM	INCHES	CM	INCHES	CM
⅛	3	0.3	9	22.9	30	76.2
¼	6	0.6	10	25.4	31	78.7
⅜	10	1.0	11	27.9	32	81.3
½	13	1.3	12	30.5	33	83.8
⅝	16	1.6	13	33.0	34	86.4
¾	19	1.9	14	35.6	35	88.9
⅞	22	2.2	15	38.1	36	91.4
1	25	2.5	16	40.6	37	94.0
1¼	32	3.2	17	43.2	38	96.5
1½	38	3.8	18	45.7	39	99.1
1¾	44	4.4	19	48.3	40	101.6
2	51	5.1	20	50.8	41	104.1
2½	64	6.4	21	53.3	42	106.7
3	76	7.6	22	55.9	43	109.2
3½	89	8.9	23	58.4	44	111.8
4	102	10.2	24	61.0	45	114.3
4½	114	11.4	25	63.5	46	116.8
5	127	12.7	26	66.0	47	119.4
6	152	15.2	27	68.6	48	121.9
7	178	17.8	28	71.1	49	124.5
8	203	20.3	29	73.7	50	127.0

YARDS TO METRES

YARDS	METRES	YARDS	METRES	YARDS	METRES	YARDS	METRES	YARDS	METRES
⅛	0.11	2⅛	1.94	4⅛	3.77	6⅛	5.60	8⅛	7.43
¼	0.23	2¼	2.06	4¼	3.89	6¼	5.72	8¼	7.54
⅜	0.34	2⅜	2.17	4⅜	4.00	6⅜	5.83	8⅜	7.66
½	0.46	2½	2.29	4½	4.11	6½	5.94	8½	7.77
⅝	0.57	2⅝	2.40	4⅝	4.23	6⅝	6.06	8⅝	7.89
¾	0.69	2¾	2.51	4¾	4.34	6¾	6.17	8¾	8.00
⅞	0.80	2⅞	2.63	4⅞	4.46	6⅞	6.29	8⅞	8.12
1	0.91	3	2.74	5	4.57	7	6.40	9	8.23
1⅛	1.03	3⅛	2.86	5⅛	4.69	7⅛	6.52	9⅛	8.34
1¼	1.14	3¼	2.97	5¼	4.80	7¼	6.63	9¼	8.46
1⅜	1.26	3⅜	3.09	5⅜	4.91	7⅜	6.74	9⅜	8.57
1½	1.37	3½	3.20	5½	5.03	7½	6.86	9½	8.69
1⅝	1.49	3⅝	3.31	5⅝	5.14	7⅝	6.97	9⅝	8.80
1¾	1.60	3¾	3.43	5¾	5.26	7¾	7.09	9¾	8.92
1⅞	1.71	3⅞	3.54	5⅞	5.37	7⅞	7.20	9⅞	9.03
2	1.83	4	3.66	6	5.49	8	7.32	10	9.14

ABOUT THE AUTHOR

Patrick Spielman's love of wood began when, as a child, he transformed fruit crates into toys. Now this prolific and innovative woodworker is respected worldwide as a teacher and author.

His most famous contribution to the woodworking field has been his perfection of a method to season green wood with polyethylene glycol 1000 (PEG). He went on to invent, manufacture, and distribute the PEG-Thermovat chemical seasoning system.

During his many years as shop instructor in Wisconsin, Spielman published manuals, teaching guides, and more than 14 popular books, including *Modern Wood Technology*, a college text. He also wrote six educational series on wood technology, tool use, processing techniques, design, and wood-product planning.

Author of the best-selling *Router Handbook* (over 500,000 copies sold), Spielman has served as editorial consultant to a professional magazine, and his products, techniques, and many books have been featured in numerous periodicals.

This pioneer of new ideas and inventor of countless jigs, fixtures, and designs used throughout the world is a unique combination of expert woodworker and brilliant teacher—all of which endear him to his many readers and to his publisher.

At Spielmans Wood Works in the woods of northern Door County, Wisconsin, he and his family create and sell some of the most durable and popular furniture products and designs available.

Should you wish to write Pat, please forward your letters to Sterling Publishing Company.

Charles Nurnberg
Sterling Publishing Company

Alphabets and Designs for Wood Signs. 50 alphabet patterns, plans for many decorative designs, the latest on hand carving, routing, cutouts, and sandblasting. Pricing data. Photo gallery (4 pages in color) of wood signs by professionals from across the U.S. Over 200 illustrations. 128 pages.

Carving Large Birds. Spielman and renowned carver Bill Dehos show how to carve an array of large birds. All the tools and basic techniques used are discussed in depth, and hundreds of photos, illustrations, and patterns are provided for carving graceful swans, majestic eagles, comical-looking penguins, and scores of other birds. 16 pages in full color. 192 pages.

Gluing and Clamping. A thorough, up-to-date examination of one of the most critical steps in woodworking. Spielman explores the features of every type of glue—from traditional animal-hide glues to the newest epoxies—the clamps and tools needed, the bonding properties of different wood species, safety tips, and all techniques from edge-to-edge and end-to-end gluing to applying plastic laminates. Also included is a glossary of terms. Over 500 illustrations. 256 pages.

Making Country-Rustic Furniture. Hundreds of photos, patterns, and detailed scaled drawings reveal construction methods, woodworking techniques, and Spielman's professional secrets for making indoor and outdoor furniture in the distinctly attractive Country-Rustic style. Covered are all aspects of furniture making from choosing the best wood for the job to texturing smooth boards. Among the dozens of projects are mailboxes, cabinets, shelves, coffee tables, weather vanes, doors, panelling, plant stands and many more durable and economical pieces. 400 illustrations. 4 pages in full color. 160 pages.

Making Wood Decoys. A clear step-by-step approach to the basics of decoy carving. This book is abundantly illustrated with closeup photos for designing, selecting, and obtaining woods; tools; feather detailing; painting; and finishing of decorative and working decoys. Six different professional decoy artists featured. Photo gallery (4 pages in full color) along with numerous detailed plans for various popular decoys. 160 pages.

Making Wood Signs. Designing, selecting woods, tools, and every process through finishing is clearly covered. Hand-carved, power-carved, routed, and sandblasted processes in small to huge signs are presented. Foolproof guides for professional letters and ornaments. Hundreds of photos (4 pages in full color). Lists sources for supplies and special tooling. 144 pages.

Realistic Decoys. Spielman and master carver Keith Bridenhagen reveal their successful techniques for carving, feather-texturing, painting, and finishing wood decoys. Details that you can't find elsewhere—anatomy, attitudes, markings, and the easy step-by-step approach to perfect delicate procedures—make this book invaluable. Includes listings for contests, shows, and sources of tools and supplies. 274 closeup photos, 28 in color. 224 pages.

Router Handbook. With nearly 600 illustrations of every conceivable bit, attachment, jig, and fixture, plus every possible operation, this definitive guide has revolutionized router applications. It begins with safety and maintenance tips, then forges ahead into all aspects of dovetailing, freehanding, advanced duplication, and more. Details for over 50 projects are included. 224 pages.

Scroll Saw Handbook. This companion volume to *Scroll Saw Pattern Book* covers the essentials of this versatile tool, including the basics (how scroll saws work, blades to use, etc.) and the advantages and disadvantages of the general types and specifc brand name models available on the market. All cutting techniques are detailed, including compound and bevel sawing, making inlays, reliefs, and recesses, cutting metals and other nonwoods, and marquetry. There's even a section on transferring patterns to wood! Over 500 illustrations. 256 pages.

Scroll Saw Pattern Book. This companion book to *Scroll Saw Handbook* contains over 450 workable patterns for making wall plaques, refrigerator magnets, candle holders, pegboards, jewelry, ornaments, shelves, brackets, picture frames, signboards, and many more projects. Beginners and experienced scroll saw users alike will find something here to intrigue and challenge them. 256 pages.

Working Green Wood with PEG. Covers every process for making beautiful, inexpensive projects from green wood without cracking, splitting, or warping. Hundreds of clear photos and drawings show every step from obtaining the raw wood through shaping, treating, and finishing your PEG-treated projects. 175 unusual project ideas. Lists supply sources. 160 pages.

Index